Controversies of the
George W. Bush Presidency

CONTROVERSIES OF THE GEORGE W. BUSH PRESIDENCY

Pro and Con Documents

NANCY S. LIND AND BERNARD IVAN TAMAS

FRANKLIN SQ. PUBLIC LIBRARY
19 LINCOLN ROAD
FRANKLIN SQUARE, N.Y. 11010

GREENWOOD PRESS
Westport, Connecticut • London

Library of Congress Cataloging-in-Publication Data

Lind, Nancy S., 1958–
 Controversies of the George W. Bush presidency : pro and con documents / Nancy S. Lind and Bernard Ivan Tamas.
  p. cm.
 Includes bibliographical references and index.
 ISBN 0-313-34011-0 (alk. paper)
 1. United States—Politics and government—2001—Sources. 2. United States—Foreign relations—2001—Sources. 3. United States—Economic policy—2001—Sources. 4. War on Terrorism, 2001—Sources. I. Tamas, Bernard Ivan. II. Title.
 E902.L557 2007
 973.931092—dc22   2006029483

British Library Cataloguing in Publication Data is available.

Copyright © 2007 by Nancy S. Lind, Bernard Ivan Tamas

All rights reserved. No portion of this book may be reproduced, by any process or technique, without the express written consent of the publisher.

Library of Congress Catalog Card Number: 2006029483
ISBN: 0-313-34011-0

First published in 2007

Greenwood Press, 88 Post Road West, Westport, CT 06881
An imprint of Greenwood Publishing Group, Inc.
www.greenwood.com

Printed in the United States of America

The paper used in this book complies with the Permanent Paper Standard issued by the National Information Standards Organization (Z39.48-1984).

10 9 8 7 6 5 4 3 2 1

CONTENTS

Acknowledgments vii
Chronology of George W. Bush Presidency ix
Introduction 1

ECONOMIC POLICY
   Introduction 7
   Tax Relief Act of 2001 (May 2001) 12
   Enron (January 2002) 16
   Andean Trade Preference Act (April 2002) 20
   Jobs and Growth Tax Relief Reconciliation Act (May 2003) 24
   Steel Tariffs (November 2003) 26
   Social Security Reform (January 2005) 29
   Oil Drilling in the Alaskan National Wildlife Reserve
      (June 2005) 32
   Economic Policy Web Sites 36
   Economic Policy Reference Articles and Books 36

DOMESTIC POLICY
   Introduction 39
   Faith-based and Community Initiatives (January 2001) 44
   Stem Cell Research (August 2001) 47
   Department of Homeland Security (September 2001) 52
   USA PATRIOT Act 2001 (October 2001) 57
   No Child Left Behind (January 2002) 68
   Yucca Mountain Nuclear Waste Site (February 2002) 74
   Shuttle Columbia (February 2003) 76
   Hurricane Katrina (September 2005) 80
   Wiretaps/Domestic Spying (December 2005) 84
   Domestic Policy Web Sites 88
   Domestic Policy Reference Articles and Books 90

FOREIGN POLICY
   Introduction 93
   Navy Surveillance Plane in China (April 2001) 97

Kyoto Climate Protocol (June 2001)	100
Afghan Women and Children Relief Act of 2001 (December 2001)	105
Roadmap to Peace in the Middle East (March 2002)	108
Nuclear Arms Reduction with Russia (May 2002)	110
Withdrawal from the 1972 Anti-Ballistic Missile Treaty (June 2002)	115
Zimbabwe Sanctions (March 2003)	118
Avian Flu (November 2005)	121
Foreign Policy Web Sites	126
Foreign Policy Reference Articles and Books	127

TERRORISM AND MILITARY ACTIONS

Introduction	129
September 11 and Osama bin Laden (September 2001)	133
Attack on Afghanistan (October 2001)	139
Anthrax (November 2001)	143
Axis of Evil (January 2002)	145
Terror Alert System (March 2002)	150
Authorization of the Use of Force against Iraq (October 2002)	155
National Missile Defense (December 2002)	160
Attack on Iraq (March 2003)	164
War Is Over in Iraq (May 2003)	169
Iraq/Niger Connection (July 2003)	174
Abuse of Iraqi Prisoners at Abu Ghraib Prison (May 2004)	177
Defense of Donald Rumsfeld (April 2006)	181
Terrorism and Military Actions Web Sites	185
Terrorism and Military Actions Reference Articles and Books	186

Index   189

ACKNOWLEDGMENTS

Various individuals have directly and/or indirectly aided us in writing this book. We are indebted to our department chairperson, Jamal Nassar, who encouraged us to develop this project. We are also indebted to Mariah Gumpert, our editor at Greenwood Press, who has provided prompt responses to our many questions throughout the process. We especially appreciate the contributions of our two graduate assistants, Tanya R. Austin and Anthony Bolton, who researched and drafted some of the information for the book. We also thank the countless undergraduates, foremost among them Vanda Rajcan, for assisting the graduate students when pressures became greatest.

This book is dedicated to future generations who will be able to assess our work and evaluate the claims we have made about the influences of many policies in the Bush administration. Bernard Ivan Tamas dedicates the book to his first nephews, Stephen and Richard Fink. Nancy Lind dedicates the book to her nieces, nephews, and cousins: Mitchell, Jordan, and Claira Lind; MaKynna and Jensynn Lesinski; Reid and Kaitlyn Sroda; and the youngest, Jacob and Zackary Sroda. May their futures all be bright.

CHRONOLOGY OF GEORGE W. BUSH PRESIDENCY

2001

January 6: A joint session of the House and Senate certifies the electoral college votes awarding the presidency to George W. Bush.

January 9: Linda Chavez withdraws her name from consideration for secretary of labor after admitting to sheltering an illegal immigrant.

January 20: George W. Bush takes the oath of office to become the forty-third president of the United States.

January 29: Bush signs executive order to create the White House Office of Faith-Based and Community Initiatives.

February 8: Bush sends Congress his $1.6 trillion, ten-year tax-cut plan, arguing that broad based tax relief is needed to boost a slowing economy.

May 17: Bush unveils his administration's energy policy, which emphasizes increasing domestic oil production, including drilling in the Arctic wilderness.

June 28: A *Wall Street Journal*/NBC News poll gives President Bush a 50 percent approval rating, the lowest presidential approval rating in more than five years.

July 12: Bush announces plan to enable Medicare recipients to purchase prescription drugs at discount prices.

August 9: Bush announces that he will permit federal funding of limited research on human embryonic stem cells.

September 11: Hijackers commandeer four commercial jetliners, flying two of them into the World Trade Center and one into the Pentagon. The fourth jet crashes in a field in Shanksville, Pennsylvania.

September 12: Bush states that the acts of terrorism were "acts of war."

September 20: Bush addresses a joint session of Congress, outlines his campaign against terrorism and announces a new cabinet-level agency, the Office of Homeland Security.

December 13: Bush announces that the United States will withdraw from the 1972 Antiballistic Missile (ABM) Treaty between the United States and Russia.

December 28: Bush comments that U.S. forces will likely remain in Afghanistan for "quite a long period of time."

2002

January 8:	Bush signs a sweeping education reform measure into law.
January 29:	Bush delivers his first State of the Union address, calling North Korea, Iran, and Iraq "an axis of evil."
March 12:	A new system of color-coded terrorism alerts is unveiled.
June 6:	Bush asks Congress to create a new cabinet department for homeland security, which would combine twenty-two federal agencies but not include the CIA or FBI.
July 30:	In response to corporate scandals, Bush signs a law increasing penalties for accounting fraud.
September 12:	Bush takes his case against Iraq to the United Nations.
September 19:	Bush asks Congress for authority to "use all means" to disarm Iraq.
October 11:	Congress approves use of U.S. military force against Iraq.
November 5:	Republicans regain the Senate and add six seats to their margin in the House. GOP wins are seen as a major victory for Bush.
November 8:	The UN Security Council unanimously approves a new resolution, warning of "serious consequences" if Iraq fails to comply with strict new weapons inspections. The Bush administration promises "zero tolerance" if Iraq fails to disarm.
November 25:	Bush signs legislation creating a new Department of Homeland Security to fight against domestic terrorism.
December 7:	Iraq submits arms declaration to the United Nations.

2003

February 3:	Space Shuttle *Columbia* breaks up during reentry killing all seven astronauts aboard.
March 17:	Bush gives Iraqi president Saddam Hussein and his sons forty-eight hours to leave Iraq before military action begins.
May 2:	Bush announces that "major combat operations in Iraq have ended."
July 25:	Bush orders troops to positions off Liberia.
November 20:	Massive anti-Bush protest occurs in London.

2004

January 15:	Bush unveils vision for moon and beyond; seeks $1 billion more in NASA funding.
January 20:	Bush makes State of the Union address.
February 11:	Bush names panel to study weapons of mass destruction intelligence failure.
May 24:	Bush announces five-step Iraq plan.
August 10:	Bush appoints new CIA director.
September 21:	Bush defends U.S. Iraq policy before the United Nations.
November 2:	Bush is reelected.
December 3:	Bush retains Donald Rumsfeld as secretary of defense.

2005

January 20:	Bush is sworn in for the second term.
February 2:	Bush lays out his second-term agenda in his State of the Union address and indicates he will consider any proposal to reform Social Security.

February 17:	Bush names John Negroponte as intelligence chief.
March 4:	Bush urges Syria to get out of Lebanon.
May 26:	Bush pledges aid to Palestinians.
July 3:	Bush rejects Kyoto-style G8 deal.
July 19:	Bush names John Roberts to Supreme Court.
August 29:	Hurricane Katrina batters gulf coast.
September 2:	Bush condemns Hurricane Katrina aid effort.
September 7:	Bush seeks $50 billion for hurricane relief.
October 31:	Bush nominates Samuel Alito to Supreme Court.
November 1:	Bush unveils pandemic flu strategy.
November 30:	Bush outlines Iraq victory plan.
December 17:	Bush admits he authorized spying.
December 22:	Bush suffers Patriot Act defeat by extending it only for a month.

2006

January 31:	Bush makes State of the Union address.
February 18:	Bush works to reenergize nuclear energy.
February 21:	Bush faces pressure to block port deal, which would give a United Arab Emirates country control over six major U.S. seaports.
March 2:	The United States and India agree to a nuclear pact.
March 10:	Bush indicates that Iran is a "grave security threat."
April 14:	Bush rebuffs attacks on Secretary of Defense Donald Rumsfeld.

INTRODUCTION

The Bush administration has garnered both successes and failures in its initiation and implementation of public policies. President Bush has confronted natural disasters of unprecedented magnitude, such as Hurricane Katrina, and acts of international terrorism on the soils of the United States. There have been excellent responses that seem responsive to public opinion, and instances of mediocre responses that have revealed miscommunication in the White House, as well as instances of poor responses that have demonstrated a lack of knowledge by the president. And there have been supporters and critics of each decision of the Bush administration.

This book represents our best judgments about which issues, initiatives, and events were the most important in the George W. Bush administration. At the very least, the issues and events covered have attracted considerable media attention and a wide range of criticism and praise. As with most current events, the true judge of our assertions will be time. Future scholars will assess the successes and failures of the Bush administration and will critique whether or not the policies we identified were key events in the actions of the president.

SCOPE, ORGANIZATION, SELECTION CRITERIA, AND METHODOLOGY

The readings and issues confronted by President Bush are divided into four main sections: Economic Policy, Domestic Policy, Foreign Policy, and Terrorism and Military Actions. They cover the most central and controversial issues faced by the Bush administration. Every president emphasizes some issues and downgrades the significance of others. Additionally, the push of external events often lead to international attention on the issues the president may seek to downplay or avoid. Both types of issues shape what is important in any presidential administration and will be covered in this book.

Additionally, external events often occur that demand presidential responses, and political circumstances may change in ways that may or may not reflect the president's position on issues of public policy. Accordingly, we surveyed the record of President Bush's first six years in office and focused on events that influenced citizen judgment of the president's actions. We also used our professional judgment in examining which issues led to the most controversies in the Bush presidency.

This approach allowed us to develop a list of core issues that were central to President George W. Bush and to find and analyze opposing positions to these issues. This volume focuses on the arguments of President Bush and his opponents to advance their own positions and to critique those of the opposition, and it seeks to place these arguments in the larger political context of the new millennium. For each issue area, a pro and a con speech was provided, the former by President Bush and the latter by an opponent of the policy. These opponents were always Democratic politicians who were members of the U.S. Senate or House of Representatives at the time. When more appropriate, presidential documents or the answers to journalist questions were included. Each section also cites print and electronic resources that can be used for further reference, and the book ends with a selected, general bibliography.

THE CONTEXT: POLITICAL, SOCIAL, AND ECONOMIC CHANGES IN THE NEW MILLENNIUM

Popular discussions of politics tend to emphasize the role of the president in shaping events and responding to unintended and unpredicted events. Supporters of the president credit him with successful programs that strive to improve the conditions of society, whereas critics of the president blame him for the failed programs that leave people in the same conditions or worse off than before the implementation of the programs. There is a tendency of presidential supporters to overestimate the successes of the president and to underestimate his failures. At the same time, critics tend to overemphasize the president's role in unsuccessful policies and calamitous world events.

The president is but one actor on the national and international scene, and his actions must always be evaluated in the larger context of external events, factors often beyond his control. The president is hampered or helped in his objectives by other elected officials such as Congress in its enactment of laws, or the Supreme Court in its interpretation of laws, as well as by the action or inaction of the bureaucracy.

This introduction focuses on several contexts that can be seen to have shaped the choices and actions of President George W. Bush. These include the impact of the economy, the influence of war and peace on policies regarding terrorism, the role of culture in assessing the needs and demographics of citizens, the impact of natural disasters, and the role of global power. Each of these factors has influenced what President Bush has been able to achieve, and hence each deserves some discussion prior to addressing the individual issues that confronted the president.

Political Culture and Elections

During the 2000 presidential election, commentators and political scientists began noticing a shift in the way Americans are divided politically. Rural areas, which had often voted Democratic in previous decades, became solidly Republican, and urban areas, especially port cities, were becoming heavily Democratic. This became expressed by the red state/blue state phenomenon, whereby more rural, red states tended to vote for Bush while more urban, blue states voted for Al Gore.

This phenomenon, combined with an extremely close presidential election in 2000, produced the odd situation in which Al Gore won the popular vote but George W. Bush won the presidency. The election was decided by less than 600 votes in Florida, a critical battleground state. Electoral irregularities seemed to have helped Bush win the election there. A poorly designed ballot, known as the "butterfly ballot," confused voters and apparently led many Gore supporters to accidentally vote for Pat Buchanan, a right-wing candidate nominated by the Reform Party. Florida also had laws that excluded most ex-felons from voting, but the lists were drawn up in such a way that, allegedly, they kept a large number of African Americans, who were never convicted of a crime, from voting. Since African Americans overwhelmingly support Democratic candidates, this also helped Bush win Florida and the presidency.

With the election so close in Florida, the state began a hand recount of the results. When it became clear that some counties would not be able to complete the recount by November 14 (the date Florida law requires all counties to certify and report election results), the Gore campaign appealed to the Florida Supreme Court, which ruled that the recount should not be stopped. The political and legal battles continued for over a month. Protestors, often party activists, came to Florida from around the country. On December 12, the Florida state legislature, controlled by a Republican majority, voted to certify Bush as the winner. A few hours later, the Florida Supreme Court, largely considered pro-Democratic, ordered the recount to continue. Then, in a five-four vote, the Supreme Court ruled that a recount requires consistent standards, which were lacking in Florida. Since there was insufficient time to develop and implement these standards, the court effectively decided that the certification of Bush as the winner would stand, granting him the White House. Al Gore conceded soon afterward.

While Bush had won this difficult battle, it had hurt the legitimacy of his administration. Accusations that he had been appointed by a court selected primarily by Republican presidents, including his father, lingered. The shadow of difficult and contested election did not lift until after the terrorist attacks in September 2001.

The State of the Economy

Going into 2000, the government prepared for a Y2K event that never happened, by infusing the budget with new dollars. This increased capital had no place to go except the stock market, producing "stock inflation." Facing a weak economy, the federal government opted for an expansionist fiscal policy. It also cut taxes and increased unemployment insurance benefits. But the economy was slow to recover, experiencing negative growth just before Bush took office and for two quarters in 2001. There seemed to be various causes, including the burst of the technology bubble as many overvalued dot-com companies quickly went out of business. Economic scandals, like the Enron and World Com bankruptcies, may have also fueled the problem. The shock of the 9/11 attacks also hurt the economy. Consumer confidence dropped dramatically, travel and tourism declined, and insurance companies gave out huge payoffs to victims of the attacks.

The sluggish economy also meant that the government was receiving less revenues from taxes. That problem was made worse by the Bush tax cuts of 2001, which translated into considerable revenue loss to the government. The president has argued that the economic downturn had nothing to do with his policies, but was instead a product of unexpected and unavoidable events, like the terrorist attacks, corporate scandals, and the War on Terror. Nonetheless, White House projections have consistently underestimated budget deficits and expenses. Before the War in Iraq, the administration even claimed that the invasion and occupation would practically pay for themselves.

The War on Terror

The 2000s have been marked by issues that include a rising threat of terrorism, the rapid globalization of the economy, and an explosive expansion of computer-based technologies. The most significant political developments, however, can be seen in the War on Terror and the War in Iraq. After the 9/11 attacks, President Bush declared that the United States was entering a "new era," and that if other countries were not with us in the War on Terror, then they were against us. The War on Terror by the U.S. government and some of its allies has become controversial for a range of reasons, including the threat of a new imperial presidency and the concern that this war opens the door for violating the civil rights of Americans and the basic human rights of detainees.

The War on Terror enhanced the powers of the U.S. federal government, some would argue, by reducing the civil liberties of some citizens. Investigations have been started in many branches of numerous governments, pursuing millions of tips. Thousands of people have been detained, arrested, or questioned by border patrol. Many have been detained secretly in undisclosed locations and been denied access to an attorney. Among those secretly detained are U.S. citizens. Several laws, notably the USA PATRIOT Act, were passed that expanded the ability of law enforcement agencies to investigate individuals. The military, intelligence, and security branches of the federal bureaucracy were reorganized, and most of these functions were put under the new Department of Homeland Security.

Following the September 11, 2001 terrorist attacks against the United States, the Bush administration argued that it was necessary to invade Iraq in order to remove Saddam Hussein from power. The Hussein regime was a grave threat, it claimed, because it was a supporter of the al-Qaeda terrorist organization and it was stockpiling weapons of mass destruction. According to the administration, the Iraqi government was even attempting to develop nuclear weapons. Initially, the invasion was successful; the government collapsed rapidly, and coalition troops quickly entered and took over Baghdad. But, then, an insurgency broke out, and the U.S. military found itself in what many have called a quagmire. At the same time, evidence against the justifications for war grew steadily stronger. The war in Iraq, and not the larger War on Terror, may well become the defining event of the Bush administration.

Natural Disasters

A terrorist attack was not the only devastating crisis that the Bush administration faced. The federal government's response to Hurricane Katrina led to a range of accusations against the president. His administration was accused of ignoring the crisis because the main victims were poor. The fiasco of the "evacuation" before the storm revealed a complete lack of planning and a total failure to provide resources to the most vulnerable sectors of society. It also reinforced the impression many had that this administration was more concerned about the images it projects than the actual work of government. It was the political team that could produce an exceptional "Mission Accomplished" photo event, the argument went, while the war itself was mismanaged and ongoing. In the same way, to many, the administration's response to Katrina seemed driven more by an attempt to control the media image than to save lives. At the same time, supporters of the president point out that responses of the state of Louisiana and the city of New Orleans, respectively led by a Democratic governor and mayor, were equally bad, though they did not receive the same accusations of class bias and obsession with image control.

Global Power

Finally, the Bush administration is attempting to function in a period of globalization, a time when countries are becoming more economically and culturally intertwined. While the Bush administration was certainly never protectionist, it did believe that the United States, as the world's leading democracy, could function more unilaterally and should avoid international entanglements. The Bush team was critical of the Clinton administration's involvement in the conflicts within the former Yugoslavia, for example, and they were opposed to "nation building" as a U.S. policy. Many in the administration also believed that the United Nations had too much power and needed significant reform.

Global pressures, including the realities of the War on Terror, forced the administration to change these stands significantly. After attacking Afghanistan and Iraq, the administration effectively began a process of nation building. The administration also went to the United Nations to plead its case for war before attacking Iraq, and it attempted to build a broad coalition of allies before the invasion. Demonstrating the limits of its power, especially with a taxed military, the Bush administration also had to negotiate with hostile regimes like Iran.

In many ways, the problems of globalization reflect a problem mentioned above: presidents do not choose and cannot control their political environments. The economy began failing near the end of the Clinton administration, though many held Bush responsible. Terrorists had been attempting to attack the United States well before Bush took office, and while some would argue that the administration ignored ample warnings of a looming crisis, it is not clear that the plot could have been stopped. Bush also inherited the problems with foreign governments such as North Korea, and has no choice but to contend with the rising power of China. In other words, President Bush has to function within a complex political arena with many factors beyond his control.

CONCLUSION

In sum, this volume represents our understanding of the critical issues of the policies of 2000–2006, how President Bush acted on these policies, and how his opponents sought to discredit his arguments and responses. We also provide a framework for further analysis of the remaining years of the George W. Bush presidency.

ECONOMIC POLICY

INTRODUCTION

Given a consistent surge toward globalization throughout most of the industrialized world, many issues spring forth as examples of the difficulties of economic management. These issues illustrate the "bumps in the road" along the way to a smoothly functioning global economy. Specific issues worthy of consideration are corruption within the economy, international trade openness (free trade), and domestic economic strengthening policy. These issues outline some of the major challenges facing economic growth and stability worldwide, as well as within the United States. These issues also serve to illustrate the concept of political involvement in the economy, which, in this case, will be analyzed under the political influence of President Bush. However, before starting this analysis, it is vital for people to understand that the actual influence of a president on most economic issues is difficult to determine and measure over a short period (ten or less years, typically), especially in a broad-spectrum macroeconomic setting like the United States.

President Bush has had limited involvement in pure economic policies. However, he has had an impact on various issues that involve the U.S. economy. A major concern for his policies has been the impact of corruption in various major companies and accounting firms. A few notable cases spring to mind, mainly Enron and WorldCom.

Enron is a relatively new company, coming into the market after the merger of two natural gas companies in 1985. It gradually built up its share of the natural gas market and other domestic energy resources, hitting its high at $90 a share in 2000. However, trouble loomed on the horizon for Enron. During the California energy crisis, Enron deliberately manipulated the energy market in California, selling the state electricity at vastly inflated prices. As this practice was revealed to the public, unethical and illegal accounting practices were also discovered in the company. Enron had previously posted enormous revenues, but at the expense of hiding short- and long-term debts. As these debts eventually came due, various executives in the company sold their stock early and watched as the company's stock price dropped to less than $1 a share. By October 2001, the Securities and Exchange Commission had announced an investigation into Enron. This investigation found even more illegal practices at Enron and its official accounting firm, Arthur Andersen, which had shredded literally tons of incriminating Enron documents to hide them from investigators, resulting in their indictment in 2002.

WorldCom is another example of massive corruption, in which a lack of corporate accountability and shoddy accounting work led to the fall of a huge telecommunications company. Successful from its beginnings in the mid-1980s, the company reached its high in 1999, posting a $61.99 per stock price. However, its attempt to buy out a large rival, Sprint, failed when U.S. and European antitrust regulators objected. Previous and subsequent investigations into WorldCom's loans and accounting practices found illegal and unethical procedures, resulting in a trial against various WorldCom executives, including the CEO Bernard Ebbers. Numerous witnesses professed that they had carried out orders from their superiors in illegal accounting practices. Various executives were convicted, capping the largest accounting scandal ever in the United States. Ebbers was sentenced to twenty-five years in prison, the longest of various sentences against him and his fellow executives.

As a result of these cases of corruption, President Bush supported the Sarbanes-Oxley Act in 2002 in an attempt to curtail the corruption in accounting and reporting practices found in Enron, WorldCom, and other companies. This act requires more reporting and accountability from CEOs regarding their company's finances. It (Sarbanes-Oxley) is an example of President Bush's attempts to establish economic accountability to the people that companies serve. This act has been popular politically, though various analysts have commented that it may be overly harsh.

The Sarbanes-Oxley Act serves as an example of policy action by President Bush in supporting increased controls and accountability among companies to which various members of his own administration had links. These cases served to highlight the bleak economic mood after the attacks of September 11 and the brief economic recession during that year. It could be argued that economic recovery could have progressed much more quickly had companies acted ethically, since Enron's actions in illegally bilking California for money and WorldCom's shoddy accounting practices certainly lowered consumer confidence in the economy.

FREE TRADE (OR INTERNATIONAL OPEN TRADE)

The next economic area over which President Bush has had some influence relates to American endorsements of international open trade, or free trade. Of special interest is the renewal of the Andean Trade Preference Act in 2002. Also worth mentioning is the impact of the controversy over steel tariffs in 2003. These two issues describe the effects of presidential political influence over international trade and subsequent domestic policies.

The Andean Trade Preference Act directs U.S. funding to various corporations in Bolivia, Colombia, Ecuador, and Peru, as well as monetary assistance to workers in these corporations, and monetary assistance and expertise to allow these foreign corporations more ability to adapt and advance their trade with the United States. Of particular interest concerning President Bush is his ability to influence tariffs on foreign goods. This ability allows him to act according to public sentiment against foreign companies.

In conjunction with this renewal of tariff power and influence, the brief decision to raise steel tariffs illustrates how presidential power over tariffs can be used to further political ends at the expense of economic rationality. The issue over steel tariffs was that as U.S. producers faced increased foreign competition that produced an equivalent amount of steel at lower prices, they pressured politicians to act in their interests. To this end, President Bush supported increased tariffs on steel imports in 2003. This is a prime example of the disconnect between politics and good economic policy, as this decision was condemned by numerous economists. Put simply, tariffs set an artificially high price ceiling, encouraging more output than is usable by steel buyers. In addition, the higher prices are inevitably passed on to steel buyers, most notably, vehicle manufacturers. In turn, this price increase is absorbed into the cost of new vehicles, forcing the consumer to suffer. This economic aftermath, however, was politically undesirable at the time for President Bush, as he (like many other presidents before him) attempted to satisfy a large and powerful industry. However, the lack of wisdom involved in this decision was gradually acknowledged by most people, and the tariffs were reduced. In part, this was due to threats from the World Trade Organization (WTO), who felt that the United States had set up an economically unfeasible tariff that inhibited competition and threatened reciprocal tariffs on a variety of U.S. exported goods. This case is remarkably similar to an older case of tariff enactment for political rather than economic justification. Consider the Hawley-Smoot tariff enacted immediately prior to the Great Depression in the late 1920s to late 1930s. In this case, a tariff designed to protect U.S. interests was reciprocated by foreign countries with their own tariff increases, prolonging one of the worst economic crises in U.S. history.

It is apparent, then, that President Bush has acted in some cases more in line with transitory political interests than with a purely economic rationale. In defense of the steel tariffs, there was also a motivation to save U.S. jobs in steel manufacturing, which were threatened by cheaper steel. However, the cost to consumers for securing jobs for a few people would have been much more expensive than the potential layoffs. However, Bush has also pushed policies to maintain and improve relations with new entrants into the global market, as seen in the Andean Trade Preference Act. This legislation is very attractive politically, as it allows President Bush to reach out to a Latino constituency, a key group not usually carried by Republicans. This policy stance clearly attempts to curry favor in South America in the face of vociferous anti-American leaders such as Hugo Chavez of Venezuela and Fidel Castro of Cuba.

Of particular interest currently is the issue of tightening, slackening, or maintaining immigration policy. While various politicians and Hispanic constituencies have advocated dismissal of a recent immigration bill that would more strongly enforce standing U.S. policy, President Bush is in a rather difficult position. On one hand, an open immigration policy featuring, among other things, an amnesty toward illegal immigrants has definite economic potential. Currently, people from around the world have immigrated to America to work at jobs that most Americans choose not to do. Most of these jobs are menial in nature but are necessary for continued economic prosperity (construction, food services, etc.). On the other hand, an open immigration policy increases the likelihood of smuggling weapons and people into the United States. It is far too early to predict that a terror attack will result because of open borders, but it is a source of concern for people favoring a tightening of American border security.

Overall, these issues illustrate various causes of concern with a free trade policy and open trade/borders in general. President Bush has, for the most part, been open in his endorsement of free trade options. This openness and support has resulted in an improving economy and better political relations with various countries in Central and South America, though more work still needs to be done.

DOMESTIC ECONOMIC POLICY

President Bush has had a definite impact on domestic economic policy, but it is important to realize that some economic factors of success are perhaps mistakenly attributed to him. The two major governmental agencies that have an impact on the U.S. economy are the Department of Commerce and the Department of Treasury, which also includes the Federal Reserve, led until recently by Alan Greenspan. The Federal Reserve maintains the ability to adjust the interest rates of their loans to banks, dictating in effect the interest offered by banks on loans to consumers. This ability directly affects the economy by slowing growth before it overheats and triggers inflation. However, this is not the only ability of government to affect the economy. President Bush has advocated or supported various proposals and initiatives that have had powerful political and economic effects.

One major economic issue that the president supported early in his presidency was the Tax Relief Act of 2001. The basis for this act is the belief in the consumer's power to improve the economy. Ideally, as consumers pay less in taxes, they have more money to spend, save, or pay off debts. This being the case, the general idea is that consumers who pay fewer taxes will spend more money overall, injecting money into the economy and potentially easing a recession, such as that which occurred in 2001. This act was very popular with many Conservatives, but was looked on with disdain by most Democrats. However, it was passed and became law, allowing President Bush to take credit for subsequent economic successes. This policy has changed little over the six years of his term thus far.

Another economic issue on the domestic front was the debate over Social Security reform in 2005. This debate occurred over the issue of introducing private savings/investment accounts in conjunction with Social Security. These new accounts would invest some money that would have normally gone into the Social Security slush fund, the general fund for retiree benefits. This issue caused a massive debate over what was often classified as "robbing Social Security." However, the proposal to introduce private accounts into Social Security has significant economic merit. The current return on government investment of money in the Social Security fund is much less compared to various private investment funds. Admittedly, private funds introduce the possibility of risk, as the money put into them is not guaranteed by the federal government. However, a nuanced approach to this issue could introduce various forms of government oversight and stipulations for private investment funds.

An additional domestic economic issue that President Bush had influence over was the increased domestic oil drilling and the search for oil in Florida and Alaska. This issue was one of a few defeats for the president, though the economics were mildly attractive. At the heart of the economic issue was the profitability of increased oil exploration and drilling, that is, the likely profit realized after the expense incurred searching for new sources of oil. Given limited knowledge of the actual amounts of oil waiting to be drilled in Florida and in the proposed area of Alaska, the economics of increased drilling in these areas did not have much promise. However, it is quite possible that the oil found could be much more than expected, perhaps more than enough to cover the costs of exploration. As mentioned previously, this was a defeat for President Bush, as the proposed drilling was defeated and abandoned by the U.S. Congress. Since that time, the Bush administration has chosen to focus on other matters of economic importance.

Unemployment benefit increases were another topic of consideration within the Bush economic agenda. From an economic standpoint, increasing unemployment benefits has dubious potential. A standard economic argument against increases is that such increases in benefits encourage more people to accept unemployment, and those in unemployment to stay there. Given that this issue was brought to the fore around 2003, the argument against benefit increases is weakened somewhat, as businesses were not hiring as much as in 2006, leaving a gap in employment for people seeking jobs. Job seekers were left with less money to cover a longer time spent unemployed. In addition, given that inflation was growing, though slowly, the benefits were not covering as much in expenses as previously envisioned. Republican opposition to this increase was strong. They suggested that support of tax relief measures for consumers and for businesses to hire more workers was a more effective approach to lower unemployment and improve the economy. For President Bush, this legislation brought some focus to his economic agenda of encouraging more jobs and lowering taxes to fuel economic growth. This agenda has remained unchanged in many ways, and has been shown to be effective in combating the minor recession of 2000–2001, including the effects of the September 11 terrorist attacks.

It is informative to next look at the alternative to increasing unemployment benefits, the Jobs and Growth Tax Relief Reconciliation Act of 2003. This act was composed of many varying parts, all designed to foster economic growth. With President Bush's actions in support of it, this act was a useful stimulant to the economy. It especially corresponds with supporting business and consumer interests, key constituencies for Republicans and President Bush, specifically. In effect, this act reduced capital gains taxes (taxes on profits from investments), encouraging increased investment by consumers. In addition, this act set up increased tax credits for families and businesses, the latter of which were then in a position to hire more workers, further alleviating unemployment and benefiting the economy. This policy is in line with President Bush's agenda of supporting economic growth through lowering taxes and encouraging investment in the economy, whether in the stock market or through private enterprise (new business openings, etc.). A policy of tax relief suits a political landscape of Republican openness toward business interests and subsequent political support through contributions and votes.

Finally, it is useful to consider the political and economic ramifications of the debate over the 2005 federal government budget. The debate over budgetary allocations has consistently been a source of conflict between Republicans and Democrats. In the case of the 2005 budget, this was not an issue that President Bush had a great amount of control over, at least in the formulation stages in Congress. However, given that he had to approve the final version, President Bush did exert a great deal of influence over Congress to reach consensus over the budget. Recently, the impact of his influence over the budget has perhaps lessened due to his waning influence as his time in office comes to a close. Overall, his advocacy of the budget corresponded to his principles of supporting economic growth and consumer power. This put him at odds with various legislators who viewed the budget as an instrument for effecting social issues rather than economic issues with social impact. Except for funding of institutions that have some effect at the macroeconomic level, such as the U.S. Department of Commerce and the U.S. Department of Treasury, the economic impact of the budget is small compared with other policies championed by President Bush. However, his stance on securing economic growth policy and other constants was unaffected by the budget debate.

CONCLUSIONS

It is apparent that President Bush has limited power over the economic development and activity of the United States. However, his advocacy of specific issues and economic rationales for specific agendas of economic development has been shown to have definite effects on the economy. These effects range from limited usefulness, as is seen in the budget battle for 2005, to much more direct influence, as seen in his support for revised tax policy. The economic policy of the Bush administration has translated into continued support from numerous industries and business interests in general. This support clearly fits into the political landscape as a Republican constant, encouraging business interests, though perhaps at the loss of union and other nonbusiness groups. Overall, his policies have maintained business growth (after the brief recession of 2000–2001) and have resulted in continued business support for his policies. In addition, consumers have benefited from his support for certain economic policies, and this has been evidenced by his reelection to a second term. As such, President Bush's economic policies fit neatly into his political agenda and have changed little over the years of his presidency.

TAX RELIEF ACT OF 2001 (MAY 2001)

In his first year as president, Bush favored some controversial legislation, particularly with regard to taxes. The Tax Relief Act provided consumers with a tax rebate based on income. The plan of the administration was to put money back into the hands of the taxpayers because of a projected surplus for ten years down the road. Economic advisors and the Federal Reserve both said that these estimates and projections could not be counted on and that mass action like the Tax Relief Act should not occur.

Republicans and the president pushed for the passage of this legislation, and with dual majorities it passed. Most households received a check for $300. In addition to the objection that there was no guaranteed surplus, criticism also arose because of the high tax relief it gave to the richest 10 percent of the nation. The tax relief checks were seen as a ploy to achieve temporary economic growth. Democrats objected because of a fear of a deficit.

BUSH'S REMARKS ON PASSAGE OF THE ECONOMIC GROWTH AND TAX RELIEF RECONCILIATION ACT OF 2001 (MAY 26, 2001)

...Today, for the first time since the landmark tax relief championed 20 years ago by President Ronald Reagan, and 40 years ago by President John F. Kennedy, an

American President has the wonderful honor of letting the American people know significant tax relief is on the way. What is especially significant about the tax relief passed by the United States House and Senate today is that it cuts income taxes for everyone who pays them. Nothing could be more profound, and nothing could be more fair. No more wondering whether you're targeted in or whether you meet all the fine print requirements to qualify for one special tax break or another. No, this tax relief is straightforward and fair. If you pay income taxes, you get relief.

And for this year's first installment of the tax cut, the check will literally be in the mail. Late this summer and into the fall, every single American who pays income taxes will receive a check. Single taxpayers will receive a check of $300. Single parents who are heads of household will receive a check of $500. And married couples will receive a check of $600.

That immediate tax relief will provide an important boost at an important time for our economy. And what is more is you can feel comfortable using it because more tax relief is on the way. The checks are the first installment of lasting, long-term reductions in tax rates. As a result, when this tax relief plan is fully implemented, a typical family of four will see their taxes cut by about half.

Ultimately, tax rates will be reduced from the current 28 to 25, from 31 down to 28, from 36 to 33, and from 39.6 to 35 percent. Over the next 10 years, the child credit will double from last year's $500 per child to $600 per child this year to $1,000 by the year 2010. The marriage penalty will be dramatically reduced, and the unfair death tax will be completely abolished by the year 2010.

This tax relief helps all taxpayers. It especially helps those at the low end of the economic ladder. It helps American workers by letting them keep more money. And it helps small businesses, so that family-owned restaurants and startup software companies can hire more workers and provide more jobs for Americans. The tax relief package honors marriage and family by reducing the unfair marriage penalty and doubling the credit for children. It does away with one of the most unfair aspects of the Tax Code, a death tax that taxes earnings when you make them, the interest when you save them, and one more time when you die.

I, once again, thank and applaud the Members of Congress, both Republicans and Democrats, who joined together to get results on behalf of the American people. The tax relief package that was voted on today was agreed on last night, after this week's change in the balance of power in the United States Senate. And it can be a model for the work that is ahead. Tax relief was based on important principles, principles that are compassionate and conservative and principles that were preserved during the legislative process of give-and-take.

We listened to the voices of those in my party and in the Democratic Party who wanted additional help for those at the lowest end of the economic ladder. We listened, and as a result, this plan has even more help for lower income Americans. The earned-income credit is expanded for low income married couples, and the child credit is refundable for parents, providing the most help for those who earn between $10,000 and $25,000 a year.

We acted on principle. We worked together to build consensus and to get results. This is significant, and this is only the beginning.

Source: *Public Papers of the Presidents of the United States: George W. Bush* (Washington, DC: Government Printing Office), 816–817.

CRITICISM OF THE ECONOMIC GROWTH AND TAX RELIEF ACT OF 2001 (MARCH 8, 2001)

Mr. Patrick J. Kennedy (D-RI). Mr. Speaker, I rise in strong opposition to this Reaganesque, trickle-down tax cut that will not spur the economy and will further deficits.

I believe that the President's tax plan is a betrayal of the rhetoric he has used to cloak himself as a moderate. He claims that he is determined to leave no child behind, but he will leave millions behind if his plan becomes law. He talks about instilling a sense of responsibility, but proposes to saddle future generations with tremendous deficit. He touts help for working Americans while dramatically widening the income gap.

This bill, and the tax plan of which it is a part, is bad for America. I understand the House leadership's desire to pass it as quickly as possible, before the American people take a close look.

Because if they examine it, they will see that it rests on pie-in-the-sky economic forecasts. No responsible family would commit itself to spending patterns based on guesses about its income in ten years, and neither should the government.

They will realize that we have been here before, we have experimented with enormous tax cuts with disastrous consequences. The country cannot afford a return to the discredited supply-side, trickle-down economics of the 1980s.

They will notice, as the Republicans wish they wouldn't, that the tax cuts are appallingly tilted to the wealthy. Our nation has rarely been as polarized between rich and poor as it is today, yet the Bush plan would direct 43 percent of the tax cuts to people earning more than $300,000 per year.

And they will, I believe, agree that we have higher priorities as a nation than unfair, economically suspect tax cuts that will return the country to deficits and prevent investment in our people and our future.

The language of this debate is tax policy, but the substance of it runs much deeper. This debate is about priorities. It is about the sort of community we choose to make for ourselves. It is about our young children and our elderly parents, about the working poor and the uninsured, about creating an America we can be proud of.

We live in a national community that allows forty-three percent of its children to grow up poor enough to qualify for free or reduced lunches. Forty million of our citizens go without health insurance. Our public education system frequently consigns children to classes of thirty or more in crumbling buildings, without textbooks, where everyone including the students knows they will not learn what they need to know to escape poverty.

How can we possibly look at our society and conclude that addressing poverty and health insurance and education are less important than huge tax cuts? If we as a nation do reach that decision, what does it say about our American community? What does it say about us?

This choice is real. President Bush and the majority may try to spin it otherwise, but there is not room for both massive tax cuts and plans to address needs like health care, education, and Social Security in any meaningful way.

Underlying this new tax-cutting mania is the famous surplus. Let's look at that surplus. The Congressional Budget Office recently estimated the ten year surplus at five-point-six trillion dollars.

But nobody, including the CBO, knows what will happen five or ten years in the future....

It's also important to realize that more than half of the surplus predicted by the CBO belongs to the Social Security system and to Medicare. We shouldn't spend that money on tax cuts.

And we need to be prepared for future growth. The CBO estimates and the Bush tax plan assume that spending will increase only at the rate of inflation. This assumption is unrealistic because the population keeps growing. Every year there are more cars on the road, more travelers in airports, more students in college, more children eligible for Head Start, more kids in our public schools. We need to increase spending just to keep up with the increasing demand on government services.

The Bush tax plan ignores these considerations. Not only does it rely on untrustworthy numbers, it threatens to dip into Social Security and Medicare and it ignores the need for increased spending.

And nobody in Washington is talking about the ripple effect that this will have at the state level. As federal taxes are cut, state and local taxes, which are often at least partially tied to the federal tax rate, are going to have to be increased to make up the difference. In addition, because the federal government will have to cut back even further on services, pressure will mount on the states to pick up the slack. In a small state like Rhode Island, that prospect is particularly ominous.

So this bill and the Bush tax plan, first, rely on numbers nobody in their right mind would count on, and, second, spend even more than those numbers estimate to be available. If this sounds eerily familiar, that's because it is.

It unfortunately appears, however, that George W. Bush missed the lesson about the folly of supply-side economics. Not only is he going back to the supply-side policies that brought on massive deficits, he is advertising this tax cut plan as tonic for the economy. But this is just old wine in a new bottle. Long before the warning flags went up about the slowdown of the economy, he was saying gargantuan tax cuts were needed.

You can tell his plan is not intended to be an economic stimulus by its structure. If you wanted to help the economy now, you would put more money in the pockets of working class people, the people who are having trouble meeting their bills, as soon as possible. Not only are the Bush tax cuts mostly backloaded, due to take effect six or more years down the road, but they are heavily tilted towards the wealthy. They are not economic medicine, they are economic poison.

And if we do cut taxes, we must ask for whom? Under the Bush tax plan, 43 percent of the tax savings would go to the wealthiest one percent of Americans. That means people earning more than $319,000 are receiving a huge windfall. What about working folks, the forty percent of our citizens who earn less than $25,000? They get a measly 4.3 percent of the President's largesse.

The President touts his big income tax rate cuts, but four out of five American workers pay more in payroll taxes than they do in income tax. In fact, most workers earning under $35,000 per year don't pay any income tax at all. Therefore, a typical family who could really benefit from a tax cut is left out. Even the Wall Street Journal, hardly the mouthpiece of the left, has written that the affluent stand the most to gain from the Bush tax cuts.

Another pillar of the Bush tax plan is the elimination of the estate tax, or inheritance tax. This tax is currently paid only by the wealthiest two percent of families. If a couple's estate is worth less than $1.3 million, they pay no estate tax. In other words, one of the Republicans' highest priorities is $50 billion per year in tax relief for millionaires.

Even provisions that could help working people if done right are skewed towards more affluent taxpayers. The Republican plan to eliminate the marriage penalty in the last Congress was structured in such a way that 89 percent of the benefits would go to those making more than $75,000 per year. The increase in the child tax credit the President proposes is nonrefundable, which means most working class families will not see the benefit of it.

The Republicans justify this reverse Robin Hood approach by saying that the affluent get the biggest share because they pay the most in taxes. Well I say that they also gained the most from this economic expansion. The wealthy have already received the upside of the economic growth. It's time that the working men and women who made this surplus possible saw some of the benefit.

Twenty years ago we closed our eyes to hopelessly optimistic economic predictions, and allowed an affable President to gamble our future on a dubious economic theory that promised us the moon. He told us we could afford to eat dessert before dinner, we could get big tax cuts and a balanced budget. We made some decisions about priorities that led to trillions of dollars in national debt, the biggest deficits in our nation's history, more poverty, and fewer federal investments in people. Are we going to make those decisions again?

Source: *Congressional Record*, March 8, 2001, H 761–809.

ENRON (JANUARY 2002)

One of the most controversial moves of the Bush presidency has been the president's and Vice President Dick Cheney's ties to big business. No connection has been bigger and more influential than their dealings with the energy industry. When the full effects of the bankruptcy of Enron became evident, the majority of the media spent its time focusing on the administration's ties to energy corporations. In prior months, the vice president had met with various energy executives in an attempt to solve the problems of rolling blackouts in California and across America. When Enron collapsed, thousands of employees lost their pensions and their children's college funds because these were intrinsically tied to Enron's stock. In addition, twenty-one thousand people lost their jobs.

For six years straight, Enron had been *Fortune* magazine's most innovative company. Upon filing for bankruptcy, the most systematic and well-documented accounting fraud scheme was unmasked. Arthur Andersen was also convicted for its dealings with Enron. In speaking of Enron, the president only said that justice will be served and that the administration had no ties to the company nor prior knowledge of the events. At the majority of press conferences, the president avoided the subject. Many members of Congress called for a swift investigation, especially into the administration's ties to Enron's CEO Kenneth Lay and the corporation itself. The trials of Kenneth Lay and Geoffrey Skillings are scheduled to begin in

2006. Former CEO Andrew Fastow and his wife Lea Fastow, the former assistant treasurer, accepted guilty pleas in January 2004 as did former Enron treasurer Ben Glisan Jr. An independent investigation that could conclusively prove ties between Enron and the Bush administration has not yet been completed.

BUSH'S REMARKS FOLLOWING A MEETING WITH THE ECONOMIC TEAM AND AN EXCHANGE WITH REPORTERS (ENRON) (JANUARY 10, 2002)

One of the things we're deeply concerned about is that there have been a wave of bankruptcies that have caused many workers to lose their pensions, and that's deeply troubling to me. And so I've asked the Secretary of Treasury, Secretary of Labor, and Secretary of Commerce to convene a working group to analyze pensions, rules and regulations, to look into the effects of the current law on hardworking Americans, and to come up with recommendations how to reform the system to make sure that people are not exposed to losing their life savings as a result of a bankruptcy, for example.

As well, Secretary of Treasury, along with the SEC, the Fed, and the CFTC, are going to convene a working group to analyze corporate disclosure rules and regulations. In light of the most recent bankruptcy, Enron, there needs to be a full review of disclosure rules to make sure that the American stockholder or any stockholder is protected.

And so, I think this is an important part of, obviously, other investigations that are ongoing. The Justice Department announced and informed us late yesterday that they're in the process of investigating aspects of the Enron bankruptcy. The administration is deeply concerned about its effects on the economy. We're also deeply concerned about its effects on the lives of our citizenry.

Q. When was the last time you talked to either Mr. Lay or any other Enron official about the—about anything? And did discussions involve the financial problems of the company?

The President. I have never discussed with Mr. Lay the financial problems of the company. The last time that I saw Mr. Lay was at my mother's fundraising event to—for literacy, in Houston. That would have been last spring. I do know that Mr. Lay came to the White House in—early in my administration along with, I think, 20 other business leaders to discuss the state of the economy. It was just kind of a general discussion. I have not met with him personally.

Q. [Inaudible]——to inoculate and your administration politically from the fallout?

The President. Well, first of all, Ken Lay is a supporter. And I got to know Ken Lay when he was the head of the—what they call the Governor's Business Council in Texas. He was a supporter of Ann Richards in my run in 1994. And she had named him the head of the Governor's Business Council, and I decided to leave him in place, just for the sake of continuity. And that's when I first got to know Ken and worked with Ken, and he supported my candidacy.

This is—what anybody's going to find, if—is that this administration will fully investigate issues such as the Enron bankruptcy to make sure we can learn from the past and make sure that workers are protected.

Q. What can you do about pensioners—what can you do about pensioners now? Isn't that horse already out of the barn at Enron?

The President. Our group is meeting, and they will bring recommendations here. They'll look at—fully investigate what went on. My concern, of course, is for the shareholders of Enron. But my—I have great concern for the stories—for those I read about in the stories who put their life savings aside and for whatever reason, based upon some rule or regulation, got trapped in this awful bankruptcy and have lost life savings. And one of the things this group is going to do is take a good, hard look at it.

Source: *Public Papers of the Presidents of the United States: George W. Bush* (Washington, DC: Government Printing Office), 42–44.

CRITICISM OF INTRODUCED BILLS AND JOINT RESOLUTIONS (ENRON) (DECEMBER 18, 2001)

Mrs. Barbara Boxer (D-CA). Mr. President, today Senator Corzine and I are introducing the Pension Protection and Diversification Act of 2001 (PPDA).

I authored and Congress passed a bill in 1997 amending ERISA. That law bars employers from forcing employees to invest employee voluntary contributions to their 401(k) in the employer's real estate or equities with a couple of exceptions. I believe that what Enron did violated the law I authored. Enron "locked down" its pension fund for a period of time during which the company's stock plummeted. That lockdown effectively forced Enron employees to have their voluntary contributions and earnings on those contributions invested in Enron's plunging stock. That said, we are introducing the PPDA today in order to protect employees from losing their retirement savings in the future the way that Enron employees lost theirs.

Enron employees were naturally drawn to Enron stock because of its meteoric rise. But when the stock crashed, it took many Enron employees' savings down with it. There are two lessons we should learn from this situation. First, Enron workers had far too much of their individual 401(k) account plans invested in Enron stock. And second, Enron forced its employees to hold its matching contribution in Enron stock to the employee's 401(k) account for far too long.

Unfortunately, Enron employees are not alone in their 401(k) investment habits. There are far too many workers in far too many companies disproportionately investing their retirement savings in employer stock.

The "Pension Protection and Diversification Act of 2001," PPDA, will encourage workers to diversify their retirement savings and to encourage employers to give workers the power to diversify their retirement plans.

Toward that end, the bill limits to 20 percent the investment an employee can have in any one stock across their individual account plans with an employer. Studies show that employees do not diversify their investments sufficiently even when they have the power to diversify. In the Enron case, too many workers followed their employer's lead and invested too much of their own money in Enron stock. This provision, based on the opinions that financial management experts have expressed in numerous articles over the last few years, is designed to discourage that gamble.

The PPDA also limits to 90 days the time that an employer can force an employee to hold a matching employer stock contribution. Too often, the current holding period on stock ownership in a retirement plan is prohibitive because it requires participants to keep their shares far longer than might suit their needs.

There are typically two types of structures. Either the participant is required to hold the stock until a certain age, for example, at Enron they had to hold it until they were at least 50 years old or older, or the participant is required to hold the stock for a certain period of time, for example, for 5 years or longer. These mandatory holding periods require investors to hang on to their company stock for 5 to 25 years or more before they can properly divest themselves to a more diversified portfolio. This bill will put an end to that practice.

To encourage cash matching contributions rather than matching contributions in stock, the PPDA limits to 50 percent, instead of 100 percent, the tax deduction that an employer can take on a matching contribution if that contribution is made in stock. Employees often report that the employer match in employer stock to their 401(k) plans is seen as a tacit recommendation to put their voluntary contributions in employer stock as well. By encouraging cash over stock contributions, this bill gives employees the power to determine where their funds are invested.

And, last, the PPDA lowers to 35 years of age and 5 years of service the triggers that allow an employee to diversify his or her investments in an Employee Stock Ownership Plan, ESOP. The current diversification rules are too restrictive and leave employees too exposed.

ESOPs currently are required to allow employees to diversify only a portion of their employer stock; they can diversify only during limited window periods; and they can diversify only after they reach age 55 with 10 years of plan participation. So, most employees most of the time don't have current diversification rights in ESOPs. By the time they are eligible to diversify, it may be too late.

There is another factor to bear in mind. A 401(k) or other defined contribution plan that holds enough employer stock can readily be converted to an ESOP. New worker protections enacted to apply to 401(k) plans could be circumvented by converting the portion of the 401(k) plan that is investing in company stock to an ESOP or by setting up an ESOP from the outset. Allowing divestiture at an earlier date will help avoid the situation.

We exempt ESOPs from the rest of this bill because there are other factors at play, such as the basic purpose of ESOPs. I think there is justification for having 401(k) diversification rights that are far broader then ESOP diversification rights; but I am including ESOP diversification requirements in this bill because in their current form, those requirements are too narrow.

Whether or not Enron broke the law in the management of its pension plan is being determined in the courts. I believe that they did, but we must make sure all workers are protected from losing their savings before an employer's stock collapses.

Source: *Congressional Record*, December 18, 2001, S 13465–13469.

ANDEAN TRADE PREFERENCE ACT (APRIL 2002)

The Andean Trade Preference Act was enacted in 1991 under President Clinton. Its goals were to combat drug production in Bolivia, Columbia, Ecuador, and Peru. In return for combating drugs, the United States would provide trade benefits for legitimate industries in these countries. In 2002, President Bush amended the act, which is now called the Andean Trade Promotion and Drug Eradication Act. The new stipulations of the program provide free trade for nearly 6,000 different items. The president justified this act by claiming that the drug trade was intrinsically tied to the war on terror and the funding of terrorism, so by helping to combat drugs, we are also helping to combat terror. He said that free trade in the Andean Trade Act would be the necessary incentive for these nations to combat illicit drugs and promote useful industry.

Opponents of the new addition to the act claim that the free trade status will simply cause these nations to remain underdeveloped. There will be environmental degradation and an exploitation of labor rights, and it will not actually promote development and growth.

BUSH'S REMARKS ON TRADE PROMOTION AUTHORITY LEGISLATION AND EXTENSION OF THE ANDEAN TRADE PREFERENCE ACT (APRIL 4, 2002)

...I need the support of Congress on two urgent matters, trade promotion authority and the Andean Trade Preference Act. Both are awaiting action in the Senate. Both sit waiting for the Senate to act, and both are essential to the economy of the United States.

And it's also in our interest to bring confidence to countries around the world, to realize we're serious about it when we speak—countries in our own neighborhood. I mean, trade promotion authority will help us establish the free trade agreement of the Americas. And that's going to be in our country's interests, in our neighborhood's interests to do that as well.

The other thing that's important about trade for our country to understand is that people who trade with America benefit. Trade is just not a one-way street. It is a positive relationship. It's important for Americans to understand that by trade, we help people, and we help poor people, and we help people get lifted out of poverty.

And it's very important for us to always remember that a—as I mentioned earlier, a prosperous neighborhood, a democratic neighborhood, and a peaceful neighborhood is in our Nation's interests. As a matter of fact, in all due respect to nations from around the world, the best foreign policy starts with making sure your own neighborhood is prosperous and safe and sound. And I—as Colin mentioned, we have just come back—or a while ago came back from a meeting with our friends in Central America and our friends in the Andean nations. And we had very constructive dialog, but let me tell you what I heard.

I heard fine, democratically elected leaders who are troubled by the fact that the United States Congress cannot yet respond to their simple desire to trade, their desire to expand and extend the Andean Trade Preference Act. It is important for these nations—and all you've got to do is ask the Prime Minister or the Ambassadors from the four countries with whom I met—ask them the facts. That's what I ask the Senate to do. What does the Andean Trade Preference Act mean to nations that protect and defend democracy and, at the same time, fight off narcotraffickers? Trade in this instance not only is important for their economies; it is important for their security.

It is important that these nations be given market access so they can develop products other than coca, that the workers in their countries are not prone to need to work in the narcotics industry. If we're serious about dealing with narcotics, not only will we work to reduce demand, as John Walters is going to do, but we've got to work in a constructive way, in a real way, with the Andean nations. And that means not only to work on interdiction, but it means helping these nations through trade and develop substitute products—products that can be substituted for the quick buck in narcotics.

I hope Congress understands that. I hope Congress understands that the Andean Trade Preference Act is a crucial part of making sure that our hemisphere is democratic and free and stable and secure. The United States Senate needs to affirm America's trade leadership and bring both measures I've talked about today, the trade promotion authority and the Andean Trade Preference Act, to the Floor by April 22d.

Source: *Public Papers of the Presidents of the United States: George W. Bush* (Washington, DC: Government Printing Office), 563–567.

CRITICISM OF THE ANDEAN TRADE PREFERENCE ACT (APRIL 30, 2002)

Mr. Paul Wellstone (D-MN). . . . The question is how to pursue these values when we are negotiating trade agreements. The Bush administration believes that commercial property rights are primary in trade agreements, and should be enforceable with trade sanctions, and that environmental and labor rights are secondary. . . .

Our trade policy should seek to create fair trading arrangements which lift up standards and people in all nations. It should foster competition based on productivity, quality and rising living standards, not competition based on exploitation and a race to the bottom. Protection of basic labor rights, environmental, and health and safety standards are just as important, and just as valid, as any other commercial or economic objectives sought by U.S. negotiators in trade agreements. We need to be encouraging good corporate citizenship, not the flight of capital and decimation of good-paying U.S. jobs. We ought not be pitting workers in Bombay against workers in Baltimore, making them compete against one another to get a decent living. Giving them ultimatums to accept an unlivable wage, or else. It is our responsibility in trade agreements to make the global trading system fair and workable.

It is the role of national governments to establish rules within which companies and countries trade. That is what trade agreements do. They set strict rules. If a country does not enforce respect for patents, trade sanctions can be invoked. If a country allows violations of commercial rules, trade sanctions can be invoked. You can bet that U.S. companies get right in the face of our negotiators to make sure that the rules in these agreements which protect their interests are iron clad and will be strictly enforced. Of course it is one of the goals of trade agreements to advance the interests of U.S. employers. But we are elected to help ensure that those agreements allow trade to benefit the interests of a majority of Americans, not only those with significant commercial interests abroad. I would go further and say that we also even have an interest in advancing the interest of a majority of people in other countries. Development abroad means more demand for products and services that we produce.

The negative effects of NAFTA, which took effect in 1994, and the WTO, created in 1995, demonstrate the harm in failure to negotiate important safeguards in trade agreements. NAFTA's damaging results have been documented by a range of reliable observers. They include loss of jobs, suppression of wages, and attacks upon and weakening of environmental and health and safety laws. Fast-track promoters want this authority to make it easier to extend NAFTA throughout the hemisphere in a proposed Free Trade of the Americas agreement and to expand the WTO in a new round of multilateral negotiation. If we repeat our past failure to include adequate labor, environmental, and health and safety provisions in new agreements, we only condemn ourselves to seeing some of NAFTA and other trade arrangements' worst consequences again.

NAFTA is a bad agreement. But I must also note briefly the tremendous weakness of this fast-track bill itself. The bill reported by the Finance Committee requires only that trading partners enforce existing labor and environmental laws. Nowhere in this bill does it state that parties must strive to ensure that their labor and environmental laws meet international standards. Nowhere in this bill do we demand that countries make progress in protecting the rights of workers and the environment. This is unacceptable. Have we learned nothing? Shouldn't we, at a minimum, require that countries try to do better?

The bill requires only that a country enforce its own laws as they stand today, and to add insult to injury, it has a loophole that allows countries to lower labor and environmental standards with impunity. It allows for strong enforcement of the provisions on intellectual property and other commercial rights, but then provides no adequate enforcement for violations of the labor and environmental provisions. In the real world, the effect of weak labor standards coupled with no enforcement mechanism means that while a U.S. company could easily bring a case against a country for not enforcing laws on copyright protection, that same country could fail to enforce minimum wage laws or even lower the minimum wage, and neither the U.S., nor a worker who is affected, could bring a case for violation of the trade agreement. I believe this provision shows exactly whose interests this bill is meant to benefit, and it's not the working man.

And unfortunately, the drafters have not learned from the mistakes of the NAFTA agreement when it comes to investor lawsuits. Just like under NAFTA, this bill does not forbid investor lawsuits that challenge domestic laws on the grounds of expropriation—expropriation that is not even limited to the long standing legal precedent that it must involve more than just a diminution in value or loss of profits....

The draft text of the FTAA, released in April, also contains no language whatsoever, not even as a proposal, linking trade benefits to workers' rights or environmental protection. If the FTAA negotiations continue on their current path, even the modest workers' provisions now included in the Generalized System of Preferences—which currently applies to virtually every Latin American country—will be rendered moot. In regard to the on-going Chile and Singapore negotiations, the Bush Administration has apparently retreated from the Jordan agreement commitments which were to be the baseline for the labor and environmental provisions of any new agreement. It has also failed to bring forth any proposals on labor and environment in the negotiations. Chilean negotiators have told reporters that the U.S. is only asking for monetary fines to enforce labor and environmental standards. This falls short of even the modest Jordan standard.

It is clear this Administration has no commitment to labor rights or the environment in its trade policy. In fact, it doesn't see them as fundamental principles necessary to achieve fairness in the global trading system—it sees them as "potential new forms of protectionism." This is what USTR Zoellick said in a speech to business associations in New Delhi last year. He also told the audience: "We can work cooperatively to thwart efforts to employ labor and environmental concerns for protectionist purposes."

All of this leads me to the final reason I oppose moving to the fast-track bill. It is obvious this nation has more urgent priorities than debating fast-track authority. America's manufacturing industry is in a deep, long-lasting crisis that threatens the future of American prosperity.

We must address the condition of the American worker first. Trade Adjustment Assistance is critical for thousands of American workers and their families, and it should not be boot-strapped to a flawed, undemocratic bill that will cause more long-term hardship. I support the trade adjustment assistance portion of this bill. It will provide important assistance that is urgently needed. But, I believe we should address TAA separately, on its own merits.

A fair increase in the minimum wage is long overdue. This body should not be proceeding to this wrong-headed fast track measure at all. But at the least we should not be doing so in advance of considering a minimum wage increase to correct some of losses suffered as the result of our shameful inaction in the past. No one who works for a living should have to live in poverty.

Let me make a second point, which is more hard hitting. When I look at past trade agreements and some of the empirical evidence, I don't want to give up my right to amend future trade agreements which I think will have the same detrimental or an even more detrimental effect on families in the State of Minnesota or, for that matter, around the country.

It breaks my heart that we are told we can lead, but we can't lead with American values. What we are hearing from the administration and some of the proponents of this is: We have to do this. We have to lead. But we dare not—and believe me, I will have an amendment on the floor that will do this—we dare not tie this to human rights or democracy. There cannot be any mention of human rights or democracy in any of these trade agreements. We are asked to lead, but not lead with our values. We are asked to lead, but not stand for human rights. We are asked to lead, but not stand for democracy. As a first-generation American, the son of a Jewish immigrant who fled persecution from Russia, I reject that proposition.

Why aren't we focusing on the basic concerns of working families? I make this appeal on the floor of the Senate. Why aren't we talking about raising the minimum wage? Why aren't we talking about minimum wage jobs? Why aren't we talking about affordable prescription drugs? Why aren't we talking about health security for all? Why aren't we talking about how to meet these exorbitant health care expenses that small businesses can't meet? Why aren't we talking about what we are going to do as more and more of our neighbors, parents, or grandparents live to be 80 and 85 to make sure they can stay at home and live at home with dignity and not be forced to go to nursing homes? Why aren't we talking to our health care providers and to our physicians about adequate Medicare? Why aren't we talking about how we can have more support for nurses and attract more teachers? Why aren't we talking about retaining more teachers? Why aren't we talking about doing more for K-12? Why aren't we talking about affordable higher education, how we can make sure that every child by kindergarten knows how to spell his names, knows the alphabet, the colors, the shapes, and the sizes when they are ready to go to school?

Why in the world are we not focusing on these issues that are so important to the vast majority of the people we represent?

Why are we talking about fast track? Why are we calling upon all of us to give up our constitutional authority to amend trade agreements; to give up our responsibility to represent the people back in our States in case these trade agreements are antithetical to their rights as workers, or to their environment, or to their safety, or to their children; or to the rights of consumers?

I don't think there is a great commitment on the part of this administration on behalf of the environment, consumers, or ordinary people who do not have all the capital and who make the huge contributions. I don't see a whole lot of commitment.

Source: *Congressional Record,* April 30, 2002, S 3530–3555.

JOBS AND GROWTH TAX RELIEF RECONCILIATION ACT (MAY 2003)

When the president signed the Tax Relief Act of 2001, many thought that it would be the end of tax reductions by the Bush administration. The terrorist attacks of September 11 and the War in Iraq have exhausted any surplus and brought the United States back into deficit spending. This situation explains why many were shocked when the president introduced the Jobs and Growth Tax Relief Reconciliation Act of 2003.

This act called for decreasing income tax, granting an additional $400 per child credit and a large reduction in capital gains. The majority of Congress agreed with the increase in child credit, but the debate ensued over capital gains and other measures that helped large corporations. The president and congressional Republicans said these measures were necessary to promote growth and create jobs. Democrats, on the other hand, said that this act would only put the United States further into debt, and allow for corporations to have even larger tax breaks.

BUSH'S REMARKS ON SIGNING THE JOBS AND GROWTH TAX RELIEF RECONCILIATION ACT OF MAY 28, 2003 (MAY 28, 2003)

... With my signature, the Jobs and Growth Tax Relief Reconciliation Act of 2003 will deliver substantial tax relief to 136 million American taxpayers.

We are helping workers who need more take-home pay. We're helping seniors who rely on dividends. We're helping small-business owners looking to grow and to create more new jobs. We're helping families with children who will receive immediate relief. By ensuring that Americans have more to spend, to save, and to invest, this legislation is adding fuel to an economic recovery. We have taken aggressive action to strengthen the foundation of our economy so that every American who wants to work will be able to find a job.

The Jobs and Growth Act reduces Federal income taxes across the board. And today the Internal Revenue Service will post new withholding tax tables so that employers can begin leaving more money in the paychecks of American workers, starting next month.

The Jobs and Growth Act increases the per-child tax credit from $600 to $1,000. So today I'm directing the Department of Treasury to issue checks of up to $400 per child to 25 million eligible families. And those checks will begin arriving in July.

The benefits of the Jobs and Growth Act will also go to investors. The top capital gains tax rate will be reduced by 25 percent, which will encourage more investment and risk taking, and that will help in job creation.

The bill also allows for dividend income to be taxed at a lower rate. This will encourage more companies to pay dividends, which in itself will not only be good for investors but will be a corporate reform measure....

We're delivering substantial tax relief to small-business owners and entrepreneurs.

This law reflects a commonsense economic principle: The best way to have more jobs is to help the people who create new jobs, and those are the small-business owners of America.

When people have more money, they can spend it on goods and services. And in our society, when they demand an additional good or a service, somebody will produce the good or a service. And when somebody produces that good or a service, it means somebody is more likely to be able to find a job.

Increased hiring happens gradually, but we're on the path to greater job creation across this country. We know that tax relief is going to help this economy because it has done so in the past. The tax relief we passed in 2001 helped make the recession one of the shallowest in American history. It gave millions of families needed relief during a difficult time for our country. It helped many entrepreneurs to pursue their dreams.

That's what America's all about, providing opportunity. The bill I'm going to sign provides opportunity for millions of Americans across this country. And the more opportunity there is, the more likely it is somebody is going to find work in this country.

And now, with this bold legislation, we're sending a clear message to the doubters, the doubters that Washington can respond. We can respond. We can respond in a positive way. We're building on the strengths of our economy so that everybody who wants to work can find a job in this great country.

Source: *Public Papers of the Presidents of the United States: George W. Bush* (Washington, DC: Government Printing Office), 666–669.

CRITICISM OF THE JOBS AND GROWTH RECONCILIATION TAX ACT OF 2003 (MAY 9, 2003)

Mr. Benjamin L. Cardin (D-MD). Mr. Speaker, I thank the gentleman from New York for yielding me this time.

Make no mistake about it, this bill is extreme and reckless. Mr. Speaker, $550 billion-plus, every dollar must be borrowed. The Republican budget, by its own numbers, doubles the national debt from $6 trillion to $12 trillion over the next 10 years. Two-thirds of the relief on the capital gains and on the dividend exclusion goes to those people who have incomes over $200,000. Yet, not one dime for the unemployed.

Yes, we have an urgent need. We have an urgent need to act to extend unemployment insurance benefits that expire at the end of this month. That is immediate, fiscally responsible. We have the money in our trust account, and it will help create jobs. Two million Americans in the next 6 months will exhaust their State unemployment insurance benefits and will get no relief.

This bill is extreme, it is reckless, and it is wrong.

Source: *Congressional Record,* May 9, 2003, H 3864–3956.

STEEL TARIFFS (NOVEMBER 2003)

In March 2002, President Bush placed tariffs on imported steel to protect the domestic steel industry. The resulting issuing, and then the lifting, of the tariffs nine months later created much controversy, not only in the United States, but in the international arena as well.

Since at least thirty U.S. steel companies had filed for bankruptcy in the recent past, Bush attempted to protect the industry by increasing the price of steel. But steel tariffs placed only an additional 8–30 percent cost on the price of foreign steel despite the fact that U.S. steel companies had wanted a 40 percent increase, and because of the North America Free Trade Agreement, Canada and Mexico were exempt from the tariffs.

Immediately after the issuance of steel tariffs by Bush, the European Union issued retaliatory tariffs on U.S. steel to protect its own steel industry. The case of the steel tariffs was brought to the World Trade Organization in late fall 2002. The WTO decided that tariffs amounted to illegal barriers against free trade and ordered both sides to lift them. Upon hearing the verdict, Bush decided to lift the tariffs at the beginning of December 2003, drawing much criticism from his opponents as well as the automobile and steel industries.

Many believed that the tariffs were counterproductive and actually decreased economic production. Although the tariffs may have saved a few companies in the short run, they would ultimately have caused more companies to file for bankruptcy.

BUSH'S REMARKS ON STEEL TARIFFS (NOVEMBER 14, 2003)

Q. Can I ask a question about trade?
The President. Please, yes. Let me guess. [Laughter]

Q. You had a ruling on Monday——
The President. We did.

Q. ——which was not favorable to the U.S. decision last year. Are you going to lift the tax?
The President. Well, let me kind of review the bidding right quick on this issue. The International Trade Commission ruled that imports were harming the industry. Therefore, I felt obligated to take a look at that ruling and make a decision based upon that ruling, which as you know, I did. And we're now in the process of looking at a lot of things. One, of course, is whether or not the respite given helped the industry to restructure and to the extent at which it did restructure.

To answer—a very short answer—I am listening, looking, and we'll decide at an appropriate time. I haven't made up my mind yet.

Source: *Public Papers of the Presidents of the United States: George W. Bush* (Washington, DC: Government Printing Office), 1601–1611.

CRITICISM OF THE STEEL TARIFFS (JULY 16, 2003)

Mr. Lamar Alexander (R-TN). The backfire could not be coming at a worse time. As our economy recovers—and I believe that it is—the last thing our country needs is a wave of plant closings in the auto and auto parts industry. But that is exactly what will happen if the steel tariffs continue. The tariffs have become a job killer in the United States and a jobs growth program for Korea, Japan, Germany, and other countries that produce quality auto parts.

In March 2002, the Bush administration imposed tariffs of up to 30 percent on 10 different categories of steel imported from Europe, Asia, and South America. The tariffs may have saved a few steel-producing jobs for the time being. But since their institution in March 2002, the steel tariffs have already destroyed nearly as many jobs in the steel-consuming companies of America as exist in the entire domestic steel-producing industry.

If these steel tariffs continue through the years 2004 and 2005, as scheduled, there will be a wave of plant closings across Tennessee and other steel-consuming States, especially among auto parts suppliers. Ironically, many of the steel-producing jobs themselves will also disappear for two reasons: One, when the tariffs eventually end, the protected and inefficient steel mills will find they are unable to compete in the world marketplace. And second, the demand in this country for this kind of steel will have dropped because automakers and auto parts suppliers will be buying parts overseas instead of buying U.S. steel to make parts in the U.S.A.

Fortunately, the President has an opportunity in September to review the decision that he made in March 2002 to impose steel tariffs. I respectfully urge him to chalk this one up to experience, to acknowledge that this exercise proves once again that protective tariffs are self-defeating and usually boomerang and to finally end the tariffs. Ending the tariffs would allow America's steel-consuming auto parts manufacturers and other American manufacturers a fair chance to make their products in the U.S.A. instead of overseas.

In addition, steel companies broke their contracts in order to charge higher prices to auto parts suppliers. The auto parts suppliers then turned to their customers, the big automobile companies, and tried to pass along these price increases. The answer from the auto companies was: Sorry, we are cutting costs; we are not increasing them. So because the auto suppliers could not raise prices to cover increased costs, they suffered losses, and they began to lay off employees. In a few instances, entire plants closed.

Both the automakers and the auto parts suppliers began to consider the next logical step: looking offshore in another country for a place to build parts where steel is cheaper and is pegged at the global market price, not an artificial price as it is here.

Most small American manufacturers live on the edge. They are constantly under pressure to cut costs, and if costs cannot be cut, they cut a job or two. And if cutting a job or two does not do it, the only option is to move all the jobs overseas where costs are lower. It is that or go out of business.

Since the United States tariffs do not apply to auto parts, only to the steel material, the auto parts suppliers will do only what they can do: Make the parts in Japan and ship them to the Nissan plant in Tennessee at a much lower cost than what they can make in Tennessee using United States steel.

This means small manufacturing plant after small manufacturing plant in small American town after small American town in State after State in 2004 will be closing their doors and shipping those good paying jobs with benefits to Korea, to Germany, to China, and to Japan. These same jobs that more than any other factor helped my State of Tennessee become prosperous will be gone, and I am afraid it will be hard to get them back.

Let me say just a word about steel-consuming jobs, like auto suppliers, versus steel-producing jobs, like steel plants. This tariff is a good-faith effort by the administration to save jobs in U.S. steel mills. There are more than 200,000 of these steel-producing jobs nationwide.

Here is the backfire. According to a study by Dr. Joseph Francois and Laura Baughman, almost 200,000 Americans in steel-consuming industries have lost their jobs in the last year since the imposition of the steel tariffs.

Our President, George Bush, is working hard to improve this economy. I am his strong supporter. I believe he is on the right track. I believe his jobs growth plan is working. I want him to succeed. I believe the economy is beginning to recover, and the last thing we need is any new cost on a major segment of American manufacturers that slows this economy's growth down.

I fear if the steel tariffs stay on as scheduled that we will see wave after wave of plant closings in the automobile industry across this State, in Tennessee, Ohio, Florida, Michigan, Pennsylvania, West Virginia, New Mexico, Illinois, Iowa, Wisconsin, Minnesota, Washington, and we do not want to see that. So I respectfully hope as the President comes to September and sees this opportunity, he will say: "I did my best. I made a good-faith effort to help save those steel-producing jobs. It has not worked. It has backfired. It is the wrong policy, and the best thing I can do for the American worker is to end the steel tariffs."

Source: *Congressional Record*, July 16, 2003, S 9484–9486.

SOCIAL SECURITY REFORM (JANUARY 2005)

A hot button topic for every presidential race in the past twenty years has been social security reform. The 2000 election was no exception: both candidates vowed to make changes that would ensure the continuation of social security benefits for future generations. Many feared that President Bush's plan would endanger the future of social security, as well as potentially deplete current funding for the system. The president proposed that every tax-paying citizen be able to use part of their FICA tax to invest into personal savings accounts. In effect, there would be a partial privatization of social security. The president and his supporters claimed that privatization would allow the youth of today to receive social security benefits when they retire while still retaining adequate funds for those who are currently receiving benefits.

Opposition to the privatization of social security was abundant. Many critics claimed that those with personal brokers and access to financial advice would have more money than hard-working blue-collar citizens. Furthermore, privatization was seen as risky in comparison to the current system. Neither side believes the current system is adequate, but this is where the agreement ends.

BUSH'S REMARKS IN A DISCUSSION ON SOCIAL SECURITY REFORM (JANUARY 11, 2005)

The President. . . . I know this is an issue that some would rather not be talking about. It's an issue that is kind of—I think some think has got too much political danger attached to it, and so therefore let's just kind of, maybe, move it down to the next group of people coming to Washington, or maybe things will get better by ignoring it. That's not what I think. And today I want to talk about why we have an issue with Social Security, why I believe those of us who have been elected to office have an obligation to do something about it, and then I want—and give some ideas, some constructive ideas to Congress as to how to deal with the issue, and then I want others to share with me their ideas.

First, let me tell you how much, I understand, Social Security has meant for generations of Americans. I mean, Franklin Roosevelt, in thinking boldly, envisioned a Social Security system where Social Security would help seniors with their retirement. And the system worked for a lot of people. And it's been a—an incredible achievement, if you think about a piece of legislation being relevant for nearly 70 years.

The problem is, is that times have changed since 1935. Then, most women did not work outside the house, and the average life expectancy was about 60 years old, which, for a guy 58 years old, must have been a little discouraging. Today, Americans, fortunately, are living longer and longer. I mean, we're living way beyond 60 years old, and most women are working outside the house. Things have shifted.

The Social Security system is not a personal savings account. The Social Security system is not an account where money is earned. The Social Security system is an account where money comes out to pay for retirees and is put in the system by people who are working. And that's changed. More and more retirees have taken out money relative to the number of people putting money in. In the fifties, there were 16 workers for every beneficiary, so the system was in pretty good shape. Today, there's three workers for every beneficiary. Relatively quickly, there's going to be two workers for every beneficiary. And that's a problem. And that's a problem because in the year 2018, in order to take care of baby boomers like me and—some others I see out there—the money going out is going to exceed the money coming in.

That's not a good thing. It means that you're either going to have to raise the taxes of people or reduce the benefits. And the longer you wait, the more severe the pain is going to be to fulfill the promise for a younger generation of workers coming up. As a matter of fact, by the time today's workers who are in their mid-twenties begin to retire, the system will be bankrupt. So if you're 20 years old, in your mid-twenties, and you're beginning to work, I want you to think about a Social Security system that will be flat bust, bankrupt, unless the United States Congress has got the willingness to act now. And that's what we're here to talk about, a system that will be bankrupt.

Now, I readily concede some would say, "Well, it's not bankrupt yet. Why don't we wait until it's bankrupt?" The problem with that notion is that the longer you wait, the more difficult it is to fix. You realize that this system of ours is going to be short the difference between obligations and money coming in by about $11 trillion, unless we act. And that's an issue. That's trillion with a "T." That's a lot of money, even for this town.

And so I'm looking forward to working with Congress to act. We've got an expert from the Social Security system that will talk about "the problem." And I'm going to talk about "the problem." You know, "the problem" is that some in Congress don't see it as "the problem." They just kind of think that maybe things will be okay. But the structure of Social Security is such that you can't avoid the fact that there is a problem. And now is the time to get something done.

Now, I've talked about this, and I want the people to clearly understand, if you're a senior receiving your Social Security check, nothing is going to change. Those days of politicizing Social Security, I hope, are in the past. A lot of people who ran for office and if they even mentioned the word Social Security, there would be TV ads and fliers and people knocking on doors saying, "So-and-so is going to ruin

Social Security for you." There is plenty of money in the system today to take care of those who have retired or near retirement. The issue really is for younger folks.

I said we're not going to run up the payroll taxes. I think running up payroll taxes will slow down economic growth.... I think we can solve the problem without increasing payroll taxes.

I also threw out another interesting idea—it's certainly not my idea, because others have talked about it—and that is to allow younger workers, on a voluntary basis, to take some of their own money and set it aside in the form of a personal savings account, a personal savings account which is their own, a personal savings account which would earn a better rate of return than the money—their money currently held within the Social Security trust, a personal savings account which will compound over time and grow over time, a personal savings account which can't be used to bet on the lottery or a dice game or the track. In other words, there will be guidelines. There will be certain—you won't be allowed just to take that money and dump it somewhere. In other words, there will be a safe way to invest, to be able to realize the compounding rate of interest.

I've heard some say, "Well, this is risky to allow people to invest their own money." It's risky to let people—say, "You can take your money that's supposed to be for a retirement account and put it on the lottery." I realize that. But it's not risky. Federal employees—the Thrift Savings Plans invest under certain guidelines, and I don't hear them screaming, "It's risky." It makes sense to try to get a better rate of return on your money, if you expect there to be a Social Security system which is going broke. And that's what we're talking about.

Owning your own personal savings account does two other things. One, it allows you to pass on your savings to whoever you choose. You can't do that in Social Security today. If you pass away earlier than expected, that money that you put in the system is gone. And at the same time that you manage your own account, you own your own account. I love promoting ownership in America. I like the idea of encouraging more people to say, "I own my own home. I own my own business. I own and manage my health accounts, and now I own a significant part of my retirement account." Promoting ownership in America makes sense to me to make sure people continue to have a vital stake in the future of our country.

... I believe it is a vital issue. And I know that if we don't address the problem now, it will only get worse with time. And I believe there is a fundamental duty, for those of us who have been given the honor of serving the American people, to solve problems before they become acute and not to pass them on to future Presidents and future generations.

... And the fundamental question confronting the people elected to the United States Congress is, will they act? I will assure you, I'm going to ask them to act. I think that one of the reasons I'm sitting here is because I said to the people of the country, "We have an issue with Social Security. We have a problem. I think it's important to be a problem-solver. Give me 4 more years, and I intend to work with people of both parties and solve problems, and there is a problem with Social Security."

I see a problem. I also see a solution. And I realize that it's going to require bipartisan cooperation. And I look forward to working with members of both political parties in both Houses to come together and do our duty. I realize it's not going to be easy. This isn't easy. If it were easy, it would have already been done. It kind of makes it fun, though, isn't it—take on the tough jobs.

Members who will work—constructively work with us will be able to look back and say, "I did my duty. I came to Washington to be more than just a placeholder.

I came to Washington to analyze a problem, to deal with a problem, and to leave a legacy behind of fixing the problem." And so I'm looking forward to working with the Members of Congress.

Source: *Public Papers of the Presidents of the United States: George W. Bush* (Washington, DC: Government Printing Office), 39–44.

CRITICISM OF THE SOCIAL SECURITY PRIVATIZATION SCHEME (JANUARY 26, 2005)

Mr. Frank Pallone Jr. (D-NJ). Mr. Speaker, this week we had another reality check on how fiscally devastating Republican fiscal policies are on our Nation. Yesterday the Bush administration announced that the budget deficit is set to hit another record this year, a whopping $429 billion.

The President also had to admit that thanks to these new projections, he is already behind in his campaign pledge to cut the deficit in half over the next 5 years. Yet the President has no plans to alter his misguided policies that took us from record surpluses when he arrived in Washington to record deficits now.

But the President is still not finished. He has a plan that would use an additional $2 trillion in Federal funds to privatize Social Security. Enough is enough. Congressional Republicans need to stop blindly following this President before it is too late, and it is time that they abandon this risky Social Security privatization scheme.

Source: *Congressional Record,* January 26, 2005, H 202–203.

OIL DRILLING IN THE ALASKAN NATIONAL WILDLIFE RESERVE (JUNE 2005)

One of the biggest concerns facing the United States in recent times has been the increase in the price of crude oil. Democrats have placed the blame on the two-front war against terror in both Afghanistan and Iraq, while the Republicans have blamed America's dependency on foreign oil. While both arguments have their merit, it is the latter of the two that facilitated the passage of a bill to permit the drilling of oil in the Alaskan National Wildlife Reserve (ANWR).

The debate concerned whether the environmental cost was worth the amount of crude oil that would be extracted. The president claimed that while the supply is not great, it would give us another avenue if oil prices became too high or if the OPEC nations decided to cut off supply. Democrats felt the environmental damage to ANWR was too great to risk for less than a month's worth of crude oil. While drilling has not begun, increased oil prices have opened up the likelihood of the drilling to commence. While alternative fuel options are being explored, the bill that would allow oil drilling in ANWR has been passed.

BUSH'S REMARKS TO THE 16TH ANNUAL ENERGY EFFICIENCY FORUM (JUNE 15, 2005)

... The primary cause of rising gasoline prices is that the global demand for oil is growing faster than global supply. Here in America, we have become too dependent—too dependent—on the increasingly limited supply of foreign oil for our own energy needs. For many years, most of the crude oil refined in American [sic]—into gasoline in America came from domestic oil fields. In 1985, 75 percent of the crude oil used in U.S. refineries came from American sources, only about 25 percent came from abroad. Today, that equation is nearly reversed. In a relatively quick period of time, only about 35 percent of the crude oil used in U.S. refineries is produced here at home—think about that—while about 65 percent comes from foreign countries like Saudi Arabia, Mexico, Venezuela, and Canada. To compound the problem, countries with rapidly growing economies like India and China are competing for more of the world oil supply, and that drives up the global price of oil, and that makes prices of gasoline here at home even higher for our families and small businesses and farmers.

Our dependence on foreign oil is like a foreign tax on the American Dream, and that tax is growing every year. My administration is doing all we can to help ease the problem. We're encouraging oil-producing countries to maximize their production, so more crude oil is on the market to meet the demands of the world. And we're going to make sure that consumers here at home are treated fairly. There's not going to be any price gouging here in America.

But people got to understand our dependence on foreign oil didn't develop overnight, and it's not going to be fixed overnight. To solve the problem, our Nation needs a comprehensive energy policy. That's why one of the first things I did when I came to office 4 years ago was to develop a new energy strategy for America....

The second step toward making America less dependent on foreign oil is to produce and refine more crude oil here at home in environmentally sensitive ways. By far the most promising site for oil in America is the Arctic National Wildlife Refuge in Alaska. Technology now makes it possible to reach the oil reserves in ANWR by drilling on just 2,000 of the 19 million acres. Developing this tiny area could eventually yield up to a million barrels of oil a day, and that million barrels of oil a day would be—would make us less dependent on foreign sources of energy. Thanks to technology, we can reach ANWR's oil with almost no impact on land or local wildlife. To make America less dependent, Congress needs to pass a pro-growth, pro-jobs, pro-environment development of ANWR. It makes sense. It is an important part of a comprehensive strategy.

We also need to improve our ability to refine crude oil into gasoline and other products. Do you realize this? There hasn't been a single new refinery built in America since 1976. To meet our growing demand for gasoline, America now imports about a million barrels of refined gasoline every day. That means about one out of every nine gallons of gas you get at the pump is refined in a foreign country. Not only are we dependent on foreign sources of oil, we're becoming more dependent on foreign sources of gasoline.

The third step toward making America less dependent on foreign oil is to develop new alternatives to gasoline and diesel. . . .

Source: *Public Papers of the Presidents of the United States: George W. Bush* (Washington, DC: Government Printing Office), 999–1003.

CRITICISM OF THE DEFICIT REDUCTION OMNIBUS RECONCILIATION ACT OF 2005 (NOVEMBER 2, 2005)

Ms. Maria Cantwell (D-WA). I think it is important that we have a continued debate on drilling in Alaska that meets the environmental and permit processes that any drilling in America would have to meet. And that is not what we are discussing in the underlying bill.

I appreciate that this debate over the Arctic Refuge coastal plain has continued for more than 2 decades. I know the Presiding Officer and my other colleague from Alaska have spent many hours on this legislation. But this issue has continued to stir the passions of many and polarized communities across our country. That is because this debate is more than just about the Arctic Wildlife Refuge. It is not simply about protecting one of America's last remaining great treasures. Rather, it is a debate that forces us to confront our priorities. It forces us to ask basic critical questions: Where do we go from here on the future of our energy policy? What inheritance do we want to leave our children from an environmental perspective?

We all must realize that God only granted the United States less than 3 percent of the world's remaining oil reserves and we as Americans need to do more with our own ingenuity to become less dependent on foreign oil.

Imagine a future where we don't turn a blind eye to oppressive regimes in the Middle East only because they happen to control the majority of the world's remaining oil reserves, or a future where Americans can drive hybrid or hydrogen-powered SUVs that get 40, 50, or even 100 miles per gallon. That is how we want to see our future. That is how we are going to save consumers who are being hurt at the gas pump today by these unbelievably high prices.

In the future we want Americans to have the opportunity to enjoy and appreciate this unique part of Alaska. That is why I believe the amendment I am offering today talks about our national priorities. That is why this is too important a question to slide into the budget bill. This bill circumvents the processes for permitting and environmental safeguards.

It is ironic that if this legislation passes we will actually be opening up drilling in a wildlife refuge with less protections than any other drilling in any other site in America. So instead of going to greater extremes to protect a particular wildlife refuge, we are going to have the weakest standard. The American people expect more.

I hope my colleagues appreciate that there are many flawed assumptions inherent in this drilling proposal. The simple act of putting a policy on a budget bill itself, I believe, is disingenuous.

But that is not all because section 401 will almost certainly never raise the $2.4 billion that drilling proponents claim it will. That is because the measure presumes to generate these funds by splitting revenues between Alaska and the Federal Government on an even 50-50 basis. But I think my colleagues might be surprised to learn that this 50-50 legislative language may not hold up in court. We just don't know right now. We do know the State of Alaska has long maintained it is due 90 percent of all the natural resource development revenue generated from Federal land within its boundaries, and we know this remains a controversial issue. Some have suggested this proposed 50-50 split in this legislation is merely a ploy to win passage. Some have suggested that once it passes, it will be followed by a court battle from the State of Alaska to force the Federal Government into a 90-10 split of revenue. So this $2.4 billion the United States might receive would be a much different picture.

I am also concerned that many Senators may not support my amendment because they believe drilling in the refuge can be done in an environmentally benign way. They actually believe we should move forward because they think drilling in ANWR can be done in a way that is environmentally sensitive.

I think they are wrong. There is no real way to sugarcoat the fact that the oil company records on the adjacent Prudhoe Bay have been shameful. The facts speak for themselves.

According to the Alaska Department of Environmental Conservation, the Prudhoe Bay oilfields and Trans-Alaska Pipeline have caused an average of 504 spills annually—annually—on the North Slope since 1996. Through last year, these spills included more than 1.9 million gallons of toxic substances, most commonly diesel, crude oil, and hydraulic oil. It takes one spill to permanently destroy a section of this fragile arctic ecosystem. The people know this.

I also want the American people to know that the tradeoff for destroying our Nation's last great wild frontier will not be relief from skyrocketing gas prices. Our sacrifice will do little to decrease our reliance on foreign oils from countries that don't have our best intentions in mind. Here is why. The Energy Department's latest analysis estimates that even when the refuge oil hits peak production 20 years from now, it will lower gas prices by just one penny. A penny, Mr. President. That is not an estimate that I have come up with, that is the Department of Energy's own estimate.

That is not very impressive considering the fact that the constituents in my State of Washington are now paying twice as much for a gallon of gas as they did just 3 years ago.

I understand that some of my colleagues believe it is appropriate to sacrifice this area for what will amount to about 6 months' oil supply, but I think all Senators today agree that these are questions that are not part of a budget policy. They are more fundamental about the discussions of what our national energy policy should be and the future of our country.

I hope my colleagues will also begin to finally start focusing on energy policies to diversify off fossil fuel, to recognize that God gave us only 3 percent of the world's oil reserves and that the best interest of the United States is to diversify off fossil and plan for a future that lowers gas prices, plan for a future that makes us more secure on an international basis.

Source: *Congressional Record*, November 2, 2005, S 12149–12219.

ECONOMIC POLICY WEB SITES

Barnes, Fred. "The Four Horsemen of Bush Economic Policy." *The International Economy*, January 20, 2003. http://www.weeklystandard.com/Content/Public/Articles/000/000/002/122qtfrk.asp

Barro, Robert. "Bush's Economic Policies: The Bull's Eyes and Busts." *Businessweek Online*, November 4, 2002. http://www.businessweek.com/magazine/content/02_44/b3806035.htm

Bush, George W. "Jobs and Economic Growth." January 6, 2006. http://www.whitehouse.gov/infocus/economy/

CBS News. "Bush Dumps Economic Team." December 6, 2002. http://www.epi.org/content.cfm/pm20060216

CNN. "Bush Defends His Economic Policy." May 5, 2004. http://www.cnn.com/2004/ALLPOLITICS/03/10/bush.ohio/index.html

Democratic Policy Committee. "Recent Economic Data Reflect Continued Failure of President Bush's Economic Policies." October 2, 2003. http://democrats.senate.gov/dpc/dpc-new.cfm?doc_name=fs-108-1-351

"The Dismal Science Bites Back." *The Economist*, October 7, 2004. http://www.economist.com/world/na/displayStory.cfm?story_id=3262965

Edwards, Chris. "The Economic Policies of Bush and Kerry." *Cato Institute*, June 22, 2004. http://www.cato.org/dailys/06-22-04.html

Gale, William, and Samara Potter. "The Bush Tax Cut: One Year Later." *Brookings Institute Policy Brief 101*, June 2002. http://www.brookings.edu/comm/policybriefs/pb101.htm

Ifill, Gwen, "The State of the Economy." *Online News Hour*, August 13, 2002. http://www.pbs.org/newshour/bb/economy/july-dec02/forum_8-13.html

Irons, John, and Lee Price. "Bush's Tax and Budget Policies Fail to Promote Economic Growth." *Economic Policy Institute*, February 16, 2006. http://www.epi.org/content.cfm/pm20060216

Lindsey, Lawrence. "Bush Administration Economic Policy." February 21, 2001. http://fpc.state.gov/fpc/7464.htm

"Not Exactly Major League: George Bush's Economic Team Still Looks Weak." *The Economist*, March 17, 2005. http://www.economist.com/displaystory.cfm?story_id=3773191

Sawicky, Max. "Collision Course: The Bush Budget and Social Security." *Economic Policy Institute*, March 25, 2006. http://www.epinet.org/content.cfm/bp156

Solman, Paul, and Glenn Hubbard. "Bush Economics." *A News hour with Jim Lehrer Transcript*, August 30, 2004. http://www.pbs.org/newshour/bb/economy/july-dec04/bushecon.html

Trei, Lisa. "Experts Spar Over Merits of Bush, Kerry Economic Plans during Recent Debate." *Stanford Review*, October 12, 2004. http://newsservice.stanford.edu/news/2004/october13/econdebate-1013.html

ECONOMIC POLICY REFERENCE ARTICLES AND BOOKS

Altman, Daniel. *Neoconomy: George Bush's Revolutionary Gamble with America's Future*. New York: Public Affairs, 2004.

Conniff, Ruth. "The Budget Surrender." *The Progressive* 65, no. 6 (June 2001): 12.

Galuszka, Peter. "Where Is Our Economic Policy." *The Chief Executive*, June 2005.

Hilliard, Bryan, Tom Lansford, and Robert P. Watson, eds. *George W. Bush: Evaluating the President at Midterm*. Albany, NY: SUNY Press, 2004.

Hughes, Kent. *Building the Next American Century: The Past and Future of American Economic Competitiveness*. Baltimore, MD: Johns Hopkins University Press, 2005.

Judis, John. "Bush League Economics." *The American Prospect* 12, no. 2 (January 28, 2002): 10.

McIntrye, Robert. "Supply-Siders Go to War." *The American Prospect* 12, no. 19 (November 5, 2001): 9.

Office of Management and Budget. "A Blueprint for New Beginnings: A Responsible Budget for America's Priorities." Washington, DC: Executive Office of the President, 2001.

Ruffin, David. "What the Next Election Means for You: Our Economists Review the Impact of Bush's Economic Policies and Offer Their Outlook on the Presidential Race." *Black Enterprise*, June 1, 2004.

Schier, Steve, ed. *High Risk and Big Ambition: The Presidency of George W. Bush*. Pittsburgh, PA: University of Pittsburgh Press, 2004.

Snepper, Jeff. "Analyzing the Bush Savings Proposals." *USA Today* 132 (July 2003): 59.

DOMESTIC POLICY

INTRODUCTION

In January 2001, President George W. Bush issued Executive Order 13199, which established the White House Office of Faith-Based and Community Initiatives. This office was intended to help expand the role of faith-based and other nonprofit organizations trying to meet social needs in their communities. Bush argued that faith-based organizations are critical in meeting the needs of the poor. The goal, according to the Bush administration, was to make these organizations a partner of, and not a replacement for, the government. The primary purpose of the policy change was to permit religious groups to compete on a level playing field with nonreligious organizations for federal funds if those funds were to be used for promoting welfare by supporting families or neighborhoods or fighting public ills like crime, addiction, and poverty. The Bush administration also hoped that this policy change would stimulate private contributions to nonprofit, faith-based organizations by expanding possible tax deductions and creating other incentives.

The president was advocating lifting government barriers to faith-based and other community service programs. Specifically, he proposed to accomplish this by expanding the Charitable Choice principle. Charitable Choice was part of the Welfare Reform Act of 1996. Administration over social service programs for the poor was moved from the federal government to the states, and the states, in turn, were allowed to hand over responsibility for these services to religious organizations. With the Bush plan, these groups could now also compete directly for federal government funds.

By 2005 President Bush was hailing the progress of the Faith Based Initiatives Act. In fiscal year 2004, for example, the federal government awarded $2 billion in competitive grants to faith-based nonprofit organizations. Bush also proposed further tax incentives to faith-based organizations. He also proposed expanding the Charitable Choice provision in another way: he argued that faith-based organizations should be allowed to use the religious backgrounds of applicants as a criterion for determining hiring decisions, something many consider to be a violation of nondiscrimination employment laws. He also argued that religious organizations should not have to give up their religious mission to receive federal funds, even as it influences the spending of that money. In 2006 President Bush signed an executive order creating the Center for Faith-Based and Community Initiatives in the Department of Homeland Security (DHS). The Center is meant to remove obstacles to faith-based and other community organizations from participating in Homeland Security operations, such as providing disaster relief and recovery services.

Additionally, President Bush created the USA Freedom Corps (USAFC), which was intended to build on the charitable outpouring of Americans after the 9/11 terrorist attacks. Like the Peace Corps, but focused on United States, the USA Freedom Corps is intended to build an American culture of service and volunteering. Bush announced the formation of the USAFC in his 2002 State of the Union address, a few months after the attacks, calling on Americans to serve a cause greater than themselves. He also called on Americans to make a commitment of at least two years to service.

On a different front, President George W. Bush initially banned stem cell research, but a few months later partially reversed this position by allowing research on the few existing lines of stem cells. Opponents of this policy considered this compromise far from adequate. Among these opponents was the family of former Republican president Ronald Reagan. Nancy Reagan believed that this research could be used to find a cure for Alzheimer's, the disease that slowly killed her husband, and she argued that President Bush should relax restrictions on this research. Many in Congress backed her stand. Fifty-eight senators, primarily Democrats, sent the president a letter making the same argument.

This polarizing issue gained significant attention in Congress, but there did not appear to be sufficient majorities to either tighten or loosen the current restrictions. In 2005, a bill to loosen the restrictions gained significant support, and was even backed by the Republican Senate majority leader, Bill Frist. But it failed to pass. With Congress effectively deadlocked, the issue has shifted to the state legislatures. Several states have begun to allow stem cell research, bypassing restrictions at the federal level.

President Bush was much more successful in instituting policies intended to fight terrorism. One of the critical failures that led to the attacks of 9/11 was the lack of effective communication between federal agencies like the CIA and FBI about the developing threat. The Department of Homeland Security was established to bring dozens of agencies with missions related to homeland security under a single roof in addition to administering the federal government's efforts to avoid another terrorist attack. The agency was also responsible for the federal response to all major emergencies, including those caused by natural forces.

The USA PATRIOT Act was also enacted to improve the ability of the United States to stop another terrorist attack. An enormous piece of legislation, the act included a number of highly controversial provisions such as increasing the ability of law enforcement agencies to wiretap individuals suspected of possible terrorist activities, beginning a program for monitoring foreign students, and allowing the FBI to obtain information on peoples' library or bookstore records if they were being investigated for possible terrorist activities. Despite its detractors, the act was renewed in 2006 with overwhelming support in the House and Senate. It raced through Congress with little dissent and remarkable speed.

Nonetheless, critics of this act have been vocal. Dennis Kucinich, a member of Congress who ran for the Democratic presidential nomination in 2004, introduced legislation that would have repealed more than ten sections of the act. Calling it the "Benjamin Franklin True Patriot Act," the Kucinich bill would have outlawed "sneak and peak" wiretapping, searches of library and other records without a warrant, and the detention or deportation of noncitizens without proper judicial review. The bill never gained much support in Congress.

The American Civil Liberties Union, or ACLU, filed a lawsuit challenging provisions of the Electronic Communications Privacy Act, which allows the FBI to obtain customer records from Internet and telephone companies if the information is being used for a counterterrorism investigation. In *ACLU vs. Ashcroft* (2004), the ACLU argued successfully that the act violated the First and Fourth Amendments to the Constitution. Specifically, it was argued that these companies should be able to disclose that they received a subpoena, and that their right to do so outweighs the government's need for secrecy in an investigation.

Along with criticisms of the USA PATRIOT Act came complaints about the handling of presidential papers. According to the Presidential Records Act, passed in 1978, the government is required to release presidential papers to the public twelve years after the end of an administration. In 2001, President Bush signed an executive order that allowed sitting and former presidents to block this release. Even in a case in which the former president wants the records released, the executive order allows the sitting president to prevent it. The White House has defended this decision by arguing that the restrictions balance the public's right to know with national security concerns. Critics counter that the public's right to know has been replaced by presidents' choice to suppress information. Congress has begun consideration of a bill to overturn the executive order.

Before the September 11 terrorist attacks, President Bush had made education reform a top priority. He argued that the federal government should define standards for schools, hold people accountable based on those standards, and provide school districts resources to meet those standards. Toward this end, Bush signed the No Child Left Behind legislation in January 2002. The administration argued that the legislation gives more freedom to state and local communities and provides more choice to parents, and at the same time promotes proven education methods. Republicans tend to praise the law, saying that it toughens standards for schools, teachers, and students. Democrats generally disagree. They argue that the rules are too rigid and that the federal government has not allocated enough funds to make the requirements feasible. Critics also argue that the law is unrealistic because it requires yearly progress from every subgroup of students, including those with disabilities or who speak English as a second language.

Since it is argued that there is a relationship between drug use and school failure, it is no surprise that President Bush also unveiled a National Drug Control Policy in 2002. This policy is based on three core principles: discouraging drug use, healing addicts, and disrupting the drug trade. Part of the strategy is education. Bush argues that outreach programs have helped teach Americans that recreational drugs can harm an individual's health as well as society at large. Part of the strategy is to cut the availability of drugs, therefore making them both harder to locate and more expensive.

The environment has been a difficult issue for the second Bush administration, as seen with the Yucca Mountain proposal. In 1983, the Department of Energy listed the mountain in Nevada as one of nine possible sites to store waste from commercial nuclear power plants. Nevada officials loudly opposed the idea from the beginning. Bush's energy secretary, Spencer Abraham, reopened the issue by arguing that a repository there would serve a compelling national interest for a stable energy supply, homeland security, and national defense. Nevada lawmakers have responded negatively to the Yucca Mountain proposal, and have threatened lawsuits claiming that transporting nuclear waste is dangerous, that the safety of storage at the site has not been well established, and that the plan's implementation would harm business in Las Vegas.

President Bush nonetheless went ahead with the proposal, asking Congress to select Yucca Mountain to store 77,000 tons of highly radioactive nuclear waste. With a 306 to 117 vote, the House of Representatives accepted the Yucca Mountain plan. The Senate followed, voting sixty to thirty-nine in a key procedural vote in favor of the project. By 2010, storage of nuclear waste at the site might begin.

President Bush also signed a new round of campaign finance reform into law, though he argued that the bill was far from perfect. The previous law had imposed limits on the size of "hard money" contributions, or money that would be spent directly on campaigning. However, individuals, unions, and corporations could give unlimited amounts in "soft money" contributions, which was money earmarked for party building, voter registration, and get-out-the-vote efforts. The new bill, generally referred to as the "McCain-Feingold Act" in the Senate, raised the limits on hard money contributions, but it also eliminated soft money contributions.

The campaign finance reform measures signed into law by President Bush have a wide range of opponents, including both liberal and conservative interest groups. One of the most common arguments against this law is that it is unconstitutional; opponents argue that limiting money to campaigns is a violation of the right to free speech. However, in 2003, the Supreme Court upheld the main provisions of the law, effectively upholding the right of Congress to limit contribution to candidates.

An unexpected crisis that the Bush administration had to confront was that of the Shuttle Columbia. Columbia disintegrated during its reentry just minutes before its scheduled landing at the Kennedy Space Center in Florida. With seven crewmembers lost in the crash, questions were raised about the future of the International Space Station. NASA officials immediately began an investigation.

The Columbia Accident Investigation Board quickly recognized that the accident was likely not an anomaly, but rather a product of the culture of the space program as well as NASA's history. The report focused on changes to organizational characteristics that could improve the safety of the inherently risky Space Shuttle program. They also offered a list of other recommendations, including that the space program focus more on external warnings of potential danger.

A key crisis for the Bush administration was the Valerie Plame affair. In his 2003 State of the Union address, President Bush justified a possible invasion of Iraq on the grounds that, according to British intelligence, the Hussein regime had attempted to buy uranium from Niger that could be used for creating nuclear weapons. The evidence for this statement was based partially on the research of Joseph Wilson. At the time that the alleged attempt to buy uranium occurred, Ambassador Wilson was sent to Niger to determine if the reports were true. He reported that the evidence of this claim was weak at best. After the invasion, Wilson made his report public, claiming that the administration had ignored the evidence in order to bolster its case for war. Soon after Wilson made this damning claim, conservative columnist Robert Novak published an article revealing that Valerie Plame, Wilson's wife, is a CIA agent.

The investigation into the leak of this classified information quickly pointed toward central officials in the Bush administration. Karl Rove, Bush's key political advisor, was repeatedly brought before a grand jury to explain his role, though in the end he was not indicted. Lewis Libby, the vice president's chief of staff, was not so lucky. He was indicted on five counts of obstruction of justice and perjury. Others pointed to Vice President Cheney as a possible co-conspirator. Regardless of how the information was leaked to Novak, the affair gave many the impression that this administration was willing to go so far as to break the law in order to achieve its political goals.

In another appointment, President Bush named John Negroponte, the U.S. ambassador to Iraq, as the government's first national intelligence director. As intelligence director, Negroponte's primary job is to prevent the types of intelligence failures that kept the government from stopping the September 11 terrorist attacks. To accomplish this, his responsibilities include bringing together fifteen spy agencies that have a history of being highly competitive with each other. At the same time, Negroponte has to vie for power against Secretary of Defense Donald H. Rumsfeld, CIA Director Porter Goss, and other intelligence leaders. The choice of Negroponte drew praise from the high-ranking Democratic and Republican members of the House and Senate intelligence committees.

One of the major responsibilities of the intelligence director is to oversee domestic spying and wiretaps. In 2002, the president signed a secret order that authorized the National Security Agency to wiretap telephone conversations between people living in America—both U.S. citizens and foreign nationals—as well as people overseas. The administration defended its actions, arguing that the program was necessary for monitoring conversations and other communications between potential terrorists in the United States and operatives of al Qaeda. Instead of following standard due process, the NSA's domestic spying program was monitored by a secret court that met at the Department of Justice and approved requests for wiretaps and searches. Opponents argued loudly that this type of program is clearly illegal, since it violates Americans' basic civil rights, including their right to privacy.

Hurricane Katrina was another critical, and damaging, moment for the Bush administration. After the September 11 attacks, the administration argued vigorously that it was more capable of handling large-scale emergencies than its Democratic rivals could. Katrina called that claim into question. As the storm approached, Bush directed the secretary of homeland security, Michael Chertoff, to coordinate a federal response. Chertoff designated Michael Brown, head of the Federal Emergency Management Agency (FEMA), to lead that operation. However, the storm devastated large sections of Louisiana and Mississippi, including New Orleans, when rising flood waters breached the levees separating the city from a neighboring lake. Thousands are dead or missing because of the storm, and the damage amounted to billions of dollars.

The federal response was sluggish and appeared both incompetent and indifferent. President Bush was recorded on television congratulating Brown for his excellent job, which was followed by news reports that he had little background in emergency management. Bush had also argued that no one could have predicted that the levees would be breached—eerily similar to his claims a few years earlier that no one could imagine terrorists hijacking planes and flying them into buildings—but videos were subsequently leaked to the press showing Bush being briefed about the storm, including the likelihood of a levee breach.

Appointments to the Supreme Court brought mixed results for President Bush. After Sandra Day O'Connor announced her plan to retire from the court, Bush appointed Judge John Roberts to replace her. Then, after Chief Justice William Rehnquist passed away, Bush withdrew Roberts's nomination and then nominated him again, this time to replace Rehnquist as the head of the court. The Senate Judiciary Committee voted thirteen to five in support of Roberts, and the nomination passed the Senate floor easily, with Republicans unified behind him and Democrats split.

After withdrawing the Roberts nomination to replace O'Connor, Bush nominated Harriet Miers for this position. The Miers' candidacy was suggested by Harry Reid, the minority leader of the Senate, but it ran into problems almost immediately. Opponents argued that she was simply a Bush confidant, not someone with the background to hold a position on the Supreme Court. While an attorney, she had never even been a judge. Early meetings with senators went badly; the ranking Democrat and Republican on the Senate Judiciary Committee also sent back her questionnaire, complaining that her answers were insufficient and even insulting. The key pressure, though, seemed to be coming from the right. Many conservatives were particularly upset that Bush chose Miers, someone without a legal record, instead of a seasoned jurist who would clearly vote along conservative lines on the court.

After the administration hastily withdrew the Miers candidacy, Bush selected Judge Samuel Alito as his nominee for associate justice. Alito was a known conservative judge with firm views on abortion, federalism, and religion in the public sphere. Liberal groups accused Bush of bowing to the most extreme elements of his party, and Democrats chose to fight this nomination much harder than that of Roberts. Reflecting a partisan split, Alito was confirmed as the Supreme Court's 110th justice by a Senate vote of fifty-eight to forty-two.

CONCLUSIONS

It is clear that the Bush administration faced its share of domestic controversies in his first six years in office. They range from responses to the terrorist attacks on the World Trade Center to natural disasters such as Hurricane Katrina. The controversies often revolve around what the president knew about these situations, when he knew it, and how he acted on the information he had. President Bush also proposed major reforms to the nation's intelligence structure and its handling of senior citizens through the Social Security program. Since the results of these decisions will take time to come to fruition, it will not be possible to fully evaluate many of his initiatives for years to come.

FAITH-BASED AND COMMUNITY INITIATIVES (JANUARY 2001)

The first action that President Bush took on entering office was to enact the Faith-based Initiatives policy. Faith-based Initiatives are subsidies by the government to religious groups to provide social services and represent the first time that federal monies were used for religious affiliated organizations. The initiative required that faith-based organizations follow nondiscriminatory regulations and the Equal Opportunity Act. President Bush felt that the Faith-based Initiatives were a good way to more heavily involve the community while providing federal funds for much-needed social programs.

The opposition to this came in two forms: from the Christian right and from House Democrats. The objections by the Christian right focused on taking away religious organizations' ability to combine Scripture with social programs. They argued that these programs have always had a religious connotation, providing spiritual guidance as well as practical aid. Under the new federal statute, groups could no longer incorporate their religious faith with their community service. House Democrats objected for a different reason. They believed that Faith-based Initiatives would drain away money for federal social welfare programs such as Medicaid, Medicare, and Social Security. They also felt that Faith-based Initiatives were a breach between the church and the state.

BUSH'S REMARKS ANNOUNCING THE FAITH-BASED INITIATIVE (JANUARY 29, 2001)

It is one of the great goals of my administration to invigorate the spirit of involvement and citizenship. We will encourage faith-based and community programs without hanging their mission. We will help all in their work to change hearts while keeping a commitment to pluralism. I approach this goal with some basic principles. Government has important responsibilities for public health or public order and civil rights, and Government will never be replaced by charities and community groups. Yet when we see social needs in America, my administration will look first to faith-based programs and community groups, which have proven their power to save and change lives. We will not fund the religious activities of any group, but when people of faith provide social services, we will not discriminate against them.

As long as there are secular alternatives, faith-based charities should be able to compete for funding on an equal basis and in a manner that does not cause them to sacrifice their mission. And we will make sure that help goes to large organizations and to small ones, as well. We value large organizations with generations of experience. We also value neighborhood healers, who have only the scars and testimony of their own experience.

Tomorrow I will begin turning these principles into a legislative agenda. I will send to Congress a series of ideas and proposals. Today I want to raise the priority and profile of these issues within my own administration. I want to ensure that faith-based and community groups will always have a place at the table in our deliberations.

In a few moments, I will sign two Executive orders. The first Executive order will create a new office, called the White House Office of Faith-Based and Community Initiatives. The head of this office will report directly to me and be charged with important responsibilities. He will oversee our initiatives on this issue. He will make sure our Government, where it works with private groups, is fair and supportive. And he will highlight groups as national models so others can learn from them.

The second Executive order will clear away the bureaucratic barriers in several important agencies that make private groups hesitate to work with Government. It will establish centers in five agencies—Justice, HUD, HHS, Labor, and Education—to ensure greater cooperation between the Government and the independent sector. These centers will report back on regulatory barriers to working with nonprofit groups, and make recommendations on how those barriers can be removed.

I have put this broad effort into the hands of two exceptional people—first, Steve Goldsmith, known as one of the most innovative mayors in America, who pioneered ways to promote community efforts. He will continue to advise me on these issues.

And I have asked Steve to serve on the board of the Corporation for National Service. This organization has done some good work in mobilizing volunteers of all ages. I've asked Steve to report to me on how we can make the Corporation do better and to get help where it's most needed.

And secondly, Professor John DiIulio will head the new office I am announcing today. He is one of the most influential social entrepreneurs in America. I can't tell you how honored I am for him to leave his post in academia to join us. He is the author of a respected textbook on American Government. He has a servant's heart on the issues that we will confront. He's worked with disadvantaged children. He has been a major force in mobilizing the city of Philadelphia to support faith-based and community groups.

It's a fantastic team. I'm honored to have them on my team. I look forward to hearing from them, as well as I look forward to working with the people in this room and the social entrepreneurs all across America who've heard the universal call to love a neighbor like they'd like to be loved themselves, to exist and work hard, not out of the love of money but out of the love of their fellow human beings. I'm absolutely convinced the great fabric of the Nation exists in neighborhoods, amongst unsung heroes who do heroic acts on a daily and hourly basis.

It's the fabric of the country that makes America unique. It is the power of promise that makes the future so promising—is the power of the missions that stand behind me.

This is an effort that will be an effort from now, the second week of my administration, to the last week of my administration, because I am confident that this initiative when fully implemented will help us realize the dream that America—its hopes, its promise, its greatness—will extend its reach throughout every single neighborhood all across the land.

Source: *Public Papers of the Presidents of the United States: George W. Bush* (Washington, DC: Government Printing Office), 232–233.

CRITICISM OF THE FAITH-BASED INITIATIVE (JUNE 13, 2001)

Mr. Ron Paul (R-TX). Mr. Speaker, I recommend to my colleagues the attached article, "The Real Threat of the Faith-Based Initiative" by Star Parker, founder and president of the Coalition on Urban Renewal and Education (CURE). Miss Parker eloquently explains how providing federal monies to faith-based institutions undermines the very qualities that make them effective in addressing social problems. As Miss Parker points out, religious programs are successful because they are staffed and funded by people motivated to help others by their religious beliefs. Government funding of religious organizations will transform them into adjuncts of the federal welfare state, more concerned about obeying federal rules and regulations than fulfilling the obligations of their faith.

If religious organizations receive taxpayer monies, they will have an incentive to make obedience to the dictates of federal bureaucrats their number-one priority.

Religious entities may even change the religious character of their programs in order to avoid displeasing their new federal paymaster. This will occur in large part because people who currently voluntarily support religious organizations will assume they "gave at the (tax) office" and thus will reduce their level of private giving. Thus, religious charities will become increasingly dependent on federal funds for support. Since "he who pays the piper calls the tune" federal bureaucrats and Congress will then control the content of "faith-based" programs.

Those who dismiss these concerns should consider that funding religious organizations will increase federal control of religious programs; in fact the current proposal explicitly forbids proselytizing in federally-funded "faith-based" programs. While religious organizations will not have to remove religious icons from their premises in order to receive federal funds, I fail to see the point in allowing a Catholic soup kitchen to hang a cross on its wall or a Jewish day center to hang a Star of David on its door if federal law forbids believers from explaining the meaning of those symbols.

Miss Parker points out that the founding fathers recognized the danger that church-state entanglement poses to religious liberty, which is why the First Amendment to the United States Constitution protects the free exercise of religion and forbids the federal government from establishing a national church. As Miss Parker points out, the most effective and constitutional means for Congress to help those in poverty is to cut taxes on the American people so that they may devote more of their resources to effective, locally-controlled, charitable programs.

In conclusion, Mr. Speaker, I hope all my colleagues will read Miss Parker's article and join her in supporting a return to a constitutional policy that does not put faith in federal programs but instead in the voluntary actions of a free and compassionate people.

Source: *Congressional Record*, June 13, 2001, E 1089.

STEM CELL RESEARCH (AUGUST 2001)

Embryonic stem cell research has been a topic in recent years that has polarized the United States. Stem cells are undifferentiated cells that have the ability to transform into any type of cell in the human body. The medical advantage of stems cells originates in their remarkable ability to repair the body. It is believed that if this science could be mastered it could possibly lead to the cures for diseases such as diabetes, Alzheimer's, and Lou Gehrig's disease.

In August of 2001, President Bush gave his first speech concerning embryonic stem cell research and the policy he would like to see enacted. The dilemma he faced was deciding whether embryonic stem cells were equivalent to human life. The president, relying on his strong religious values, came to the conclusion that embryonic stem cells were indeed the earliest form of human life. In order to prohibit the destruction of this proto life, President Bush decided that federal funds would only be available for research on existing lines of embryonic stem cells. He concluded that the more than sixty lines of embryonic stems cells along with nonembryonic stem cells gave the medical community a vast area to research for the cure of many diseases.

In September of 2001, Senator Harry Reid, Senate minority whip, raised his objections to President Bush's plan for embryonic stem cell research. Senator Reid feared that the president's restrictions on embryonic stem cell research would cripple the research. He pointed out that only about twenty-five of the sixty stem cell lines that were known met the limitations President Bush placed on federal funding for research. Senator Reid said he believed that the United States should lead the world in embryonic stem cell research. He argued that, in this way, we could have oversight on the world's progress in stem cell research and could thereby insure that the research was being done in an ethical manner.

BUSH'S ADDRESS TO THE NATION ON STEM CELL RESEARCH FROM CRAWFORD, TEXAS (AUGUST 9, 2001)

...The issue of research involving stem cells derived from human embryos is increasingly the subject of a national debate and dinner table discussions. The issue is confronted every day in laboratories as scientists ponder the ethical ramifications of their work. It is agonized over by parents and many couples as they try to have children or to save children already born. The issue is debated within the church, with people of different faiths, even many of the same faith, coming to different conclusions. Many people are finding that the more they know about stem cell research, the less certain they are about the right ethical and moral conclusions.

My administration must decide whether to allow Federal funds, your tax dollars, to be used for scientific research on stem cells derived from human embryos. A large number of these embryos already exist. They are the product of a process called in vitro fertilization, which helps so many couples conceive children. When doctors match sperm and egg to create life outside the womb, they usually produce more embryos than are implanted in the mother. Once a couple successfully has children, or if they are unsuccessful, the additional embryos remain frozen in laboratories. Some will not survive during long storage; others are destroyed. A number have been donated to science and used to create privately funded stem cell lines. And a few have been implanted in an adoptive mother and born and are today healthy children.

Based on preliminary work that has been privately funded, scientists believe further research using stem cells offers great promise that could help improve the lives of those who suffer from many terrible diseases, from juvenile diabetes to Alzheimer's, from Parkinson's to spinal cord injuries. And while scientists admit they are not yet certain, they believe stem cells derived from embryos have unique potential.

You should also know that stem cells can be derived from sources other than embryos, from adult cells, from umbilical cords that are discarded after babies are born, from human placentas. And many scientists feel research on these types of stem cells is also promising. Many patients suffering from a range of diseases are already being helped with treatments developed from adult stem cells. However, most scientists, at least today, believe that research on embryonic stem cells offer the most promise because these cells have the potential to develop in all of the tissues in the body.

Scientists further believe that rapid progress in this research will come only with Federal funds. Federal dollars help attract the best and brightest scientists. They ensure new discoveries are widely shared at the largest number of research facilities and that the research is directed toward the greatest public good.

The United States has a long and proud record of leading the world toward advances in science and medicine that improve human life. And the United States has a long and proud record of upholding the highest standards of ethics as we expand the limits of science and knowledge. Research on embryonic stem cells raises profound ethical questions, because extracting the stem cell destroys the embryo and thus destroys its potential for life. Like a snowflake, each of these embryos is unique, with the unique genetic potential of an individual human being.

As I thought through this issue, I kept returning to two fundamental questions: First, are these frozen embryos human life and, therefore, something precious to be protected? And second, if they're going to be destroyed anyway, shouldn't they be used for a greater good, for research that has the potential to save and improve other lives?

I've asked those questions and others of scientists, scholars, bioethicists, religious leaders, doctors, researchers, Members of Congress, my Cabinet, and my friends. I have read heartfelt letters from many Americans. I have given this issue a great deal of thought, prayer, and considerable reflection. And I have found widespread disagreement.

On the first issue, are these embryos human life? Well, one researcher told me he believes this 5-day-old cluster of cells is not an embryo, not yet an individual, but a pre-embryo. He argued that it has the potential for life, but it is not a life because it cannot develop on its own. An ethicist dismissed that as a callous attempt at rationalization. "Make no mistake," he told me, "that cluster of cells is the same way you and I, and all the rest of us, started our lives. One goes with a heavy heart if we use these," he said, "because we are dealing with the seeds of the next generation."

And to the other crucial question, if these are going to be destroyed anyway, why not use them for good purpose, I also found different answers. Many argue these embryos are byproducts of a process that helps create life, and we should allow couples to donate them to science so they can be used for good purpose instead of wasting their potential. Others will argue there's no such thing as excess life and the fact that a living being is going to die does not justify experimenting on it or exploiting it as a natural resource.

At its core, this issue forces us to confront fundamental questions about the beginnings of life and the ends of science. It lies at a difficult moral intersection, juxtaposing the need to protect life in all its phases with the prospect of saving and improving life in all its stages.

As the discoveries of modern science create tremendous hope, they also lay vast ethical minefields. As the genius of science extends the horizons of what we can do, we increasingly confront complex questions about what we should do. We have arrived at that brave new world that seemed so distant in 1932, when Aldous Huxley wrote about human beings created in test tubes in what he called a "hatchery." In recent weeks, we learned that scientists have created human embryos in test tubes solely to experiment on them. This is deeply troubling and a warning sign that should prompt all of us to think through these issues very carefully.

Embryonic stem cell research is at the leading edge of a series of moral hazards. The initial stem cell researcher was at first reluctant to begin his research, fearing it might be used for human cloning. Scientists have already cloned a sheep. Researchers are telling us the next step could be to clone human beings to create individual designer stem cells, essentially to grow another you, to be available in case you need another heart or lung or liver.

I strongly oppose human cloning, as do most Americans. We recoil at the idea of growing human beings for spare body parts, or creating life for our convenience. And while we must devote enormous energy to conquering disease, it is equally important that we pay attention to the moral concerns raised by the new frontier of human embryo stem cell research. Even the most noble ends do not justify any means.

My position on these issues is shaped by deeply held beliefs. I'm a strong supporter of science and technology and believe they have the potential for incredible good, to improve lives, to save life, to conquer disease. Research offers hope that millions of our loved ones may be cured of a disease and rid of their suffering. I have friends whose children suffer from juvenile diabetes. Nancy Reagan has written me about President Reagan's struggle with Alzheimer's. My own family has confronted the tragedy of childhood leukemia. And like all Americans, I have great hope for cures.

I also believe human life is a sacred gift from our Creator. I worry about a culture that devalues life and believe as your President I have an important obligation to foster and encourage respect for life in America and throughout the world. And while we're all hopeful about the potential of this research, no one can be certain that the science will live up to the hope it has generated.

Eight years ago, scientists believed fetal tissue research offered great hope for cures and treatments, yet the progress to date has not lived up to its initial expectations. Embryonic stem cell research offers both great promise and great peril. So I have decided we must proceed with great care.

As a result of private research, more than 60 genetically diverse stem cell lines already exist. They were created from embryos that have already been destroyed, and they have the ability to regenerate themselves indefinitely, creating ongoing opportunities for research. I have concluded that we should allow Federal funds to be used for research on these existing stem cell lines, where the life and death decision has already been made.

Leading scientists tell me research on these 60 lines has great promise that could lead to breakthrough therapies and cures. This allows us to explore the promise and potential of stem cell research without crossing a fundamental moral line by providing taxpayer funding that would sanction or encourage further destruction of human embryos that have at least the potential for life.

I also believe that great scientific progress can be made through aggressive Federal funding of research on umbilical cord, placenta, adult, and animal stem cells which do not involve the same moral dilemma. This year, your Government will spend $250 million on this important research.

Source: *Public Papers of the Presidents of the United States: George W. Bush* (Washington, DC: Government Printing Office), 1149–1151.

CRITICISM OF THE PRESIDENT'S POSITION ON STEM CELL RESEARCH (SEPTEMBER 10, 2001)

Mr. Harry Reid (D-NV). Mr. President, 3 years ago a young man by the name of Steve Rigazio, president and chief operating officer for the largest utility in Nevada, Nevada Power—a fine, fine young man—was diagnosed with Lou Gehrig's disease. It is a devastating illness that affects the nerve cells in the spinal cord and causes muscles to wither and die very quickly. He has lived longer than people expected. The normal time from the time of diagnosis, when you are told you have this disease, until the time you die, is 18 months. He has lived 3 years. He no longer works. He finally had to give up his job.

Because Lou Gehrig's disease attacks the body but leaves the mind intact, this vibrant man has had to watch his body deteriorate around him. He is a man of great courage, and I hope he lives much longer than people expect. He deserves it.

I have had visiting me for a number of years now two beautiful little girls from Las Vegas. They are twins. They are now 12 years old. One of the twins, Mollie Singer, has struggled with juvenile diabetes since she was 4 years old. She has had thousands of pricks of her skin—thousands. She is a beautiful little girl who believes that we in Washington can help her not have to take all these shots. As do the million Americans who suffer from this illness, Mollie fears that her kidneys will fail, she will get some kind of infection and have one of her limbs amputated or even lose her sight as a result of this diabetes.

There is something that gives Mollie and Steve hope, and that is stem cell research. It gives hope to tens of millions of Americans and their families who, like Steve Rigazio and Mollie Singer, suffer from Lou Gehrig's disease, diabetes, or Alzheimer's, Parkinson's, lupus, heart disease, spinal cord injuries, and other illnesses. Since stem cells can transform into nearly all the different tissues that make up the human body, they can replace defective or missing cells. Scientists are really very optimistic that one day stem cells will be used to replace defective cells in children with juvenile diabetes or even to create rejection-free organs.

Knowing that stem cells may have the power to save and improve lives, we cannot deny researchers the tools they need to fully realize the potential of stem cells. If we fail to seize promising research opportunities, we will fail millions of Americans and their families and people all over the world.

Early last month, President Bush announced he would limit Government funding for research to the stem cell lines that already existed at the time of his announcement. This was obviously a political compromise. I am pleased that the President left the door open for Federal funding of stem cell research in some capacity, but I am very concerned that he has not opened the door far enough to allow scientists to fully realize the life-saving potential of stem cells.

Last week, Secretary Thompson announced that no more than 25 of the 64 stem cell lines the National Institutes of Health listed as falling under the President's criteria are fully developed. We still do not know whether the remaining 40 stem cell lines would be useful to science. What we do know about the 25 viable stem cell lines that fall under the President's guidelines is very troubling. Why? Most, if not all, of the existing stem cell lines have been mixed with mouse cells. As a result, these cells could transfer deadly animal viruses to people, human beings.

It is also unclear whether these cells will be suitable for transplanting into people. Just last week, Dr. Douglas Melton, a professor of molecular and cellular biology at Harvard, testified that cells derived from mice "have proven unreliable over time for research, either dying out or growing into diseased forms." Even though scientists are working on ways to grow human embryonic cell lines without using mouse cells, they will not be eligible for Federal research money because they will be created after President Bush's arbitrary August 12 deadline. Last week the administration confirmed it would not reconsider this deadline, even if it were later discovered that none of these cell lines was suitable for long-term research.

If we fail to fund research for the new stem lines that are created without mouse cells, foreign scientists will still conduct research on stem cell lines that fall outside his guidelines. This research is going to go forward. Shouldn't it go forward under the greatest scientific umbrella in the history of the world, the National Institutes of Health? The answer is yes, that is where it should go forward, not in the little communities throughout the world that are trying to get a step up on the United States. This research is going to go forward. Let's do it the right way.

As a result of the guidelines of the President, we will not have the ability to provide any oversight of this research, if it is done overseas, to ensure that it is conducted by ethical means. Not only will we risk losing our most talented scientists to foreign countries, but we also jeopardize our potential as a nation to remain a world leader in stem cell research.

Over the course of the next several months, scientists will continue to determine whether President Bush's policy will allow stem cell research to advance at a reasonable pace. As we continue to evaluate the President's funding guidelines, we need to keep in mind that millions of Americans who suffer from devastating illnesses do not have the luxury of time—Steve Rigazio as an example. We cannot continue to dangle the hope of cure or the promise of scientific breakthrough before these patients and their families without adequately supporting research to allow scientists to achieve these very important discoveries.

Source: *Congressional Record*, September 10, 2001, S 9209.

DEPARTMENT OF HOMELAND SECURITY (SEPTEMBER 2001)

The concept of homeland security has taken on a different meaning in the United States since the attacks of September 11, 2001. Following these attacks, the United States and President Bush found the need to establish the Department of Homeland Security to prevent future attacks from occurring. The broad scope under its creation gave the department various responsibilities, ranging from terrorist attack prevention to natural disaster response. Established through the passing of the Homeland Security Act of 2002, the department comprises twenty-two federal agencies and employs more than 180,000.

President Bush has been a firm supporter of creating the Department of Homeland Security. In the days following the September 11 attacks, Bush pointed out that the perceived notion of American immunity from terrorist attack on its homeland was false; he thus urged Congress to create a department that would not only prevent further attacks from happening, but also protect American people in times of peace. President Bush acknowledged that information sharing between federal agencies must improve in the future and felt that placing the agencies under one department would facilitate this aim.

Although most people agreed that some reorganization of the federal government was necessary, critics argued that the creation of yet another department would create more bureaucracy. Concerns about the true intentions of the administration began to surface as Congress questioned the issues of privacy and the limitations imposed on this newly created governmental structure. Critics questioned the administration's timing on the formation of this department and urged their fellow members of Congress to truly examine its future implications.

BUSH'S ADDRESS BEFORE A JOINT SESSION OF THE CONGRESS ON THE UNITED STATES' RESPONSE TO THE TERRORIST ATTACKS OF SEPTEMBER 11 (SEPTEMBER 20, 2001)

...Our Nation has been put on notice: We are not immune from attack. We will take defensive measures against terrorism to protect Americans. Today dozens of Federal departments and agencies, as well as State and local governments, have responsibilities affecting homeland security. These efforts must be coordinated at the highest level.

So tonight I announce the creation of a Cabinet-level position reporting directly to me, the Office of Homeland Security. And tonight I also announce a distinguished American to lead this effort to strengthen American security, a military veteran, an effective Governor, a true patriot, a trusted friend, Pennsylvania's Tom Ridge. He will lead, oversee, and coordinate a comprehensive national strategy to safeguard our country against terrorism and respond to any attacks that may come.

These measures are essential. But the only way to defeat terrorism as a threat to our way of life is to stop it, eliminate it, and destroy it where it grows. Many will be involved in this effort, from FBI agents to intelligence operatives to the reservists we have called to active duty. All deserve our thanks, and all have our prayers. And tonight, a few miles from the damaged Pentagon, I have a message for our military: Be ready. I've called the Armed Forces to alert, and there is a reason. The hour is coming when America will act, and you will make us proud.

Tonight we face new and sudden national challenges. We will come together to improve air safety, to dramatically expand the number of air marshals on domestic flights, and take new measures to prevent hijacking. We will come together to promote stability and keep our airlines flying, with direct assistance during this emergency.

We will come together to give law enforcement the additional tools it needs to track down terror here at home. We will come together to strengthen our intelligence capabilities, to know the plans of terrorists before they act and find them before they strike. We will come together to take active steps that strengthen America's economy and put our people back to work.

Great harm has been done to us. We have suffered great loss. And in our grief and anger, we have found our mission and our moment. Freedom and fear are at war. The advance of human freedom, the great achievement of our time and the great hope of every time, now depends on us. Our Nation—this generation—will lift a dark threat of violence from our people and our future. We will rally the world to this cause by our efforts, by our courage. We will not tire; we will not falter; and we will not fail.

It is my hope that in the months and years ahead, life will return almost too normal. We'll go back to our lives and routines, and that is good. Even grief recedes with time and grace. But our resolve must not pass. Each of us will remember what happened that day and to whom it happened. We'll remember the moment the news came, where we were, and what we were doing. Some will remember an image of a fire or a story of rescue. Some will carry memories of a face and a voice gone forever.

And I will carry this: It is the police shield of a man named George Howard, who died at the World Trade Center trying to save others. It was given to me by his mom, Arlene, as a proud memorial to her son. It is my reminder of lives that ended and a task that does not end. I will not forget this wound to our country and those who inflicted it. I will not yield; I will not rest; I will not relent in waging this struggle for freedom and security for the American people.

The course of this conflict is not known, yet its outcome is certain. Freedom and fear, justice and cruelty have always been at war, and we know that God is not neutral between them.

Source: *Public Papers of the Presidents of the United States: George W. Bush* (Washington, DC: Government Printing Office), 1319–1355.

CRITICISM OF HOMELAND SECURITY (JULY 31, 2002)

Mr. Robert C. Byrd (D-WV). Mr. President, in response to the terrorist acts of September 11, the Bush administration—like so many other administrations before it—has chosen to demonstrate its tough stand against something. In the case of the Bush administration, it is a tough stand against terrorism and its concern for the safety and well-being of the American people by boldly maneuvering the Federal chess pieces to create a new Department called Homeland Security.

It is an impressive move, Mr. President—this reorganization of the Government. Many say that it is the greatest reorganization during the past half century. I think it could very well be said that it is the greatest reorganization since the Founding Fathers reorganized the Government in 1787.

As to the current proposal, it is no wimpy reorganization. To check terrorism within our borders, the administration has proposed to establish a massive new Department of Homeland Security. It will be a Department so large that it will affect an estimated 170,000 Federal employees and will constitute the largest Department—the third largest—after the Departments of Defense and Veterans Affairs.

From what I have read, the thousands of workers of this proposed Department will be doing essentially the same job they are already doing, but they will be doing it under a different newly consolidated roof with different lines of authority. Why the administration seems to think that these workers will perform their duties better just because they are transferred to a new agency has both bothered and baffled me until late last week.

Last week, President Bush let it be known that if any version of the Department of Homeland Security passes the Congress which ensures Civil Service protections, collective bargaining rights, and other provisions to safeguard Federal workers' rights and protections, he will veto it.

At first, I thought this was simply another of the usual pokes at Federal workers. There is the unfortunate implication in the President's veto threat that the current Federal workforce is so full of slackers—there are some there, no doubt—but it is so full of slackers and ineptitude that he may need to get rid of them all and hire a new Federal force.

But then as I thought about the President's claims that the Secretary of the Department of Homeland Security will need the ability—get this—to act "without all kinds of bureaucratic rules and obstacles," I began to have other concerns about the Bush administration's intentions.

It may be that this White House crowd, comprised of CEOs, corporate managers, and other wealthy business elites, may be seeking to use the Department of Homeland Security to further their efforts to run the Federal Government more like a corporation, seeking freedom to hire and fire dedicated public servants, many of them experts in their fields, at will.

By the way, the actions of CEOs are not exactly models—and I am not talking about all CEOs, of course. But the actions of CEOs we have been reading about recently are not exactly models on which to run much of anything these days, and I hope that I am not detecting the same cavalier attitude about Federal pensions that we have seen in press accounts detailing the horrific pension ripoffs by some of our large corporations.

President Bush is currently pushing the Congress to subject 425,000 Federal jobs to contractor competition by the end of his term. This administration has made it a goal to take Federal jobs and dole them out like candy to private firms, apparently.

In drafting its proposed reorganization, the administration started with a panel of four—four white collar political players; four white collar political players in the bowels of the White House, in the subterranean caverns of the White House.

Who were the geniuses behind this idea? Mr. Andrew Card, a fine gentleman—I like him, a very able man; former Gov. Tom Ridge, a fine gentleman, a very able official, who has had great experience in running the Governor's office in one of our larger States in the Union, . . . Then there is the White House counsel, I believe his name is Gonzales. I am not sure I know him very well. And then the fourth in this quartet of master planners is none other than Mr. Mitch Daniels, the Director of the Office of Management and Budget.

So there is the quartet. Not quite the caliber, I would say—although one may wish to debate it—it may be worthy of argumentation—not quite the caliber of the committee of five that wrote the Declaration of Independence: Thomas Jefferson, Benjamin Franklin, John Adams, William Livingston, and Roger Sherman. Roger Sherman is the only one of the five who signed all of the founding documents of this great Nation. Now there was a committee of five.

So while there may be some argument as to how one would stack up against the other, I would put my bets on the committee of five that wrote the Declaration of Independence. I will stay with them. No disrespect intended, of course, to the White House committee of four, but they operated in secret in the bowels of the White House. I understand that when the President unveiled this massive monstrosity, some of the Department heads in the Government had not been in on the deal until the day that it was sprung.

...It was conceived in secret and was born in secret, and there we are.

So the administration has given these white-collar political players—there were four of them in the beginning—free rein to move Federal workers around from one agency to the other in the name of homeland defense. That same administration now appears poised to sabotage the pay, the health benefits, and the retirement benefits of the very Federal workers it wants to involve with safeguarding our homeland security.

There is nothing like threatening jobs and health benefits to give a boost, of course, to the morale of the employees of a new and very important Department. This is just what we need to energize our new Homeland Security Department, is it not? They will like that—jeopardize their benefits and their pay and their jobs. Imagine the concentration level of nail-biting employees concerned about where their next paycheck is coming from. Think about that. And what will happen to their families if the Bush administration prevails in freeing itself from the normal restrictions which safeguard Federal workers' rights?

...They are the Border Patrol agents. Federal workers are the Border Patrol agents guarding our 6,000-mile-long borders when we think of both borders with Mexico and Canada. All day, and all night while the rest of us are sleeping, they are guarding those borders, guarding us. Those are Federal workers. They are the Customs Service inspectors who have been working around the clock since September 11 to prevent weapons of mass destruction from being carried in containers through our ports of entry. Those are Federal workers. They are the postal workers who have to think about delivering packages of anthrax. They are the Federal workers who have had to deal with the anthrax threat. What about the Center for Disease Control workers who must confront the hard reality of a possible bioterrorist attack every day?

Federal employees are the rank-and-file workers who do the bulk of the work in securing the homeland, and they will continue to do the bulk of the work in securing this country from sea to shining sea. They are the workers who will do the bulk of the work in securing the homeland but who will receive little of the credit and the glory that go to the administration's political appointees.

The President has asked these Federal employees to be the frontline soldiers in the war on terrorism. They are out there at every hour of the day and the night, somewhere, guarding the ports of this country, guarding the borders of this country, guarding the airports of this country, standing on guard. And the President would reward them by trying to take away their basic labor, civil service rights, and job protections?

I was especially alarmed by OMB Director Mitch Daniels' explanation for stripping Federal workers of their rights. Mr. Mitch Daniels said:

> Our adversaries are not encumbered by a lot of rules. Al-Qaida does not have a three-foot-thick code. This department is going to need to be nimble.

This is a startling, as well as frightening, remark. Since when did al-Qaida become our role model for labor-management relations? I thought we were out to destroy al-Qaida, not emulate them. Ha, ha, ha, ha, ha. No, they do not have a 3-foot code of rules. Al-Qaida also does not have this code which I hold in my hand, the Constitution of the United States, but we do. We have this code, this Constitution.

It is rank-and-file Government workers, who are on the job every day and night, keeping Government operating, protecting you, Mr. President, protecting me, protecting our friends in the fourth estate there in the gallery. These are the Government workers who make the Government function, and they are the Government workers upon whom we now depend to protect us.

... Let's slow this proposed legislation down. I am not saying today that I am against a Department of Homeland Security. But what is the rush? What is the rush? Consider carefully a veto threat of any bill setting up a Department of Homeland Security which does not give this White House sweeping new powers, sweeping new powers to abolish workers rights and workers protections.

Imagine that; imagine a veto that would do that. I think the agenda of this White House is becoming very, very clear. And we had better pause, we had better stop, we had better look, and we had better listen. Talk about passing this massive new law, creating a massive, monstrous behemoth by September 11, by an artificial deadline! This legislation would emasculate certain portions of this Constitution which I hold in my hand—emasculate it! Trample it into the dirt!

... Let's slow down. We don't know what the unintended consequences will be of the passage of this legislation. Study the House bill. Study the House-passed bill. The House passed a bill after 2 days of debate. I believe there were 132 Members of the House who voted against that bill. Were they against homeland security? No! Those Members of the House who voted against that bill were as much for homeland security as I am, as much as the President of the United States is. They were for homeland security. I am for homeland security. I defy anyone to say that the Senator in the chair, that the Senator who sits just behind me, or any other Senator, is against homeland security.

Source: *Congressional Record*, July 31, 2002, S 7728–7731.

USA PATRIOT ACT 2001 (OCTOBER 2001)

After the terrorist attacks of September 11, 2001, all parties called for a comprehensive review of intelligence and national security. The USA PATRIOT Act, or Uniting and Strengthening America by Providing Appropriate Tools Required to Intercept and Obstruct Terrorism, was introduced in hopes of securing America's freedom. The argument made by the president was that giving up a few civil liberties in exchange for security was a small price to ask. He claimed that the USA PATRIOT Act was necessary to ensure the quick identification and removal of terrorists who would otherwise threaten the security of the nation.

Many groups, including the American Civil Liberties Union, complained about the law's infringement on the Constitution, yet it was passed with most senators and members of Congress having never read the legislation. It allows for search and seizure without warrants, secret courts, and the possibility that the government can obtain warrants without any burden of probable cause. It also called for the immediate deportation of all who had overstayed their student or travel visas. As more and more Democrats read over the legislation under the strong suggestion of the ACLU, they began to take issue with it. The first chance that legislators had of repealing the USA PATRIOT Act was in 2005, when a long and arduous battle over the merits and flaws of this legislation ensued.

While the president and the Republicans claim that we cannot fight terror without the USA PATRIOT Act, Democrats continuously argue that the USA PATRIOT Act takes away too many freedoms and does not allow for oversight of the Department of Homeland Security and other intelligence agencies. Awaiting a final decision, the USA PATRIOT Act is currently on a six-month continuum until it will be debated in Congress again.

BUSH'S REMARKS ON SIGNING THE USA PATRIOT ACT OF 2001 (OCTOBER 26, 2001)

...The bill before me takes account of the new realities and dangers posed by modern terrorists. It will help law enforcement to identify, to dismantle, to disrupt, and to punish terrorists before they strike.

For example, this legislation gives law enforcement officials better tools to put an end to financial counterfeiting, smuggling, and money laundering. Secondly, it gives intelligence operations and criminal operations the chance to operate, not on separate tracks, but to share vital information so necessary to disrupt a terrorist attack before it occurs.

As of today, we're changing the laws governing information-sharing. And as importantly, we're changing the culture of our various agencies that fight terrorism. Countering and investigating terrorist activity is the number one priority for both law enforcement and intelligence agencies.

Surveillance of communications is another essential tool to pursue and stop terrorists. The existing law was written in the era of rotary telephones. This new law that I sign today will allow surveillance of all communications used by terrorists, including e-mails, the Internet, and cell phones. As of today, we'll be able to better meet the technological challenges posed by this proliferation of communications technology.

Investigations are often slowed by limit on the reach of Federal search warrants. Law enforcement agencies have to get a new warrant for each new district they investigate, even when they're after the same suspect. Under this new law, warrants are valid across all districts and across all States.

And finally, the new legislation greatly enhances the penalties that will fall on terrorists or anyone who helps them. Current statutes deal more severely with drug-traffickers than with terrorists. That changes today. We are enacting new and harsh penalties for possession of biological weapons. We're making it easier to seize the assets of groups and individuals involved in terrorism. The Government will have wider latitude in deporting known terrorists and their supporters. The statute of limitations on terrorist acts will be lengthened, as will prison sentences for terrorists.

This bill was carefully drafted and considered. Led by the Members of Congress on this stage and those seated in the audience, it was crafted with skill and care, determination and a spirit of bipartisanship for which the entire Nation is grateful. This bill met with an overwhelming—overwhelming—agreement in Congress because it upholds and respects the civil liberties guaranteed by our Constitution.

This legislation is essential not only to pursuing and punishing terrorists but also preventing more atrocities in the hands of the evil ones. This Government will enforce this law with all the urgency of a nation at war. The elected branches of our Government and both political parties are united in our resolve to find and stop and punish those who would do harm to the American people.

Source: *Public Papers of the Presidents of the United States: George W. Bush* (Washington, DC: Government Printing Office), 1550–1552.

CRITICISM OF THE USA PATRIOT ACT OF 2001 (OCTOBER 25, 2001)

Mr. Russell D. Feingold (D-WI). Mr. President, I have asked for this time to speak about the antiterrorism bill, H.R. 3162. As we address this bill, of course, we are especially mindful of the terrible events of September 11 and beyond, which led to this bill's proposal and its quick consideration in the Congress.

This has been a tragic time in our country. Before I discuss this bill, let me first pause to remember, through one small story, how September 11 has irrevocably changed so many lives. In a letter to the Washington Post recently, a man, as he went jogging near the Pentagon, came across the makeshift memorial built for those who lost their lives. He slowed to a walk as he took in the sight before him, the red, white, and blue flowers covering the structure. Off to the side, was a smaller memorial with a card that read: "Happy birthday, Mommy. Although you died and are no longer with me, I feel as if I still have you in my life. I think about you every day."

After reading the card, the man felt as if he were "drowning in the names of dead mothers, fathers, sons, and daughters." The author of this letter shared a moment in his own life that so many of us have had, the moment where televised pictures of the destruction are made painfully real to us. You read a card, see the anguished face of a loved one, and then, suddenly, we feel the enormity of what has happened to so many American families and to all of us as a people.

We also had our initial reactions to the attack. My first and most powerful emotion was a solemn resolve to stop these terrorists. That remains my principal reaction to these events. But I also quickly realized, as many did, that two cautions were necessary. I raised them on the Senate floor the day after the attacks.

The first caution was that we must continue to respect our Constitution and protect our civil liberties in the wake of the attacks.

As the chairman of the Constitution subcommittee of the Judiciary Committee I recognize fully that this is a different world, with different technologies, different issues, and different threats.

Yet we must examine every item that is proposed in response to these events to be sure we are not rewarding these terrorists and weakening ourselves by giving up the cherished freedoms that they seek to destroy.

The second caution I issued was a warning against the mistreatment of Arab Americans, Muslim Americans, South Asians, or others in this country. Already, one day after the attacks, we were hearing news reports that misguided anger against people of these backgrounds had led to harassment, violence, and even death.

I suppose I was reacting instinctively to the unfolding events in the spirit of the Irish statesman John Philpot Curran, who said:

"The condition upon which God hath given liberty to man is eternal vigilance."

During those first few hours after the attacks, I kept remembering a sentence from a case I had studied in law school. Not surprisingly, I didn't remember which case it was, who wrote the opinion, or what it was about, but I did remember these words:

"While the Constitution protects against invasions of individual rights, it is not a suicide pact."

I took these words as a challenge to my concerns about civil liberties at such a momentous time in our history; that we must be careful to not take civil liberties so literally that we allow ourselves to be destroyed.

But upon reviewing the case itself, Kennedy v. Mendoza-Martinez, I found that Justice Arthur Goldberg had made this statement but then ruled in favor of the civil liberties position in the case, which was about draft evasion. He elaborated:

> It is fundamental that the great powers of Congress to conduct war and to regulate the Nation's foreign relations are subject to the constitutional requirements of due process. The imperative necessity for safeguarding these rights to procedural due process under the gravest of emergencies has existed throughout our constitutional history, for it is then, under the pressing exigencies of crisis, that there is the greatest temptation to dispense with fundamental constitutional guarantees which, it is feared, will inhibit governmental action.

The Justice continued:

> The Constitution of the United States is a law for rulers and people, equally in war and peace, and covers with the shield of its protection all classes of men, at all times, and under all circumstances... In no other way can we transmit to posterity unimpaired the blessings of liberty, consecrated by the sacrifices of the Revolution.

I have approached the events of the past month and my role in proposing and reviewing legislation relating to it in this spirit. I believe we must, we must, redouble our vigilance. We must redouble our vigilance to ensure our security and to prevent further acts of terror. But we must also redouble our vigilance to preserve our values and the basic rights that make us who we are.

The Founders who wrote our Constitution and Bill of Rights exercised that vigilance even though they had recently fought and won the Revolutionary War. They did not live in comfortable and easy times of hypothetical enemies. They wrote a Constitution of limited powers and an explicit Bill of Rights to protect liberty in times of war, as well as in times of peace.

Of course, there have been periods in our nation's history when civil liberties have taken a back seat to what appeared at the time to be the legitimate exigencies of war. Our national consciousness still bears the stain and the scars of those events: The Alien and Sedition Acts, the suspension of habeas corpus during the Civil War, the internment of Japanese-Americans, German-Americans, and Italian-Americans during World War II, the blacklisting of supposed communist sympathizers during the McCarthy era, and the surveillance and harassment of antiwar protesters, including Dr. Martin Luther King Jr., during the Vietnam War. We must not allow these pieces of our past to become prologue.

Even in our great land, wartime has sometimes brought us the greatest tests of our Bill of Rights. For example, during the Civil War, the Government arrested some 13,000 civilians, implementing a system akin to martial law. President Lincoln issued a proclamation ordering the arrest and military trial of any persons "discouraging volunteer enlistments, or resisting militia drafts." Wisconsin provided one of the first challenges of this order. Draft protests rose up in Milwaukee and Sheboygan. And an anti-draft riot broke out among Germans and Luxembourgers in Port Washington, WI. When the government arrested one of the leaders of the riot, his attorney sought a writ of habeas corpus. His military captors said that the President had abolished the writ. The Wisconsin Supreme Court was among the first to rule that the President had exceeded his authority.

In 1917, the Postmaster General revoked the mailing privileges of the newspaper the Milwaukee Leader because he felt that some of its articles impeded the war effort and the draft. Articles called the President an aristocrat and called the draft oppressive. Over dissents by Justices Brandeis and Holmes, the Supreme Court upheld the action.

We all know during World War II, President Roosevelt signed orders to incarcerate more than 110,000 people of Japanese origin, as well as some roughly 11,000 of German origin and 3,000 of Italian origin.

Earlier this year, I introduced legislation to set up a commission to review the wartime treatment of Germans, Italians, and other Europeans during that period. That bill came out of heartfelt meetings in which constituents told me their stories. They were German-Americans, who came to me with some trepidation. They had waited 50 years to raise the issue with a member of Congress. They did not want compensation. But they had seen the Government's commission on the wartime internment of people of Japanese origin, and they wanted their story to be told, and an official acknowledgment as well with regard to what had happened to them. I hope, that we will move to pass this important legislation early next year. We must deal with our nation's past, even as we move to ensure our nation's future.

Mr. FEINGOLD. Now some may say, indeed we may hope, that we have come a long way since those days of infringements on civil liberties. But there is ample reason for concern. And I have been troubled in the past 6 weeks by the potential loss of commitment in the Congress and the country to traditional civil liberties.

As it seeks to combat terrorism, the Justice Department is making extraordinary use of its power to arrest and detain individuals, jailing hundreds of people on immigration violations and arresting more than a dozen "material witnesses" not charged with any crime. Although the Government has used these authorities before, it has not done so on such a broad scale. Judging from Government announcements, the Government has not brought any criminal charges related to the attacks with regard to the overwhelming majority of these detainees.

For example, the FBI arrested as a material witness the San Antonio radiologist Albader Al-Hazmi, who has a name like two of the hijackers, and who tried to book a flight to San Diego for a medical conference. According to his lawyer, the Government held Al-Hazmi incommunicado after his arrest, and it took 6 days for lawyers to get access to him. After the FBI released him, his lawyer said:

"This is a good lesson about how frail our processes are. It's how we treat people in difficult times like these that is the true test of the democracy and civil liberties that we brag so much about throughout the world."

I agree with those statements.

Now, it so happens—and I know the Presiding Officer is aware of that because she has been very helpful on this issue—that since early 1999, I have been working on another bill that is poignantly relevant to recent events: legislation to prohibit racial profiling, especially the practice of targeting pedestrians or drivers for stops and searches based on the color of their skin. Before September 11, people spoke of the issue mostly in the context of African-Americans and Latino-Americans who had been profiled. But after September 11, the issue has taken on a new context and a new urgency.

Even as America addresses the demanding security challenges before us, we must strive mightily also to guard our values and basic rights. We must guard against racism and ethnic discrimination against people of Arab and South Asian origin and those who are Muslim.

We who do not have Arabic names or do not wear turbans or headscarves may not feel the weight of these times as much as Americans from the Middle East and South Asia do. But as the great jurist Learned Hand said in a speech in New York's Central Park during World War II:

"The spirit of liberty is the spirit which seeks to understand the minds of other men and women; the spirit of liberty is the spirit which weighs their interests alongside its own without bias...."

Was it not at least partially bias, however, when passengers on a Northwest Airlines flight in Minneapolis a month ago insisted that Northwest remove from the plane three Arab men who had cleared security?

Of course, given the enormous anxiety and fears generated by the events of September 11, it would not have been difficult to anticipate some of these reactions, both by our government and some of our people. Some have said rather cavalierly that in these difficult times we must accept some reduction in our civil liberties in order to be secure.

Of course, there is no doubt that if we lived in a police state, it would be easier to catch terrorists. If we lived in a country that allowed the police to search your home at any time for any reason; if we lived in a country that allowed the government to open your mail, eavesdrop on your phone conversations, or intercept your email communications; if we lived in a country that allowed the government to hold people in jail indefinitely based on what they write or think, or based on mere suspicion that they are up to no good, then the government would no doubt discover and arrest more terrorists.

But that probably would not be a country in which we would want to live. And that would not be a country for which we could, in good conscience, ask our young people to fight and die. In short, that would not be America.

Preserving our freedom is one of the main reasons we are now engaged in this new war on terrorism. We will lose that war without firing a shot if we sacrifice the liberties of the American people.

That is why I found the antiterrorism bill originally proposed by Attorney General Ashcroft and President Bush to be troubling.

The administration's proposed bill contained vast new powers for law enforcement, some seemingly drafted in haste and others that came from the FBI's wish list that Congress has rejected in the past. You may remember that the Attorney General announced his intention to introduce a bill shortly after the September 11 attacks. He provided the text of the bill the following Wednesday, and urged Congress to enact it by the end of the week. That was plainly impossible, but the pressure to move on this bill quickly, without deliberation and debate, has been relentless ever since.

It is one thing to shortcut the legislative process in order to get Federal financial aid to the cities hit by terrorism. We did that, and no one complained that we moved too quickly. It is quite another to press for the enactment of sweeping new powers for law enforcement that directly affect the civil liberties of the American people without due deliberation by the peoples' elected representatives.

Fortunately, cooler heads prevailed at least to some extent, and while this bill has been on a fast track, there has been time to make some changes and reach agreement on a bill that is less objectionable than the bill that the administration originally proposed.

As I will discuss in a moment, I have concluded that this bill still does not strike the right balance between empowering law enforcement and protecting civil liberties. But that does not mean that I oppose everything in the bill. By no means. Indeed many of its provisions are entirely reasonable, and I hope they will help law enforcement more effectively counter the threat of terrorism.

For example, it is entirely appropriate that with a warrant the FBI be able to seize voice mail messages as well as tap a phone. It is also reasonable, even necessary, to update the federal criminal offense relating to possession and use of biological weapons. It made sense to make sure that phone conversations carried over cables would not have more protection from surveillance than conversations carried over phone lines. And it made sense to stiffen penalties and lengthen or eliminate statutes of limitation for certain terrorist crimes.

There are other non-controversial provisions in the bill that I support—those to assist the victims of crime, to streamline the application process for public safety officers benefits and increase those benefits, to provide more funds to strengthen immigration controls at our Northern borders—something that the Presiding Officer and I understand—to expedite the hiring of translators at the FBI, and many other such provisions.

In the end, however, my focus on this bill, as Chair of the Constitution Subcommittee of the Judiciary Committee in the Senate, was on those provisions that implicate our constitutional freedoms. And it was in reviewing those provisions that I came to feel that the administration's demand for haste was inappropriate; indeed, it was dangerous. Our process in the Senate, as truncated as it was, did lead to the elimination or significant rewriting of a number of audacious proposals that I and many other members found objectionable.

For example, the original administration proposal contained a provision that would have allowed the use in U.S. criminal proceedings against U.S. citizens of information obtained by foreign law enforcement agencies in wiretaps that would be illegal in this country. In other words, evidence obtained in an unconstitutional search overseas was to be allowed in a U.S. court.

Another provision would have broadened the criminal forfeiture laws to permit—prior to conviction—the freezing of assets entirely unrelated to an alleged crime. The Justice Department has wanted this authority for years, and Congress has never been willing to give it. For one thing, it touches on the right to counsel, since assets that are frozen cannot be used to pay a lawyer. The courts have almost uniformly rejected efforts to restrain assets before conviction unless they are assets gained in the alleged criminal enterprise. This proposal, in my view, was simply an effort on the part of the Department to take advantage of the emergency situation and get something that they've wanted to get for a long time.

As I have indicated, the foreign wiretap and criminal forfeiture provisions were dropped from the bill that we considered in the Senate. Other provisions were rewritten based on objections that I and others raised about them. For example, the original bill contained sweeping permission for the Attorney General to get copies of educational records without a court order. The final bill requires a court order and a certification by the Attorney General that he has reason to believe that the records contain information that is relevant to an investigation of terrorism.

So the bill before us is certainly improved from the bill that the administration sent to us on September 19, and wanted us to pass on September 21. But again, in my judgement, it does not strike the right balance between empowering law enforcement and protecting constitutional freedoms. Let me take a moment to discuss some of the shortcomings of the bill.

First, the bill contains some very significant changes in criminal procedure that will apply to every federal criminal investigation in this country, not just those involving terrorism. One provision would greatly expand the circumstances in which law enforcement agencies can search homes and offices without notifying the owner prior to the search. The longstanding practice under the fourth amendment of serving a warrant prior to executing a search could be easily avoided in virtually every case, because the government would simply have to show that it had "reasonable cause to believe" that providing notice "may" seriously jeopardize an investigation. This is a significant infringement on personal liberty.

Notice is a key element of fourth amendment protections. It allows a person to point out mistakes in a warrant and to make sure that a search is limited to the terms of a warrant. Just think about the possibility of the police showing up at your door with a warrant to search your house. You look at the warrant and say, "yes, that's my address, but the name on the warrant isn't me." And the police realize a mistake has been made and go away. If you're not home, and the police have received permission to do a "sneak and peek" search, they can come in your house, look around, and leave, and may never have to tell you that ever happened.

That bothers me. I bet it bothers most Americans.

Another very troubling provision has to do with the effort to combat computer crime. I want the effort to stop computer crime. The bill allows law enforcement to monitor a computer with the permission of its owner or operator, without the need to get a warrant or show probable cause.

I want to tell you, Mr. President, I have been at pains to point out things I can support in this bill. I think that power is fine in a case of a so-called denial of service attack. What is that? That is plain old computer hacking. You bet. We need to be able to get at that kind of crime.

Computer owners should be able to give the police permission to monitor communications coming from what amounts to a trespasser on the computer, a real trespasser.

But we tried to point out as calmly and as constructively as possible on the floor that, as drafted in this bill, the provision might permit an employer to give permission to the police to monitor the e-mails of an employee who has used her computer at work to shop for Christmas gifts. She violated the rules of her employer regarding personal use of the computer. Or someone who uses a computer at a library or at a school and happens to go to a gambling or pornography site in violation of the Internet use policies of the library or the university might also be subjected to Government surveillance—without probable cause and without any time limit at all. With this one provision, fourth amendment protections are potentially eliminated for a broad spectrum of electronic communications.

I am also very troubled by the broad expansion of Government power under the Foreign Intelligence Surveillance Act, known as FISA. When Congress passed FISA in 1978, it granted to the executive branch the power to conduct surveillance in foreign intelligence investigations without having to meet the rigorous probable cause standard under the fourth amendment that is required for criminal investigations. There is a lower threshold for obtaining a wiretap order from the FISA court because the FBI is not investigating a crime, it is investigating foreign intelligence activities. But the law currently requires that intelligence gathering be the primary purpose of the investigation in order for this much lower standard to apply.

The bill changes that requirement. The Government now will only have to show that intelligence is a "significant purpose" of the investigation. So even if the primary purpose is a criminal investigation, the heightened protections of the fourth amendment will not apply.

It seems obvious that with this lower standard, the FBI will be able to try to use FISA as much as it can. And, of course, with terrorism investigations, that won't be difficult because the terrorists are apparently sponsored or at least supported by foreign governments. So this means the fourth amendment rights will be significantly curtailed in many investigations of terrorist acts.

The significance of the breakdown of the distinction between intelligence and criminal investigations becomes apparent when you see other expansions of Government power under FISA in this bill.

Another provision that troubles me a lot is one that permits the Government, under FISA, to compel the production of records from any business regarding any person if that information is sought in connection with an investigation of terrorism or espionage.

I want to be clear here, as well, we are not talking about travel records directly pertaining to a terrorist suspect, which we can all see obviously can be highly relevant to an investigation of a terrorist plot. FISA already gives the FBI the power to get airline, train, hotel, car rental, and other records of a suspect.

But this bill does much more. Under this bill, the Government can compel the disclosure of the personal records of anyone—perhaps someone who worked with, or lived next door to, or went to school with, or sat on an airplane with, or had been seen in the company of, or whose phone number was called by—the target of the investigation.

Under this new provision, all business records can be compelled, including those containing sensitive personal information, such as medical records from hospitals or doctors, or educational records, or records of what books somebody has taken out from the library. We are not talking about terrorist suspects, we are talking about people who just may have come into some kind of casual contact with the person in that situation. This is an enormous expansion of authority under a law that provides only minimal judicial supervision.

Under this provision, the Government can apparently go on a fishing expedition and collect information on virtually anyone. All it has to allege, in order to get an order for these records from the court, is that the information is sought for an investigation of international terrorism or clandestine intelligence gathering. That is it. They just have to say that. On that minimal showing, in an ex parte application to a secret court, with no showing even that the information is relevant to the investigation, the Government can lawfully compel a doctor or a hospital to release medical records or a library to release circulation records. This is truly a breathtaking expansion of police power.

Let me turn to a final area of real concern about this legislation, which I think brings us full circle to the cautions I expressed on the day after the attacks. These are two very troubling provisions dealing with our immigration laws in the bill.

First, the administration's original proposal would have granted the Attorney General extraordinary powers to detain immigrants indefinitely, including legal permanent residents. The Attorney General could do so based on mere suspicion that the person is engaged in terrorism. I believe the administration was really overreaching here. I am pleased that our distinguished chairman of the Judiciary Committee, Senator Leahy, was able to negotiate some protections. The bill now requires the Attorney General to charge the immigrant within 7 days with a criminal offense or immigration violation. In the event the Attorney General does not charge the immigrant, the immigrant must be released.

This protection is an improvement, but the provision remains fundamentally flawed. Even with this 7-day charging requirement, the bill would nevertheless continue to permit the indefinite detention in two situations. First, immigrants who win their deportation cases may be continued to be held if the Attorney General continues to have suspicions. Second, this provision creates a deep unfairness to immigrants who are found not to be deportable for terrorism but have an immigration status violation, such as overstaying a visa. If the immigration judge finds that they are eligible for relief from deportation, and therefore can stay in the country—for example, if they have longstanding family ties here—nonetheless, the Attorney General can continue to hold them indefinitely.

I am pleased that the final version of the legislation includes a few improvements over the bill that passed the Senate. In particular, the bill would require the Attorney General to review the detention decision every 6 months. And it would only allow the Attorney General or the Deputy Attorney General—not lower level officials—to make that determination.

While I am pleased these provisions are included in the bill, I believe it still falls short of meeting even basic constitutional standards of due process and fairness.

The bill continues to allow the Attorney General to detain persons based on mere suspicion. Our system normally requires higher standards of proof for a deprivation of liberty. For example, deportation proceedings themselves are subject to a clear and convincing evidence standard. And, of course, criminal convictions require proof beyond a reasonable doubt. The bill also continues to deny detained persons a trial or a hearing where the Government would be required to prove that that person is, in fact, engaged in terrorist activity. I think this is unjust and inconsistent with the values of our system of justice that we hold dearly.

Another provision in the bill that deeply troubles me allows the detention and deportation of people engaging in innocent associational activity. It would allow for the detention and deportation of individuals who provide lawful assistance to groups that are not even designated by the Secretary of State as terrorist organizations but instead have engaged in something vaguely defined as "terrorist activity" sometime in the past. To avoid deportation, the immigrant is required to prove a negative: That he or she did not know, and should not have known, that the assistance would further terrorist activity.

I think this language creates a very real risk that truly innocent individuals could be deported for innocent associations with humanitarian or political groups that the Government later chooses to regard as terrorist organizations. Groups that could fit this definition could include Operation Rescue, Greenpeace, and even the Northern Alliance fighting the Taliban in northern Afghanistan. So this really amounts to a provision of "guilt by association," which I think violates the first amendment.

Speaking of the first amendment, under this bill, a lawful permanent resident who makes a controversial speech that the Government deems to be supportive of terrorism might be barred from returning to his or her family after taking a trip abroad.

Despite assurances from the administration at various points in this process that these provisions that implicate associational activity would be improved, there have been no changes in the bill on these points since it passed the Senate.

Here is where my caution in the aftermath of the terrorist attacks and my concern about the reach of the antiterrorism bill come together. To the extent that the expansion of new immigration powers that the bill grants the Attorney General are subject to abuse, who do we think is most likely to bear the brunt of that abuse? It probably won't be immigrants from Ireland. It probably won't be immigrants from El Salvador or Nicaragua or immigrants from Haiti or Africa. Most likely it will be immigrants from Arab, Muslim and South Asian countries.

In the wake of these terrible events, our Government has been given vast new powers, and they may fall most heavily on a minority of our population who already feel particularly, acutely the pain of this disaster.

Concerns of this kind have been raised with the administration. Supporters of this bill have just told us: Don't worry, the FBI would never do that. I call on the Attorney General and the Justice Department to ensure that my fears are not borne out.

The antiterrorism bill we consider in the Senate today, of course, highlights the march of technology and how that march cuts both for and against personal liberty. But Justice Brandeis foresaw some of the future in a 1928 dissent when he wrote:

> The progress of science in furnishing the Government with means of espionage is not likely to stop with wire-tapping. Ways may some day be developed by which the Government, without removing papers from secret drawers, can reproduce them in court, and by which it will be enabled to expose to a jury the most intimate occurrences of the home.... Can it be that the Constitution affords no protection against such invasions of individual security?

We must grant law enforcement the tools that it needs to stop this terrible threats, but we must give them only those extraordinary tools that they need and that relate specifically to the task at hand.

In the play, "A Man for All Seasons," Sir Thomas More questions the bounder Roper whether he would level the forest of English laws to punish the Devil. "What would you do?" More asks, "Cut a great road through the law to get after the Devil?" Roper affirms, "I'd cut down every law in England to do that." To which More replies:

"And when the last law was down, and the Devil turned round on you—where would you hide, Roper, the laws all being flat? This country's planted thick with laws from coast to coast...and if you cut them down...d'you really think you could stand upright in the winds that would blow then? Yes, I'd give the Devil benefit of law, for my own safety's sake."

We must maintain our vigilance to preserve our laws and our basic rights. We in this body have a duty to analyze, to test, to weigh new laws that the zealous and often sincere advocates of security would suggest to us. That is what I have tried to do with the anti-terrorism bill, and that is why I will vote against this bill when the roll is called.

Protecting the safety of the American people is a solemn duty of the Congress. We must work tirelessly to prevent more tragedies like the devastating attacks of September 11. We must prevent more children from losing their mothers, more wives from losing their husbands, and more firefighters from losing their heroic colleagues. But the Congress will fulfill its duty only when it protects both the American people and the freedoms at the foundation of American society.

So let us preserve our heritage of basic rights. Let us practice as well as preach that liberty, and let us fight to maintain that freedom that we call America.

Source: *Congressional Record*, October 25, 2001, S 10990–11060.

NO CHILD LEFT BEHIND (JANUARY 2002)

During the 2000 presidential campaign, Vice President Gore and Governor George W. Bush of Texas debated heavily over the future of the American education system. The No Child Left Behind Act was President Bush's solution to the educational crisis in America. He felt that this legislation would hold schools accountable and allow the government to withhold federal education funding if schools did not meet set standards. The No Child Left Behind Act implements a national standardized test for all students, regardless of learning disabilities, mental disabilities, or ESL status.

The president felt that No Child Left Behind would be an equitable way of enforcing the standards and would allow our school system to keep pace with the rest of the developed world; while opponents have seen this piece of legislation as neglecting analytical thinking, literature, and the social sciences. Many claim that No Child Left Behind has forced schools to narrowly adapt teaching to the passing of standardized tests. Since it was signed into law, many schools have lost their funding. At the time of its introduction, it was heavily supported by the Republican Party and heavily opposed by the Democratic Party. Currently, No Child Left Behind is still heavily questioned by educators and politicians alike, and has helped to foster the debate about the school voucher program.

BUSH'S REMARKS ON SIGNING THE NO CHILD LEFT BEHIND ACT OF 2001 IN HAMILTON, OHIO (JANUARY 8, 2002)

We've got large challenges here in America. There's no greater challenge than to make sure that every child—and all of us on this stage mean every child, not just a few children—every single child, regardless of where they live, how they're raised, the income level of their family, every child receive a first-class education in America.

And we owe the children of America a good education. And today begins a new era, a new time in public education in our country. As of this hour, America's schools will be on a new path of reform and a new path of results.

Our schools will have higher expectations. We believe every child can learn. Our schools will have greater resources to help meet those goals. Parents will have more information about the schools and more say in how their children are educated. From this day forward, all students will have a better chance to learn, to excel, and to live out their dreams.

I want to thank the Secretary of Education, Rod Paige, for being here and for his leadership. I asked Rod to join my administration because I wanted somebody who understood what it meant to run a school district in Washington, DC. I didn't need somebody that based his knowledge on theory; I wanted somebody who based his knowledge on experience. And Rod was a teacher, a school board member, and the superintendent of the Houston Independent School District. He did a fine job there, and he's doing a fine job in Washington.

First principle is accountability. Every school has a job to do, and that's to teach the basics and teach them well. If we want to make sure no child is left behind, every child must learn to read, and every child must learn to add and subtract. So in return for Federal dollars, we are asking States to design accountability systems to show parents and teachers whether or not children can read and write and add and subtract in grades three-through-eight.

The fundamental principle of this bill is that every child can learn, we expect every child to learn, and you must show us whether or not every child is learning. I read a quote one time from a young lady in New York. She said, "I don't ever remember taking an exam. They just kept passing me along. I ended up dropping out in the seventh grade. I basically felt nobody cared."

The story of children being just shuffled through the system is one of the saddest stories of America. "Let's just move them through." It's so much easier to move a child through than trying to figure out how to solve a child's problems. The first step to making sure that a child is not shuffled through is to test that child as to whether or not he or she can read and write or add and subtract.

The first way to solve a problem is to diagnose it. And so, what this bill says, it says every child can learn. And we want to know early, before it's too late, whether or not a child has a problem in learning. I understand taking tests aren't fun. Too bad. We need to know in America. We need to know whether or not children have got the basic education.

No longer is it acceptable to hide poor performance. No longer is it acceptable to keep results away from parents. One of the interesting things about this bill, it says that we're never going to give up on a school that's performing poorly, that when we find poor performance, a school will be given time and incentives and resources to correct their problems. A school will be given time to try other methodologies, perhaps other leadership, to make sure that people can succeed. If, however, schools don't perform, if, however, given the new resources, focused resources, they are unable to solve the problem of not educating their children, there must be real consequences. There must be a moment in which parents can say, "I've had enough of this school." Parents must be given real options in the face of failure in order to make sure reform is meaningful.

And so, therefore, this bill's second principle is, is that we trust parents to make the right decisions for their children. Any school that doesn't perform, any school that cannot catch up and do its job, a parent will have these options: a better public school, a tutor, or a charter school. We do not want children trapped in schools that will not change and will not teach.

The third principle of this bill is that we have got to trust the local folks on how to achieve standards, to meet the standards. In Washington, there's some smart people there, but the people who care most about the children in Hamilton are the citizens of Hamilton. The people who care most about the children in this school are the teachers and parents and school board members. And therefore, schools not only have the responsibility to improve; they now have the freedom to improve. The Federal Government will not micromanage how schools are run. We believe strongly—we believe strongly the best path to education reform is to trust the local people. And so the new role of the Federal Government is to set high standards, provide resources, hold people accountable, and liberate school districts to meet the standards.

I can't think of any better way to say to teachers, "We trust you." And first of all, we've got to thank all the teachers who are here. I thank you for teaching. Yours is indeed a noble profession, and our society is better off because you decided to teach. And by saying we trust local folks, we're really saying we trust you. We trust you. We want you to have as much flexibility as possible to see to it that every child that walks in your classroom can succeed. So thank you for what you do.

And a fourth principle is that we're going to spend more money, more resources, but they'll be directed at methods that work, not feel-good methods, not sound-good methods, but methods that actually work, particularly when it comes to reading. We're going to spend more on our schools, and we're going to spend it more wisely.

If we've learned anything over the last generations, money alone doesn't make a good school. It certainly helps. But as John mentioned, we've spent billions of dollars with lousy results. So now it's time to spend billions of dollars and get good results.

As John mentioned, too many of our kids can't read. You know, a huge percentage of children in poverty can't read at grade level. That's not right in America. We're going to win the war overseas, and we need to win the war against illiteracy here at home, as well. And so this bill—so this bill focuses on reading. It sets a grand goal for the country: Our children will be reading by the third grade. That's not an impossible goal. It's a goal we must meet if we want every child to succeed. And so, therefore, we tripled the amount of Federal funding for scientifically based early reading programs.

We've got money in there to make sure teachers know how to teach what works. We've got money in there to help promote proven methods of instruction. There are no more excuses, as far as I'm concerned, about not teaching children how to read. We know what works, the money is now available, and it's up to each local district to make sure it happens. It's up to you, the citizens of Hamilton, to make sure no child is left behind. And the Federal Government can spend money, and we can help set standards, and we can insist upon accountability. But the truth of the matter is, our schools will flourish when citizens join in the noble cause of making sure no child is left behind.

This is the end of a legislative process. Signing this bill is the end of a long, long time of people sitting in rooms trying to hammer out differences. It's a great symbol of what is possible in Washington when good people come together to do what's right. But it's just the beginning of change. And now it's up to you, the local citizens of our great land, the compassionate, decent citizens of America, to stand up and demand high standards, and to demand that no child—not one single child in America—is left behind.

Source: *Public Papers of the Presidents of the United States: George W. Bush* (Washington, DC: Government Printing Office), 26–29.

CRITICISM OF NO CHILD LEFT BEHIND (SEPTEMBER 4, 2002)

Mr. Edward M. Kennedy (D-MA). Mr. President, for families across this country who have school-age children, they have been involved over the period of these recent days and weeks preparing their children to attend, by and large, the public schools of our country. Over 90 percent of the children in this country go to the public schools. A little less than 10 percent go to private schools.

Over these last several months, we have had, with President Bush, a bipartisan effort which resulted in what was called the "No Child Left Behind Act." That legislation recognized that what is really needed for the neediest children in this country is school reform. But we also need investment, school reform and increased resources.

For a long time, the Title I program was criticized because it provided resources without really providing the kind of accountability that is so important. So there was a bipartisan effort to provide for that kind of accountability.

Now as parents are seeing their children going back to school and they are asking whether the Congress and this administration are meeting their responsibility. Because in that legislation, we are holding accountable the children that were going through school. We are holding accountable the schools. We are holding accountable teachers.

I was asked over the recent month of August as I went around Massachusetts, is: What is going to be the administration's response to the children being left behind with the budget that the administration recommended to the Congress for funding of No Child Left Behind? Will politicians be accountable? There are 10.3 million children who fall into what we call the Title I category. Over 6 million of those children are going to be left behind under the administration's budget. We do not expect that money in and of itself to be the answer to all of the problems, but it is a pretty good indication of the priorities of a nation and the priorities of an administration. And this chart is a pretty clear indication of the recent history of increased funding for education. We are talking here about the total education budget. In 1997, a 16 percent increase; 12 percent in 1998; 12 percent in 1999; 6 percent in the year 2000; 19 percent in 2001; and 16 percent in 2002. However, it is only 2.8 percent under this administration's budget, the lowest we have seen over the last 7 years.

Again, money is not everything, but we did make a commitment to the parents, to the families, to the schools. There is tough criteria for all of those groups.

We have seen, in the efforts made by Senator Harkin in the Appropriations Committee, the recommendation that it will be higher than this program. It will be some $4.2 billion, and it will raise this percentage up to about 6 percent. 2.8 percent is the recommendation that is being made by our Republican friends in the House of Representatives. By and large, the best judgment we have is that this will be the figure coming from the House, and we will be somewhat above, and the conference will come out lower, certainly, than what we have seen in recent years.

What has resulted from this—from the fact that we have not seen adequate funding of the program? We recognize in the No Child Left Behind Act that one of the most important necessities is a well-qualified teacher in every classroom in the country. There is virtually no increase in funding for teacher training. So the 18,000 teachers that would have been trained if there had been a cost of living increase will not receive the training.

Mr. President, 20,000 students will be cut from the college Work-Study Program; 25,000 limited-English-proficient children cut from the Federal bilingual program; 33,000 children cut from afterschool programs; there is virtually no increase in the Pell grants; and there is no increase in student loans.

What has the administration requested of the Congress? Why do I take a few moments of the Senate time today? I want to point out what is happening in this debate regarding funding of education because tomorrow in the House of Representatives, they will mark up a recommendation by this administration for $4 billion in new funding for private school vouchers. We understand, this is for private schools, 10 percent of the education, $4 billion. Yet just 2.8 percent increase for the public schools, where 90 percent of the children go.

There are a number of reasons we should be concerned. I think most of us believe that we should not be taking scarce funds from the public school children and putting them into private schools. That is in effect what this is doing. If we had the $4 billion, we would be able to increase the total number of poor children to be covered under the Title I program to about two-thirds of those that are being left behind this year. However, the administration said no; we will have $4 billion over a 5-year period to be used for the private schools, for just 10 percent of the children.

The reason we raise this issue is in case we have these resources again, we will have an opportunity, hopefully, to debate this, and it ought to be directed toward the public school system.

But beyond that, some of the things that concern us is that with the $4 billion, there is virtually no requirement that we have accountability. The administration made a great deal about accountability, to make sure that we know where the money is invested, what the results will be on the standardized systems to be able to tell if children are progressing. In my own State of Massachusetts, we have seen important progress where we have had accountability and support, including the recent announcement of the MCAS results in the past week, in which we have seen continued progress in math and continued progress made in English. Not all the problems are resolved, and there are still painful problems in terms of disparity, but we have seen progress made because of accountability.

The administration has talked about accountability. But for their $4 billion, there is no accountability to any schools to ensure that they do what all the public schools do, and that is, to have the examinations.

There is no accountability to ensure that private schools accept all the children. In the public school system there has to be acceptance of all of the children, but the private schools do not have to do that.

In private schools, there is no accountability to ensure teachers will be highly qualified teachers. We wrote in that legislation that in a 4-year period there will be highly qualified teachers in the classrooms. We fund a variety of programs regarding recruitment, training, and retention, and we give maximum flexibility to local communities to be able to do that. But there is no requirement with that $4 billion that they use those funds for highly qualified teachers in the classrooms. And there is no requirement to give the parents the critical information they need and which we have insured under this legislation.

So we are puzzled. We heard both the President and our good friends on the other side saying accountability was the key element. We agree that was enormously important—we are going to have accountability and resources. However, now we have the administration coming back with $4 billion more. Instead of allocating that to the 90 percent of the schools that will train the children of America, the public school systems which returned to school this past week—no, they will use that money, the $4 billion, in the private schools for vouchers. They have basically retreated on each and every one of these principles. It seems a very important mistake and one which we will have the opportunity, hopefully, to debate.

With those resources, if the Bush budget took that $4 billion in new funding for private schools over 5 years along with the cut in public schools, had that $4 billion been available for public schools, it would mean the upgrading of the skills of 1 million teachers across this country. It would upgrade the skills of 1 million teachers. You could provide 5.2 million more children with afterschool learning opportunities.

I just point out about the afterschool programs, because of all of the Federal programs that are out there that go through the process and are considered to be quality programs, when they get in line for the funding, the afterschool programs are No. 1. Do we understand that? There is a greater need, in terms of limited resources for these programs, than for any other federal program. People understand that if you are going to provide afterschool programs and supplementary services for the children who need them, this is the way to try to do it. We are seeing the results of success academically as well as in terms of the social progress the children have made.

This is what you would be able to do. You could provide 5.2 million more children with afterschool learning opportunities. You could provide a Pell Grant to 500,000 more college students—those students who are able, gifted, talented, motivated young people whose parents have limited resources and income. They will not go on to college because they are not eligible for the Pell Grants. With these resources, 5,000,000 more children would receive increased college aid.

As we continue this debate and discussion about funding education, it is enormously important that the American people understand whose side we are on. We on this side of the aisle believe very strongly that with scarce resources in our budget, these resources ought to be used to provide more highly qualified teachers in every classroom, smaller class sizes, afterschool programs, supplementary services, and information to parents so they know what is happening in those schools—all of those for the children in this country. We believe that is where the needs are. That is what we ought to be doing with scarce resources, not siphoning off $4 billion for the 10 percent of children who are attending private schools.

We will have an opportunity, when this comes before the Senate, to debate it further. But we want the parents of children going to public schools, who are facing increasing pressure—as we have seen all across this country as States have cut back in support and help to local communities, increasing the size of their classes, reducing the afterschool programs, cutting out a number of subjects such as music programs, and cutting back on the number of teachers' aides and teachers' assistants—to know that we understand this is not a time to abandon our public schools. This is a time to invest in our future.

One final point. We have had a great deal of discussion and debate about national security and national defense. I would like to make the point that ensuring that we are going to have well-qualified children in schools that are going to meet standards is an essential aspect of our national security and national defense. And we should not shortchange that investment any more than we do our Defense Department.

Source: *Congressional Record*, September 4, 2002, S 8150–8452.

YUCCA MOUNTAIN NUCLEAR WASTE SITE (FEBRUARY 2002)

Yucca Mountain has been a site of controversy for a long time. Located in Nye County, Nevada, the mountain is made up of volcanic material and has been proposed by many as a potential new nuclear waste site. The site is about 100 miles northwest of Las Vegas, Nevada, and is currently on land protected by the federal government.

The Department of Energy (DOE) has been studying Yucca Mountain since the 1980s and has deemed it suitable to function as a nuclear waste site. President Bush is a strong supporter of the project. Citing the need for bi-partisan cooperation and participation, he encouraged members of Congress to move on the project as soon as possible. The president believes that Yucca Mountain is an essential part of our nation's security and energy future.

Many citizens of Nevada feel that their concerns are not being addressed and strongly oppose the creation of this site. Polls consistently show that Nevada residents feel the federal government has not been honest when disclosing safety information, particularly pertaining to nuclear waste, and they do not want the site to be used. To add to their worries, the federal government has decided to ship the waste by rail, a mode of transportation that brings with it the possibility of rail accidents and is vulnerable to terrorist attack. The rail locations have not been identified and continue to be a source of discontent amongst the citizens. According to the Department of Transportation, there have been over 11,000 rail accidents in the past five years. Many critics claim that this project not only puts citizens at risk but it also places our entire nation in jeopardy.

The year 2010 is the projected year when the Yucca Mountain site will be in usage; however, it continues to be a disputed and controversial topic.

BUSH'S LETTER TO CONGRESSIONAL LEADERS RECOMMENDING THE YUCCA MOUNTAIN SITE FOR THE DISPOSAL OF SPENT NUCLEAR FUEL AND NUCLEAR WASTE (FEBRUARY 15, 2002)

...In accordance with section 114 of the Nuclear Waste Policy Act of 1982, 42 U.S.C. 10134 (the "Act"), the Secretary of Energy has recommended approval of the Yucca Mountain site for the development at that site of a repository for the geologic disposal of spent nuclear fuel and high level nuclear waste from the Nation's defense activities.

As is required by the Act, the Secretary has also submitted to me a comprehensive statement of the basis of his recommendation.

Having received the Secretary's recommendation and the comprehensive statement of the basis of it, I consider the Yucca Mountain site qualified for application for a construction authorization for a repository. Therefore, I now recommend the Yucca Mountain site for this purpose. In accordance with section 114 of the Act, I am transmitting with this recommendation to the Congress a copy of the comprehensive statement of the basis of the Secretary's recommendation prepared pursuant to the Act. The transmission of this document triggers an expedited process described in the Act. I urge the Congress to undertake any necessary legislative action on this recommendation in an expedited and bipartisan fashion.

Proceeding with the repository program is necessary to protect public safety, health, and the Nation's security because successful completion of this project would isolate in a geologic repository at a remote location highly radioactive materials now scattered throughout the Nation. In addition, the geologic repository would support our national security through disposal of nuclear waste from our defense facilities.

A deep geologic repository, such as Yucca Mountain, is important for our national security and our energy future. Nuclear energy is the second largest source of U.S. electricity generation and must remain a major component of our national energy policy in the years to come. The cost of nuclear power compares favorably with the costs of electricity generation by other sources, and nuclear power has none of the emissions associated with coal and gas power plants.

This recommendation, if it becomes effective, will permit commencement of the next rigorous stage of scientific and technical review of the repository program through formal licensing proceedings before the Nuclear Regulatory Commission. Successful completion of this program also will redeem the clear Federal legal obligation safely to dispose of commercial spent nuclear fuel that the Congress passed in 1982.

This recommendation is the culmination of two decades of intense scientific scrutiny involving application of an array of scientific and technical disciplines necessary and appropriate for this challenging undertaking. It is an undertaking that was mandated twice by the Congress when it legislated the obligations that would be redeemed by successful pursuit of the repository program. Allowing this recommendation to come into effect will enable the beginning of the next phase of intense scrutiny of the project necessary to assure the public health, safety, and security in the area of Yucca Mountain, and also to enhance the safety and security of the Nation as a whole.

Source: *Public Papers of the Presidents of the United States: George W. Bush* (Washington, DC: Government Printing Office), 239.

OPPOSE HOUSE JOINT RESOLUTION 87 AND STOP THE YUCCA MOUNTAIN PROJECT (MAY 8, 2002)

Mr. Jim Gibbons (R-NV). Mr. Speaker, today we will be deciding whether to ship high-level nuclear waste, one of the most dangerous and deadly substances known to man, across this great country by and through our roads and neighborhoods and schools and parkways.

Mr. Speaker, today we must reject this dangerous plan. Whatever Members believe, let us look at some of the startling facts.

According to the Department of Transportation itself, there have been over 11,000 train accidents in the past 5 years. It is estimated that at least one train accident occurs every 24 hours. Since 1998, 3,800 people have lost their lives and more than 45,000 people have been injured in train accidents in the United States alone. Just imagine how many more people would die or could have been injured had these trains been carrying high-level nuclear waste to Yucca Mountain.

Mr. Speaker, it takes only one antitank missile or one terrorist act to cause a catastrophic nuclear disaster, but today we can prevent that disaster. We can oppose House Joint Resolution 87 and stop the Yucca Mountain project now before we endanger the lives of thousands of innocent Americans.

Source: *Congressional Record*, May 8, 2002, H 2169.

SHUTTLE COLUMBIA (FEBRUARY 2003)

On February 1, 2003, thousands gathered at the Kennedy Space Center to watch the landing of Space Shuttle Columbia. Instead, the nation mourned the loss of all seven crew members when the shuttle disintegrated during reentry into the earth's atmosphere. Columbia was launched on January 16, 2003, on a sixteen-day scientific mission. The accident is attributed to damage on the left wing caused by a piece of foam that broke off during the launch. The break allowed hot gases to enter the wing during reentry to the earth's atmosphere, which subsequently caused the shuttle to disintegrate.

Following the crash, many focused their energy toward the examination of space travel and the safety of people involved. When adressing the nation, President Bush thanked the astronauts for their courage as well as the valuable mission that they undertook.

To ensure maximum safety possible, some members of Congress called for increased budget parameters for NASA while others wanted to suspend the space travel program indefinitely. Senator Christopher Bond (R-MO) called for a committee hearing to examine the problems of Columbia as well as to create preventable measures for future space travel. Recognizing the importance of space travel for technological advancement and scientific research, Senator Bond remembered the brave seven crew members aboard the Columbia and recognized that the best way to remember them and their legacy would be to continue with the program.

BUSH'S ADDRESS TO THE NATION ON THE LOSS OF SPACE SHUTTLE COLUMBIA (FEBRUARY 1, 2003)

My fellow Americans, this day has brought terrible news and great sadness to our country. At 9 o'clock this morning, Mission Control in Houston lost contact with our Space Shuttle Columbia. A short time later, debris was seen falling from the skies above Texas. The Columbia is lost. There are no survivors.

On board was a crew of seven: Col. Rick Husband; Lt. Col. Michael Anderson; Comdr. Laurel Clark; Capt. David Brown; Comdr. William McCool; Dr. Kalpana Chawla; and Ilan Ramon, a colonel in the Israeli Air Force. These men and women assumed great risk in the service to all humanity.

In an age when space flight has come to seem almost routine, it is easy to overlook the dangers of travel by rocket and the difficulties of navigating the fierce outer atmosphere of the Earth. These astronauts knew the dangers, and they faced them willingly, knowing they had a high and noble purpose in life. Because of their courage and daring and idealism, we will miss them all the more.

All Americans today are thinking as well of the families of these men and women who have been given this sudden shock and grief. You're not alone. Our entire Nation grieves with you. And those you loved will always have the respect and gratitude of this country.

The cause in which they died will continue. Mankind is led into the darkness beyond our world by the inspiration of discovery and the longing to understand. Our journey into space will go on.

In the skies today we saw destruction and tragedy. Yet farther than we can see, there is comfort and hope. In the words of the prophet Isaiah, "Lift your eyes and look to the heavens. Who created all these? He who brings out the starry hosts one by one and calls them each by name. Because of His great power and mighty strength, not one of them is missing."

The same Creator who names the stars also knows the names of the seven souls we mourn today. The crew of the shuttle Columbia did not return safely to Earth. Yet we can pray that all are safely home.

May God bless the grieving families, and may God continue to bless America.

Source: *Public Papers of the Presidents of the United States: George W. Bush* (Washington, DC: Government Printing Office), 151.

TRIBUTE TO THE SPACE SHUTTLE COLUMBIA ASTRONAUTS (FEBRUARY 4, 2003)

Mr. Christopher S. Bond (R-MO). Mr. President, I rise today with a heavy heart, which was lifted with the inspiring and thoughtful words of our guest Chaplain. I thank him for helping us see the greater design, the hope for the future, and the good news that we have been given by the Lord.

Even while we engage in the somber work of recovering from this terrible accident, in recovering the crew and the Columbia itself, our thoughts have already returned to the work of ensuring the safety of the U.S. manned space flight program and of the remaining shuttles. That is one of the responsibilities entrusted to us with the funding and oversight of the space agency.

Shuttle safety is not a new issue to those of us on the Appropriations Committee—or the authorizing committee—which funds the space agency and its operations. It is our job—my wonderful friend, the Senator from Maryland, Ms. Mikulski, and me—to ensure we know and understand each crucial element of the budget that safeguards the lives of our brave astronauts.

Whether during my service as chairman or under the leadership of my able colleague from Maryland, the direction of the VA-HUD and Independent Agencies Appropriations Subcommittee has been consistent throughout. Space shuttle safety is paramount.

I am proud the subcommittee I currently chair has consistently fully funded NASA's request for manned space flight program safety. Nevertheless, nothing about manned exploration of space is or will ever be free of risk. Manned space flight is, by its very nature, life threatening. Flying a space shuttle is nothing less than hurtling across the heavens where a slightest mistake guarantees instantaneous death.

No matter how successful we are, and no matter how many safe shuttle launches we have under our belts, we can never forget the dangers inherent in space travel. We can and should never be complacent.

We have an ironclad social and moral contract with our astronauts: In return for their willingness to place themselves in jeopardy on behalf of all mankind, we in return have an obligation to provide them with all the resources required for a safe flight.

While it is our goal to eliminate risk, to be quite frank, we cannot. We can only minimize risk. That is the cruel reality of manned space flight. Some element of risk haunts every mission. And in the face of such risks, we still have Americans and international partners willing—yes, anxious—to go. They know the risks. Their families understand they are in harm's way and still they dare to live a dream that very few of us can fully appreciate. It is precisely that element of human nature that inspires us to seek challenges greater than ourselves.

To those who question the value of our space program, I ask them: How can you quantify the dreams of millions of children here and across the world? How can you quantify the spirit of discovery? What value should we place on our quest to understand our place in the universe?

Those are the questions we must ask ourselves during this period of recovery. The weeks and months ahead will be filled with questions. So far, we have too few answers.

Our questions did not begin with Saturday's terrible loss of Columbia. The subcommittee has had continuing concerns about whether the budget requests from NASA accurately reflect the full safety needs of the space agency and the shuttle program. It is reflected in our reports. It is all in the public record. I know NASA has always placed the safety of our astronauts as its highest priority, we have an obligation to ensure that the analysis of safety, no matter what the cost, is fully disclosed, understood, and addressed. We have labored to do so in the past and will continue to do so in the future.

We recognize that Congress, NASA, and the administration have to live within a budget. At the same time, we cannot allow a budget to force our hand on safety decisions. We have not done so, nor will we. I do not believe NASA has done so, nor this, nor the previous administration. Nevertheless, our concerns on VA-HUD appropriations were heightened by the March 2002 NASA Aerospace Safety Advisory Panel Report which stated that the current budget projections for the space shuttle were insufficient to accommodate significant safety upgrades, infrastructure needs, and the maintenance of critical workforce skills over the long term.

Our most recent report to the appropriations bill endorsed these concerns as well as the need for additional funding for shuttle safety upgrades. Our concerns were sufficient to request that NASA conduct an assessment of future safety needs in light of the shuttle's longer than expected operational life and use. We need to know more and we need to know more now.

NASA has already responded with a request for additional shuttle upgrades and safety funding over the next few years. This was the right response, but we need to know how much more we need to do to ensure that every funding decision continues to make the lives of our astronauts the paramount priority at NASA.

Clearly, we had concerns, and those concerns remain. We must work together to gain greater confidence in NASA's budget.

Of course, we must find out what happened to the Columbia, fix the problem, and move our space program forward, as the deputy administrator for space so eloquently stated on Saturday. But this is not a simple issue. We have three international astronauts on the International Space Station, two Americans and one Russian. We need to be able to bring them home in complete safety.

The administration is moving forward with two commissions to understand what happened, and to make sure it does not happen again. In addition, I believe it is appropriate to hold a hearing in the appropriations subcommittee on shuttle funding upgrades and safety needs. This is too important an issue not to receive the full attention of the Senate. I assure my colleagues that we will work to provide whatever funding is necessary to meet the immediate needs of the space agency through the remaining months of the fiscal year.

We are currently waiting to hear back from NASA at this moment, and clearly we will provide whatever additional funds are necessary for NASA in the 2003 supplemental, as appropriate, or even if we receive a request in time in the conference report on the 2003 measure that is pending. I will convene a hearing on safety needs as soon as practicable, as soon as NASA has information for us, understanding full well that the immediate needs focus on recovery of the Columbia, the crew, and the twin investigations now underway.

At a time of such tragedy, we all function as part of a team with a single mission, to find out what went wrong, and then to take steps to make sure it never happens again. We must and we will leave no stone unturned. There are astronauts who have not yet flown but who will perhaps this year and in 10 years. They dream of carrying our hopes beyond this planet we call home. We must always keep faith with them and their families. We must honor the contract that binds us in this great endeavor.

That dream has not died with Columbia and her proud crew. Her dream lives on in the hearts of all of us who look to the heavens on a quiet night in awe and wonder, and we see the Columbia still. We mourn for the astronauts and we pray for their families. We shall always remember them, along with the Challenger and the Apollo crews. The courage of all of the astronauts shall forever inspire our dreams and brighten our hopes for the future.

Manned space exploration is a great challenge, a great opportunity. Yes, there are dangers with it, but fulfilling the hopes and the dreams of those who have gone before is our great opportunity and our obligation.

Source: *Congressional Record*, February 4, 2003, S 1847–1864.

HURRICANE KATRINA (SEPTEMBER 2005)

On August 28, 2005, Hurricane Katrina made its presence felt on the southeastern part of the United States. With winds of 175 miles per hour, Hurricane Katrina was one of the deadliest and most expensive hurricanes in the history of the United States. Katrina formed in the Bahamas as a Category 1 hurricane, but gained speed and reached Category 5 status by the time it hit U.S. shores. Financial estimates of damage from the region run to around seventy-five billion dollars. The human cost was also high: more than 1,600 people are presumed dead.

The storm was one of the largest hurricanes in U.S. history causing devastation for more than 100 miles from the storm's center. This led to major damage along the coastlines of Alabama, Mississippi, and Louisiana, where large parts of the city of New Orleans was submerged under water.

President Bush responded quickly with condolences for the affected region. He outlined his plan for hurricane relief by increasing the number of police and law enforcement officials, emergency personnel, and hospital workers in the affected region. Disaster recovery missions started immediately; however, not soon enough according to some critics.

In addition, President Bush met with the Federal Reserve Chairman Alan Greenspan to assess the economic damage caused by the Hurricane Katrina and to develop an economic strategy to relieve the survivors. President Bush acknowledged that gas prices would jump overnight as major oil and gas pipelines were shut down in the Gulf Coast area.

The response by the federal government, as well as the availability of state resources, has been under heavy criticism. Many members of Congress have questioned the quality of response to the disaster and the time needed by the federal government to mobilize and assist the victims. Furthermore, attention was called to the role of local, state, and federal governments as jurisdiction and responsibility was debated. Citing many incidents of violence and long waits for assistance, critics have questioned both state and federal leadership and their inability to improve the situation. In the days immediately after the disaster, Jerrold Nadler (D-NY) drew attention to the lack of response and coordination by several agencies involved in emergency relief. Days later, he cited that the relief efforts still lacked an effective food, water, and medicine distribution system and urged all parties involved to work together to fix the situation.

BUSH'S REMARKS FOLLOWING A MEETING WITH FORMER PRESIDENT GEORGE BUSH AND FORMER PRESIDENT WILLIAM J. CLINTON: HURRICANE KATRINA (SEPTEMBER 1, 2005)

... Our first priority, of course, is to save lives. There are over 80 FEMA teams that have been deployed to the Gulf Coast to conduct search and rescue missions. I want to thank those who are working long hours, for their dedication to saving lives. We've got Coast Guard folks and Navy and Army and Air Force and National Guardsmen from many different States that are delivering needed supplies and providing the rescue missions, trying to reach those in danger.

We're working hard to repair the breaches in the levees. Federal, State, and local agencies are also cooperating to sustain life. That means getting food and water to those who are stranded. Medical personnel and local officials are helping hospital patients and people gathered in the Superdome to evacuate. Again, I want to thank the folks in Texas for welcoming those people. Bus caravans are shuttling back and forth between Houston and New Orleans to get those folks to Houston. Law enforcement and National Guardsmen and local leaders are working to restore public order.

Earlier today, General Blum along with Mike Chertoff gave me a briefing about the number of guards-folks trained in police work that will be moving into New Orleans as well as other law enforcement officials from around the area. As we speak, people are moving into the New Orleans area to maintain law and order. I thank them for their good work. Government agencies are working with faith-based and community groups to find shelters for thousands of displaced persons.

And finally, we're moving forward with a comprehensive recovery strategy. We're working hard to restore electric power, repair transportation infrastructure, restart energy production, and of course, strategize as to how to provide housing for these folks.

I met with Chairman Greenspan at lunch as well as the economic team to evaluate the impact of Hurricane Katrina. We particularly spent a lot of time talking about the damage done to our energy infrastructure and its effect on the availability and price of gasoline. In our judgment, we view this storm as a temporary disruption that is being addressed by the Government and by the private sector. We've taken immediate steps to address the issue. The Secretary of Energy is approving loans of crude oil from the Strategic Petroleum Reserve. The EPA has provided a temporary, nationwide waiver for fuel requirements so supplies of gasoline can move more easily within our country and so that we can attract more gasoline from overseas.

We're also working with energy companies to repair and reactivate major refineries and pipelines. The good folks must understand that major refineries have been shut down, which means it's going to be hard to get gasoline to some markets. We're working to help these pipelines get up and running. Pipelines carry refined product.

And so we're working with the majors—major oil companies to get the [sic]—with Colonial Pipeline so they can carry the products of the major oil companies, the refined products. Right now the Colonial Pipeline, which is a major pipeline serving the East Coast, is back in operation but only at 50-percent capacity. We anticipate that as the days go by, more and more of that capacity will be restored. Other major pipelines are coming back online. But as I said, we're going to have a temporary disruption of gasoline product.

Another challenge we face is that the downed pipelines are causing the need to transport gasoline to needed markets by ship. Under current law, shipping between American ports can only take place on American ships, and there are currently not enough American ships to move the oil and gasoline to where it's needed. So today I've instructed Secretary of Homeland Security Chairman Chertoff to temporarily waive this requirement, so foreign ships can also help distribute oil and gasoline to where it's needed. Today's action will further help us move gasoline to accommodate the demands of the American citizens.

This recovery is going to be a long process. It's going to take a lot of hard work and patience and resolve. It's also going to require a lot of money. And the Federal Government will do its part, but the private sector needs to do its part as well. And that's why I've asked Presidents Bush and Clinton to lead a nationwide fundraising effort to help the victims of Hurricane Katrina.

In the days ahead, the former Presidents will ask Americans to open their hearts and their wallets to help those in need. And they're going to talk to large corporations and small businesses and individual citizens across the Nation. The contributions will benefit the relief organizations that are doing vital work on the ground. We're going to take a look and make sure that the money raised is money needed. Right now if our fellow citizens want to help, they ought to give a cash donation to the Red Cross...

I was so proud of the efforts that President Clinton and President Bush did to help the victims of the tsunami relief. Our country marveled at their capacity to rally our citizens and to work together. And once again, I've asked them to work to help the needs of those who hurt. And once again, I'm confident that the American people will respond.

I know this is an agonizing time, or we all know this is an agonizing time for the people of the Gulf Coast. I ask their continued patience as recovery operations unfold. I can assure them that the thoughts and prayers of the entire Nation are with them and their loved ones. I'm also confident that when it's all said and done, the efforts to rebuild the great city of New Orleans and to rebuild those communities in Mississippi and to help the folks in Alabama will make this Nation a stronger place.

Source: *Public Papers of the Presidents of the United States: George W. Bush* (Washington, DC: Government Printing Office), 1336–1338.

CRITICISM OF THE HURRICANE KATRINA RESPONSE (SEPTEMBER 2, 2005)

Mr. Jerrold Nadler (D-NY). Mr. Speaker, it is with a heavy heart that I rise in support of the emergency relief bill. I know that all of us have been held rapt by the images and stories coming out of the Gulf Coast. The sorrow and suffering there is almost unimaginable, and it is my fervent hope and prayer that relief, real relief, will come soon.

On top of our grief, there is also outrage for it is nothing short of outrageous that in this country, where we talk of 9/11 every day, we still have not dedicated enough resources to improving our emergency response capabilities.

The people of New Orleans and the Gulf Coast, as they wait day after agonizing day for help to arrive, are crying out for leadership and more simply, for help. For those who have died unnecessarily, the help is already too late. If this is the best the world's greatest power can do for its own people, or if it is not, it is a national disgrace.

There will be plenty of time in the future to assess exactly why we were so poorly prepared for this storm and why it has taken the Federal Government so long after the levees broke to get effective help to New Orleans.

Certainly the roots of the inept handling of the situation are old and deep, but in the short term we need to focus on solutions. We need real leadership, a real plan, and a much bigger contingent of emergency transportation and aid workers. Reports from every corner of embattled New Orleans are that the presence of law enforcement is at best minimal, despite the declarations of the Secretary of Homeland Security, and there is, 5 days after the hurricane and 3 days after the levees broke, still no effective distribution of food, water or medicine.

How can this be? We cannot let another hour pass without a substantive response to the glowing shortfalls in the relief and evacuation effort. I would like to join the minority leader, the gentlewoman from California (Ms. Pelosi), in her call for the creation of a Select Hurricane Relief Task Force.

Our hearts go out to all those affected as well as those doing their best to respond to this disaster. Tragically, it is evident that the Federal Government's response has been wholly inadequate. Congress must insist on immediate improvement so that we can put an end to the suffering in New Orleans and the Gulf Coast as soon as possible.

Finally, we must learn some lessons. We must not save money by not preparing to prevent or to ameliorate potential catastrophes. We did not, despite ample warning, properly build up and strengthen New Orleans' defenses against hurricanes. We are paying a frightful price for that negligence.

We should learn from this disaster. The administration and Congress cut the budget for building up the levees, and we are reaping the whirlwind. The administration has acted unbelievably lethargically in bringing relief efforts, and people have died as a result. Let us not continue our negligent disregard until we suffer a nuclear or chemical catastrophe. I am tired, Mr. Speaker, of passing post-catastrophe relief bills. It is time the administration and this Congress act to prevent the next catastrophe.

Source: *Congressional Record*, September 2, 2005, H 7635.

WIRETAPS/DOMESTIC SPYING (DECEMBER 2005)

When the USA PATRIOT Act was passed in 2001, it gave broad powers to the Department of Homeland Security, NSA, FBI, and the CIA. One method that the NSA in particular has made great use of in the government's fight against terror has been domestic wiretapping.

Domestic wiretapping requires a warrant from a federal judge if the person under suspicion is a U.S. citizen. It has come to light, however, that the NSA has been conducting illegal wiretaps of U.S. citizens without warrants. In a series of speeches, President Bush first claimed that he would never have authorized this illegal practice. Slowly, however, his rhetoric changed into a defense of the practice.

Domestic wiretapping without warrants, it is argued by critics, is unconstitutional and a violation of privacy. Democrats and Republicans alike argue over the legality of domestic wiretapping. The leak that the NSA had been wiretapping without legal authorization caused the Bush administration to quickly defend its actions as necessary for the nation's security during the War on Terror. It is interesting to note, however, that the majority of those who have been subjected to wiretapping have shown no suspicious activity whatsoever and only a handful of people have been arrested.

BUSH'S REMARKS ON INTELLIGENCE AND DOMESTIC WIRETAPS (DECEMBER 19, 2005)

So, consistent with U.S. law and the Constitution, I authorized the interception of international communications of people with known links to Al Qaeda and related terrorist organizations. This program is carefully reviewed approximately every 45 days to ensure it is being used properly. Leaders in the United States Congress have been briefed more than a dozen times on this program. And it has been effective in disrupting the enemy while safeguarding our civil liberties.

This program has targeted those with known links to Al Qaeda. I've reauthorized this program more than 30 times since the September the 11th attacks, and I intend to do so for so long as our Nation is [sic]—for so long as the Nation faces the continuing threat of an enemy that wants to kill American citizens.

Q. . . . why did you skip the basic safeguards of asking courts for permission for the intercepts?

The President. First of all, I—right after September the 11th, I knew we were fighting a different kind of war. And so I asked people in my administration to analyze how best for me and our Government to do the job people expect us to do, which is to detect and prevent a possible attack. That's what the American people want. We looked at the possible scenarios. And the people responsible for helping us protect and defend came forth with the current program, because it enables us to move faster and quicker. And that's important. We've got to be fast on our feet, quick to detect and prevent.

We use FISA still—you're referring to the FISA court in your question—of course, we use FISAs. But FISA is for long-term monitoring. What is needed in order to protect the American people is the ability to move quickly to detect.

Now, having suggested this idea, I then, obviously, went to the question, is it legal to do so? I am—I swore to uphold the laws. Do I have the legal authority to do this? And the answer is, absolutely. As I mentioned in my remarks, the legal authority is derived from the Constitution as well as the authorization of force by the United States Congress.

Q. ....why, in the 4 years since 9/11, has your administration not sought to get changes in the law instead of bypassing it, as some of your critics have said?

The President. No, I appreciate that. First, I want to make clear to the people listening that this program is limited in nature to those that are known Al Qaeda ties and/or affiliates. That's important. So it's a program that's limited, and you brought up something that I want to stress, and that is, is that these calls are not intercepted within the country. They are from outside the country to in the country or vice versa. So in other words, this is not a—if you're calling from Houston to L.A., that call is not monitored. And if there was ever any need to monitor, there would be a process to do that.

Secondly, an open debate about law would say to the enemy, "Here's what we're going to do." And this is an enemy which adjusts. We monitor this program carefully. We have consulted with Members of the Congress over a dozen times. We are constantly reviewing the program. Those of us who review the program have a duty to uphold the laws of the United States, and we take that duty very seriously.

Q. Thank you, Mr. President. You say you have an obligation to protect us. Then why not monitor those calls between Houston and L.A.? If the threat is so great, and you use the same logic, why not monitor those calls? Americans thought they weren't being spied on in calls overseas—why not within the country, if the threat is so great?

The President. We will, under current law, if we have to. We will monitor those calls. And that's why there is a FISA law. We will apply for the right to do so. And there's a difference—let me finish—there is a difference between detecting, so we can prevent, and monitoring. And it's important to know the distinction between the two.

Q. But preventing is one thing, and you said the FISA laws essentially don't work because of the speed in monitoring calls overseas.

The President. I said we use the FISA courts to monitor calls. It's a very important tool, and we do use it. I just want to make sure we've got all tools at our disposal. This is an enemy which is quick, and it's lethal. And sometimes we have to move very, very quickly. But if there is a need based upon evidence, we will take that evidence to a court in order to be able to monitor calls within the United States.

Source: *Public Papers of the Presidents of the United States: George W. Bush* (Washington, DC: Government Printing Office), 1885–1896.

CRITICISM OF PROVIDING FOR CONSIDERATION OF H.R. 5020, INTELLIGENCE AUTHORIZATION ACT FOR FISCAL YEAR 2007 (APRIL 26, 2006)

Mr. James P. McGovern (D-MA). Mr. Speaker, H.R. 5020, the Intelligence Authorization Act for Fiscal Year 2007, deals with one of the most important aspects of our national security: our ability to gather and analyze intelligence effectively so that our policies are based on fact, not fantasy or obsessive desire, so that our Federal law enforcement agencies can defend us from the threat of attack, and so that our allies can rely on our resources for timely, coordinated operations in defense of freedom abroad.

I want to commend Chairman Hoekstra and Ranking Member Harman and members of the Intelligence Committee for authorizing 100 percent of the funding required for our counterterrorism operations. Regrettably, President Bush only included 78 percent of this funding in his budget request; so I thank the committee for correcting this dangerous shortfall.

The Intelligence Authorization Act traditionally receives strong bipartisan support and will likely receive that same support this year. But despite its many attributes, this bill could have and should have been better. This bill could have and should have required a dedicated funding line for the Privacy and Civil Liberties Oversight Board. When Congress passed the Intelligence Reform and Terrorism Prevention Act in December 2004 in response to the findings and recommendations of the 9/11 Commission report, it created this board to serve as a civil liberties watchdog on the potential erosion of the basic constitutional rights of the American people in a post-9/11 world.

Now, 15 months later, we find our concerns about basic civil rights to have been well founded, but the oversight board is barely up and running. The President did not nominate the members of the board for 9 months. The Senate took 5 months to confirm the chair and vice chair. And, once again, the President's budget failed to include a single penny for the board's operation in fiscal year 2007.

This could have and should have been fixed in committee. Congressmen Hastings, Reyes, and Holt offered an amendment to provide $3 million in dedicated funding for the oversight board, an amendment that should have had bipartisan support. But the majority chose to reject this funding and abandon their promise to the American people to safeguard their most basic freedoms and rights. And last night in the Rules Committee, the Republican leadership compounded this mistake by denying Congressman Reyes the right to offer this same amendment for debate on the House floor.

And then we have the issue of the National Security Agency's spying on U.S. citizens. In committee, Representative Eshoo offered a carefully crafted amendment to withhold 20 percent of the NSA's budget until the executive branch provided the Intelligence Committee with the total cost of its surveillance program. That is all: just inform the committee of this one number. The Eshoo amendment was not looking for more operational details. It was not passing judgment on whether the NSA's domestic spying program is legal or not, even though that is a controversial matter in this House. All it was looking for is how many of our tax dollars are being spent on this surveillance program.

This is a question that should concern every single Member of this body on both sides of the aisle. But with just one exception, the Republican majority found it too much to ask and rejected the Eshoo amendment.

Yesterday in the Rules Committee, the Republican leadership went even further. The Republican Rules Committee denied Representatives Schiff, Flake, Harman, and Inglis the right to offer their bipartisan amendment for debate. This amendment would have required a classified disclosure to the Intelligence and Judiciary Committees, the two committees with jurisdiction and oversight responsibilities over the NSA and the FISA process, on which U.S. citizens have been the subject of NSA electronic surveillance, and what criteria was used to target them. Such a classified report would allow Congress to understand the program and whether any current laws need to be amended to grant the President the authority he needs to carry out this program more effectively or make any changes to safeguard against abuse. In short, these two committees need this information in order to do their jobs, in order to carry out their oversight responsibilities.

This bipartisan amendment should have received bipartisan support from the Rules Committee, but it did not; not from the Republican majority on this Rules Committee and certainly not from the Republican leadership of this House.

It is outrageous, Mr. Speaker. Many of us believe that when the President authorized the NSA surveillance of Americans, he broke the law, plain and simple. And when the Attorney General says that Congress somehow granted the authority for this program after September 11, he is just wrong.

We are talking about the most basic fundamental civil liberties that protect the American people, and the Republican leadership will not even let us debate it. What are they afraid of?

I would ask my Republican friends to re-read their Constitution. Congress was not designed to be a rubber stamp for the President. Congress was not designed to protect Members from difficult votes on controversial issues. Congress was not designed to protect the President's political rear end. But under this leadership that is exactly what Congress has become.

If my friends on the other side of the aisle believe that this President should have the ability to spy on Americans without a warrant and without going to the FISA court, then they should write that bill and bring it to the floor. They should at least show that level of respect for this House and for this Constitution.

I am willing to bet that the majority of my colleagues on both sides of the aisle believe that what the President is doing is wrong. But either way, the very least we could do is have a debate and a vote.

Mr. Speaker, 25 amendments were brought to the Rules Committee last night. They dealt with issues ranging from how the NSA carries out surveillance of American citizens to how the Intelligence Committee and other relevant committees are briefed about weapons of mass destruction or the situations in Iran, North Korea, Iraq, and other hot spots. They dealt with how information is classified or reclassified, how national security whistle-blowers are protected or punished, and whether and how the amount of funds requested and appropriated for various intelligence-related activities are reported to Congress.

These are not trivial matters, Mr. Speaker. Yet only five amendments, five amendments, Mr. Speaker, plus the manager's amendment, were made in order under this highly restrictive rule.

Why is the Republican leadership so afraid to debate these issues? Why is it so afraid to debate, period? After nearly 4 months of a lackluster Congress, are we suddenly on some tight time clock so there is no time to debate matters affecting national security? Do we need to get out of town by Thursday afternoon? I am happy to stay in town on Friday if it means we can get a full debate on the Intelligence Authorization Act.

I am tired of restrictive rules. I am tired of stifling debate. I am tired of ignoring or running away from the big issues. I urge my colleagues to vote "no" on this restrictive rule and to support an open debate on important issues facing our national security and intelligence agencies.

Source: *Congressional Record,* April 26, 2006, H 1774–1785.

DOMESTIC POLICY WEB SITES

Allen, Mike. "Why Bush Picked Alito." *Time,* March 25, 2006. http://www.time.com/time/nation/article/0,8599,1124426,00.html

American Library Association. "Chronology of the USA Patriot Act, 2001." http://www.ala.org/Template.cfm?Section=theusapatriotact&Template=/ContentManagement/ContentDisplay.cfm&ContentID=11185

Associated Press. "Alito Sworn in as Supreme Court Justice." *MSNBC,* January 31, 2006. http://www.msnbc.msn.com/id/11111624/

———. "Video Shows Bush Got Explicit Katrina Warning." *MSNBC,* March 2, 2006. http://www.msnbc.msn.com/id/11627394/

Baker, Peter. "Alito Nomination Sets Stage for Ideological Battle." *Washington Post,* November 1, 2005. http://www.washingtonpost.com/wp-dyn/content/article/2005/10/31/AR2005103100180.html

Baker, Peter, and Jim VandeHei. "Bush Chooses Roberts for Court." *Washington Post,* July 20, 2005. http://www.rasmussenreports.com/2005/Katrina_September%2018.htm

BBC News. "Columbia Puncture Theory Examined," January 27, 2006. http://news.bbc.co.uk/2/hi/in_depth/sci_tech/2003/shuttle_disaster/

Branigin, William. "Bush Nominates Negroponte to New Intel Post." *Washington Post,* February 17, 2005. http://www.washingtonpost.com/wp-dyn/articles/A31826-2005Feb17.html

"Bush Katrina Ratings Fall after Speech." *Rasmussen Reports,* September 18, 2005. http://www.rasmussenreports.com/2005/Katrina_September%2018.htm

"Campaign Finance Reform." *Almanac of Policy Issues,* March 27, 2002. http://www.policyalmanac.org/government/campaign_finance.shtml

CBS News. "Bush Defends Domestic Spying." December 19, 2005. http://www.cbsnews.com/stories/2005/12/19/politics/main1135323.shtml

———. "Bush Withdraws Miers Nomination." October 27, 2005. http://www.cbsnews.com/stories/2005/10/27/supremecourt/main987367.shtml

Chaddock, Gail. "Softening of No Child Left Behind." *Christian Science Monitor,* March 16, 2004. http://www.csmonitor.com/2004/0316/p03s01-uspo.html

CNN. "An Interview with Karl Rove." September 1, 2004. http://www.pbs.org/newshour/bb/politics/july-dec04/rove_9-01.html

———. "Bush Wants Broad 'Homeland Security' Overhaul." June 7, 2002. http://archives.cnn.com/2002/ALLPOLITICS/06/06/bush.security/

———. "Remains Thought to Be from Columbia Crew." February 1, 2003. http://www.cnn.com/2003/TECH/space/02/01/shuttle.columbia/

Connolly, Ceci. "2 GOP Senators Defend Bush on Stem Cell Research." *Washington Post,* August 13, 2004. http://www.washingtonpost.com/wp-dyn/articles/A61162-2004Aug12.html

Department of Education. "No Child Left Behind." January 8, 2002. http://www.ed.gov/nclb/landing.jhtml

Department of Justice. "Preserving Life and Liberty." March 2, 2006. http://www.lifeandliberty.gov/

Eggen, Dan. "Bush Authorized Domestic Spying." *Washington Post*, December 16, 2005. http://www.washingtonpost.com/wp-dyn/content/article/2005/12/16/AR2005121600021.html

Electronic Privacy Information Center. "The USA Patriot Act." February 27, 2006. http://www.epic.org/privacy/terrorism/usapatriot/default.html

Environmental News Service. "Bush Greenlights Yucca Mountain Nuclear Waste Dump." February 15, 2002. http://www.ens-newswire.com/ens/feb2002/2002-02-15-01.asp

The White House. Faith Based and Community Initiatives Fact Sheet. http://www.whitehouse.gov/government/fbci/

Federation of American Scientists. "National Security Presidential Directives: George W. Bush Administration." March 22, 2006. http://www.fas.org/irp/offdocs/nspd/

Fitton, Tom. "Bush Keeps Presidential Papers All in the Family." *Detroit News*, March 15, 2006. http://www.detnews.com/apps/pbcs.dll/article?AID=/20060315/OPINION01/603150334/1008

Fletcher, Michael. "White House Counsel Miers Chosen for Court: Some Question Her Lack of Experience as Judge." *Washington Post*, October 4, 2005. http://www.washingtonpost.com/wp-dyn/content/article/2005/10/03/AR2005100300252.html

Horrigan, Marie. "Bush Lauds Negroponte as National Intelligence Director." *The Washington Times*, February 18, 2005. http://www.washtimes.com/upi-breaking/20050217-015710-9887r.htm

Kiefer, Francine. "A Fight Brews Over Ex-President's Papers." *Christian Science Monitor*, November 6, 2001. http://www.csmonitor.com/2001/1106/p2s2-usju.html

Krugman, Paul. "Karl Rove's America." *The New York Times* (Op-Ed), July 15, 2005. http://www.nytimes.com/2005/07/15/opinion/15krugman.html?ex=1279080000&en=d6626b2479012841&ei=5088&partner=rssnyt&emc=rss

Lacayo, Richard. "Stem Cell Decision: How Bush Got There." *Time.com*, August 20, 2001. http://www.time.com/time/2001/stemcells/

Lardner, George Jr. "Bush Clamping Down on Presidential Papers." *Washington Post*, November 1, 2001. http://www.washingtonpost.com/ac2/wp-dyn/A20731-2001Oct31

MSNBC. "How Bush Blew It." http://www.msnbc.msn.com/id/9287434/

National Public Radio. "Like Reagan Before Him, Bush Mourns Shuttle Loss." February 1, 2003. http://www.npr.org/templates/story/story.php?storyId=960446

Nieves, Evelyn. "Yucca Mountain Looms Over Vote." *Washington Post*, October 29, 2004. http://www.washingtonpost.com/wp-dyn/articles/A7362-2004Oct28.html

Nuclear Energy Insight. "It's Official: Bush Signs Yucca Mountain Resolution." August/September 2002. http://www.nei.org/documents/insight2002_08.pdf

Perl, Raphael. "Drug Control: International Policy and Approaches." *CRS Brief for Congress*, June 7, 2005. http://www.fas.org/sgp/crs/misc/IB88093.pdf

Purdum, Todd. "In Pursuit of Conservative Stamp, Bush Nominates Roberts." *New York Times*, July 20, 2005. http://www.nytimes.com/2005/07/20/politics/politicsspecial1/20nominee.html?ex=1279512000&en=07a975aedd298b36&ei=5088&partner=rssnyt&emc=rss

"Religion and Social Welfare." *The Pew Forum on Religion and Public Life*. http://pewforum.org/social-welfare/

Richardson, Valerie. "Drug Control Strategy Launched." *The Washington Times*, February 9, 2006. http://washingtontimes.com/national/20060209-121823-4265r.htm

Risen, James, and Eric Lichtblau. "Bush Lets U.S. Spy on Callers without Courts." *New York Times*, December 16, 2005. http://select.nytimes.com/gst/abstract.html?res=F00F1FFF3D540C758DDDAB0994DD404482

Stem Cell Research. March 25, 2006. http://www.cell-stem.com/

U.S. Conference of Mayors. "President Bush Announces USA Freedom Corps." February 4, 2002. http://www.usmayors.org/uscm/us_mayor_newspaper/documents/02_04_02/freedom_corps.asp

U.S. Department of State. "President Highlights Faith Based Initiative at Leadership Conference." March 1, 2005. http://usinfo.state.gov/usa/faith/s030105.htm

USA Freedom Corps. http://www.usafreedomcorps.gov/

The White House. "Bush Signs Homeland Security Act." November 2002. http://www.whitehouse.gov/news/releases/2002/11/20021125-6.html

———. "Bush Signs USA Patriot Act: Improvement and Reauthorization Act." March 9, 2006. http://www.whitehouse.gov/infocus/patriotact/

———. "Hurricane Recovery: Rebuilding the Gulf Coast." March 8, 2006. http://www.whitehouse.gov/infocus/hurricane/

———. "President Addresses Nation on Space Shuttle Columbia Tragedy." February 1, 2003. http://www.whitehouse.gov/news/releases/2003/02/20030201-2.html

———. "President Bush Outlines Campaign Reform Principles." March 15, 2001. http://www.whitehouse.gov/news/releases/2001/03/20010315-7.html

———. "President Discusses Stem Cell Research." August 2001. http://www.whitehouse.gov/news/releases/2001/08/20010809-2.html

———. "President Nominates Harriet Miers as Supreme Court Justice." http://www.whitehouse.gov/news/releases/2005/10/20051003.html

———. "President Signs Yucca Mountain Bill." July 2002. http://www.whitehouse.gov/news/releases/2002/07/20020723-2.html

———. "The President's National Drug Control Strategy." February 2002. http://www.whitehouse.gov/news/releases/2002/02/20020212-2.html

———. "Protecting the Homeland." December 17, 2005. http://www.whitehouse.gov/infocus/homeland/index.html

———. "Transforming the Federal Role in Education so No Child Is Left Behind." http://www.whitehouse.gov/news/reports/no-child-left-behind.html

———. "USA Freedom Corps." January 2002. http://www.whitehouse.gov/news/releases/2002/01/freedom-corps-policy-book.html

White House Office of Faith Based and Community Initiatives. http://www.whitehouse.gov/government/fbci/

Will, George. "Campaign Finance 'Reform'?" March 31, 2002. http://www.townhall.com/opinion/columns/georgewill/2002/03/31/162798.html

York, Byron. "New Campaign-Finance-Reform Follies." *National Review*, April 19, 2005. http://www.nationalreview.com/york/york200504190904.asp

"Yucca Mountain: Nuclear Waste in Nevada." *Las Vegas Review Journal*. http://www.reviewjournal.com/news/yuccamtn/

DOMESTIC POLICY REFERENCE
ARTICLES AND BOOKS

Bell, Jeffrey, and Frank Cannon. "The *Bush* Realignment: Morals Matter Most." *Weekly Standard* 10, no. 9 (November 15, 2004): 9–11.

Black, Amy, Douglas L. Koopman, and David K. Ryden. *Of Little Faith: The Politics of George W. Bush's Faith-based Initiatives*. Washington, DC: Georgetown University Press, 2004.

Brady, David, and Craig Volden. *Revolving Gridlock: Politics and Policy from Jimmy Carter to George W. Bush*. Boulder, CO: Westview Press, 2006.

Campbell, Dowling, ed. *A Bird in the Bush: Failed Domestic Policies of the George W. Bush Administration*. New York: Algora Publishing, 2005.

Casse, Daniel. "Is Bush a Conservative?" *Commentary* 117, no. 2 (February 2004): 19.

Chittister, Joan. "Spy Story Highlights Presidential Overreach." *National Catholic Reporter* 42, no. 11 (January 13, 2006): 16.

Christian, Margena. "Black Leaders Sound Off: Did Race Delay Relief to Disaster Areas?" *Jet* 108, no. 13 (September 26, 2005): 20.

Goldsmith, Stephen. "What Compassionate Conservatism Is—and Is Not." *Hoover Digest*, no. 4 (2000): 27.

Greenstein, Fred. "The Contemporary Presidency: The Changing Leadership of George W. Bush: A Pre- and Post-9/11 Comparison." *Presidential Studies Quarterly* 32, no. 2 (June 2002): 387.

———. *The George W. Bush Presidency: An Early Assessment*. Baltimore, MD: Johns Hopkins University Press, 2003.

———. *The Presidential Difference: Leadership Style from FDR to George W. Bush*. New York: The Free Press, 2000.

Hiltzik, Michael. *The Plot against Social Security: How the Bush Plan Is Endangering Our Financial Future*. New York: HarperCollins Books, 2005.

Himelfarb, Richard, and Rosanna Perotti, eds. *Principle Over Politics? The Domestic Policy of the George W. Bush Administration*. Westport, CT: Praeger Publishers, 2004.

Lewis, William H. "The War on Terror: A Retrospective." *Mediterranean Quarterly* 13, no. 4 (Fall 2002): 21–37.

Marsh, Jeanne. "Bush Plan Takes Security Out of Social Security." *Social Work* 50, no. 2 (April 2005): 99.

McMahon, Kevin. *Winning the White House, 2004: Region by Region, Vote by Vote*. New York: Palgrave Macmillan, 2005.

Moore, Stephen. "Make the Tax Cuts Permanent Now." *The Weekly Standard* 10, no. 15 (December 27, 2004): 14.

Niman, Michael. "Katrina's America: Failure, Racism, and Profiteering." *The Humanist* 65, no. 6 (November 1, 2005): 11.

Piven, Frances Fox. *The War at Home: The Domestic Costs of Bush's Militarism*. New York: New Press, 2004.

Relyea, Harold. "Organizing for Homeland Security." *Presidential Studies Quarterly* 33, no. 3 (September 2003): 602.

Rothschild, Matthew. "King George." *The Progressive* 70, no. 2 (February 2006): 8.

Stover, William. "Pre-emptive War: Implications of the Bush and Rumsfeld Doctrines." *International Journal on World Peace* 21, no. 1 (March 2004): 12.

"Tongue on the Loose." *Economist* 360, no. 8232 (July 28, 2001): 36.

Treaster, Joseph. "Four Years of Bush's Drug War: New Funds but an Old Strategy." *New York Times*, July 28, 1992, A7.

FOREIGN POLICY

INTRODUCTION

The foreign policy of President Bush has been shaped by various conflicts and actions that the United States has had a part in. Therefore, it is useful to place various notable events in foreign affairs during his presidency into the context of how they directly influenced U.S. policy. To that end, a categorization of these events must be made. Certain events fall under military significance, while others are diplomatic in scope. Finally, a third category of events correspond directly to domestic influence on foreign policy.

MILITARY SIGNIFICANCE

One of the earliest events of the Bush presidency was a dispute over a naval electronics aircraft designed to survey radio and other frequencies. During maneuvers in international airspace, a U.S. naval reconnaissance plane was intercepted by a Chinese fighter jet. The jet collided with the recon plane, destroying the jet and killing the pilot. The recon plane, damaged by the collision, was forced to land in China. Upon landing, the plane and crew were taken into custody.

After eleven days, the crew was released; the plane was returned to the United States approximately four weeks after the incident. This incident occurred at a point when both China and the United States were attempting to take stronger stances against each other. It was especially worrisome, as the plane was intercepted in international airspace, a legitimate provocation for war. This extreme possibility was quickly dismissed, but led both the countries to maintain frigid relations long after the incident.

The impact of this event on President Bush's foreign policy is that it forced the United States to recognize the growing influence and self-confidence of China. As such, China asserted itself as a power to be seriously reckoned with in the East Asian region.

Another major adjustment in U.S. foreign policy was the recent (2002) agreement to reduce U.S. and Russian nuclear weapons. Though it lacked some of the provisions of the earlier START (Strategic Arms Reduction Treaty) agreements, it was an important step in the right direction. This new agreement, SORT (Strategic Offensive Reductions Treaty), dictated that the United States and Russia would reduce their deployed strategic warheads to 1,700–2,200. Admittedly, this agreement did not have a timeline for implementation, and it allows both countries to take their surplus weapons out of storage by 2013; yet it remains of military and, more importantly, political significance.

The SORT agreement is part of a continuing effort to bridge U.S. and Russian interests, as the world moves toward new definitions of war, especially in the face of modern terrorism. The threat of a terrorist organization or a rogue state acquiring nuclear weapons is a looming threat to the stability of the global order. It is vital, therefore, to work to further reduce the number of nuclear weapons, and to bring the current nuclear weapon-bearing nations of the world out of a cold war paradigm of security. However, future agreements should be tailored to definite implementation periods and significant reduction of launchers. These actions would allow future agreements to have a more definite impact and overall strength of commitment on the part of both the United States and Russia.

A shift in U.S. policy along the same lines, but with a much different impact, was the U.S. withdrawal from the Anti-Ballistic Missile (ABM) Treaty agreement of 1972. This agreement was designed to limit the use of anti-ballistic missile systems in defense of both the United States and the USSR. In the original context of the treaty initiation, improvements in ballistic missile defense would force increases in the number of nuclear ballistic missiles to counteract the defense improvements. The treaty was used to encourage limits on the number of nuclear ballistic missiles constructed.

After the fall of the USSR, controversy ensued about the continuance of the United States to abide by the rules of the ABM treaty, since legally it had dubious binding power after 1991. However, the United States generally abided by and supported it until 2002, when President Bush notified Russia six months in advance of his intentions to exit the treaty. This action brought much anger from people in the United States, but only a small response from foreign nations. Given that MIRV (Mobile Independent Rocket Vehicle) technology made most ABM technology obsolete, increased ABM research would be of minimal concern to Russia. China was also satisfied with the U.S. withdrawal, as it received assurances that the United States would not look too negatively at increasing China's strategic nuclear arsenal.

The argument in favor of pulling out of the treaty was espoused by President Bush. As the two other questionable holders of nuclear weapons, China and Russia, were satisfied by President Bush's arguments that they would not be harmed by the U.S. withdrawal, the United States would develop ABM technology to create a safeguard against a rogue state that could acquire nuclear weapons. In this event, they would be unable to "blackmail" the United States into certain economic or social agreements. In addition, if a terrorist organization were to attempt to launch a nuclear missile against the United States, it would likely be destroyed with minimal harm to U.S. citizens. Another important aspect to consider in this is that the United States' current technology in ABM is still limited and has been ineffective in some tests. Therefore, though ABM technology is viable, it is still a long way off into the future before the United States will have a working system that covers the entire U.S. mainland.

The overall impact of this action on U.S. foreign policy has been limited, as the major players in nuclear weapons development and positioning have been satisfied. This has not been a highlight, but definitely not a lowlight of the Bush administration and U.S. foreign policy in general.

DIPLOMATIC SIGNIFICANCE

The U.S. foreign policy has great reliance on diplomatic efforts. One of President Bush's most prominent diplomatic initiatives was the Roadmap to Peace in the Middle East, a diplomatic plan for reconciling Israel and Palestine. Ideally, the plan would require Israeli withdrawal from a number of occupied Palestinian territories, most notably, the West Bank and the Gaza Strip. In return, the Palestinian government would seek meaningful reform and work to end terrorist activities and support for terrorism within its borders.

However, this plan encountered resistance and difficulty. Shortly after agreeing to it, Israel attacked a car in Palestinian territory that was supposedly transporting the head of a major Palestinian terrorist organization. Two people were killed, and, shortly thereafter, a Palestinian suicide bomber killed seventeen passengers on an Israeli bus. A truce was eventually achieved, but the overall path of this policy agreement has been slow and torturous. Israel did pull out of the Gaza Strip eventually, but in recent years has continued construction on what Palestinians have called a divisive wall that has been accused of separating settlers from necessary resources of water and roads needed for commerce.

As such, the diplomatic significance of the Roadmap to Peace has been ambiguous for President Bush. Originally a promising idea, the Roadmap has quickly fragmented, with some successes along with many failures. However, the successes thus far illustrate a gradually shifting perspective by the United States in more mutual support of Palestinian interests in the region. This bilateral support will be necessary for any eventual peace to have a reasonable chance of succeeding.

From a much different angle, President Bush has supported sanctions against the Zimbabwe government. Led by Robert Mugabe, this tyrannical government stands accused of severe repressive actions against its own people, from massive election fraud to illegal land seizures and distributions. On this issue, President Bush has support from both Great Britain and the European Union (EU). Both the United States and the EU have imposed travel bans and other economic restrictions on their citizens and on Zimbabwe. However, given the massive corruption and human suffering currently in Zimbabwe, the United States and the EU have pledged humanitarian support for people starving and in severe medical need there.

This is a prime example of a common issue mutually supported by the United States and the EU. In an age of globalization and growing awareness of human rights, the repressive practices of the Zimbabwean government must be opposed by democratic governments open to the political freedoms currently denied by the Mugabe regime. It is also an example of President Bush's foreign policy initiatives to encourage representative democracies around the world. In an area of Africa long accustomed to dictatorial government, Bush's support for democratic freedom is a noteworthy and welcome change.

In what was a massive political brawl, John Bolton was appointed as U.S. ambassador to the United Nations in 2005. Derided by Democrats as a Republican stooge and war hawk, his nomination was held up by Democratic opposition until President Bush appointed him in a recess appointment. The Bolton appointment can be seen as a shift toward a less ambivalent U.S. attitude toward the United Nations. In the face of massive UN corruption during the Oil-for-Food scandal, Bolton's appointment can be seen as a U.S. attempt to strike a position toward greater accountability and responsibility in the UN bureaucracy and oversight groups.

However, Bolton's appointment illustrates the larger role the United States envisions for itself in foreign affairs. Bolton advocates that U.S. foreign policy should be taken up much more strongly by U.S. officials in this administration and the next. In the context of U.S. foreign policy, this move is an astute one for President Bush to make if he can support this action with meaningful reform of the United Nations. However, the success of this particular aspect of his foreign policy will hinge on the effectiveness of Bolton in the UN; that is, whether Bolton can advocate reform and keep enough other UN members as support to see U.S. positions taken up by the greater UN legislative body.

DOMESTIC SIGNIFICANCE

Certain foreign affairs of President Bush's administration have a unique impact on domestic concerns. In this respect, it is useful to examine the domestic influence of various foreign policy positions and practices taken up by the Bush administration. This influence ranges from economic to social to a mix of both. Under these guidelines, the issues of the Kyoto climate agreement, the Afghan Women and Children Relief Act, and Avian flu will be examined and related back to domestic/foreign policy as a whole.

In 2001, President Bush officially announced U.S. withdrawal from the Kyoto climate protocol. This action dismayed many environmentally conscious people in the United States and in nations abroad. The Kyoto Protocol would require nations to lower national emissions of certain chemicals and gases to standards from the early 1990s in an effort to lower the greenhouse gas emissions that cause global warming. However, the protocol gave virtually no suggestions or possibilities as to how to accomplish this task. As such, many people supported President Bush's withdrawal from Kyoto as a removal from a failed experimental program.

The argument that Kyoto harmed more than it helped stems from the fact that even if the United States did abide by the protocol, along with every other nation, the total global temperature reduction would only be approximately 0.05–0.10 degrees Celsius. Furthermore, the Kyoto Protocol did not touch on how to enforce its standards on developing countries such as India and China. As these are two of the largest growing economies in the world, their demand for and use of chemicals that give off greenhouse gases plays no small part in the overall problem.

However, President Bush made an astute foreign policy calculation and created the idea of an Asian technology agreement, by which United States' and other nations' technologies that reduced emissions would be offered to growing economies in Southeast Asia. Many nations are members of this agreement, which is seen as a much more viable alternative to the draconian Kyoto Protocol. The domestic implications of this policy are clear in that the economy would suffer greatly if emissions had to be reduced, due to massive industrial adjustments and reductions in consumer activity. Therefore, this foreign policy choice was supported by many people outside the environmentalist fringe.

A much different foreign policy action taken by the Bush administration was support of the Afghan Women and Children Relief Act of 2001. This act sought government funding for aid and education for Afghan women and children who were severely mistreated by the Taliban regime. Remarkably enough, this legislation received much support from a variety of groups typically opposed to each other (feminists and conservatives, for example).

This legislation reflected a nuanced attempt to build democracy in Afghanistan by training and supporting future leaders today. Through this act, women and children who had little training or knowledge of basic job and education related activities received funding and support. Also included in this were Afghan women outside Afghanistan, who in many cases had been driven out for various minor infractions of the law under the Taliban.

A final foreign policy initiative by the Bush administration is the effort to contain Avian flu and develop treatments for it. This effort necessarily entails foreign policy action, as all of the cases thus far of human infection have occurred outside the United States. However, this may not always be the case, as the advent and usage of multiple avenues of transportation have allowed people to travel quickly between borders, before they even know that they are sick. The foreign policy necessary to combat the threat of Avian flue dictates that the Bush administration must use a varied approach to gain the support and necessary resources to develop a viable cure/treatment for this dangerous disease.

Overall, the Bush administration's efforts in foreign policy have been met with success and failure. While various successes have been achieved in social and political arenas, significant failures have been seen as well. What is necessary for future initiatives by the Bush administration is a continued use of foreign policy to advocate not only U.S. interests, but also the interests and rights of people around the world.

NAVY SURVEILLANCE PLANE IN CHINA (APRIL 2001)

On April 1, 2001, a United States Navy EP-3E plane was intercepted by the People's Liberation Army Navy fighter jets. The incident occurred about seventy miles from the Hainan Island controlled by China. From the beginning, the Chinese government believed that the United States was using their intelligence to spy on Chinese military facilities. The plane was forced to land on the island of Hainan after conflicting reports of crashes took place. The Chinese claimed that the U.S. plane came into the path of the Chinese J-8, while the American government claimed that it was the Chinese plane that sought contact first. American crew members believed that the Chinese pilot was attempting to pass along a message to them. Since neither of the black boxes from the airplanes was made public, the confrontation is still left to much heated debate.

The twenty-four-member crew was detained by the Chinese government for ten days and were then released on April 11, 2001. President Bush had called for a swift conclusion to this incident and requested a prompt return of not only the crew members but also the plane itself. The president was exacerbated by the slow response of the Chinese government in returning the crew members and pledged U.S. assistance in finding the Chinese plane upon the return of the American crew.

Opposition in Congress urged President Bush to not retaliate and to keep American interests in China in mind. Incorporation of China into the world economy was of mutual benefit to both the countries. To appease both sides, the United States issued a letter in which it apologized for entering the Chinese airspace and offered its condolences for the missing Chinese pilot and the plane.

It is believed that the American plane contained advanced listening equipment and much information was gathered during the mission. Upon the plane landing on the island of Hainan, the Chinese military did enter the plane, but it is unknown if any information was taken from it. The incident strained U.S.–China relations. However, since the incident, bilateral relations between the countries have steadily improved.

BUSH'S REMARKS ON THE UNITED STATES NAVY AIRCRAFT INCIDENT IN THE SOUTH CHINA SEA (APRIL 2, 2001)

Late Saturday night in Washington, Sunday morning in China, a United States naval maritime patrol aircraft on a routine surveillance mission in international airspace over the South China Sea collided with one of two Chinese fighters that were shadowing our plane. Both our aircraft and a Chinese aircraft were damaged in the collision. Our aircraft made an emergency landing at an airfield on China's Hainan Island.

We have been in contact with the Chinese Government about this incident since Saturday night. From our own information, we know that the United States naval plane landed safely. Our Embassy in Beijing has been told by the Chinese Government that all 24 crewmembers are safe.

Our priorities are the prompt and safe return of the crew and the return of the aircraft without further damaging or tampering. The first step should be immediate access by our Embassy personnel to our crewmembers. I am troubled by the lack of a timely Chinese response to our request for this access. Our Embassy officials are on the ground and prepared to visit the crew and aircraft as soon as the Chinese Government allows them to do so, and I call on the Chinese Government to grant this access promptly.

Failure of the Chinese Government to react promptly to our request is inconsistent with standard diplomatic practice and with the expressed desire of both our countries for better relations.

Finally, we have offered to provide search and rescue assistance to help the Chinese Government locate its missing aircraft and pilot. Our military stands ready to help.

Source: *Public Papers of the Presidents of the United States: George W. Bush* (Washington, DC: Government Printing Office), 560.

CRITICISM OF U.S. POLICY TO CHINA AND TAIWAN (MAY 1, 2001)

Mr. Max Baucus (D-MT). Mr. President, these past few weeks have been eventful ones in our relationship with China.

Some of these developments are infuriating and frustrating. After our plane was downed, some in Congress called for revenge, retaliation, and retribution. Proposals include that Congress reverse its approval of PNTR, Permanent Normal Trade Relations, for China; that the United States oppose holding the 2008 Summer Olympics in Beijing; and that we reduce or cease military-to-military relations with China.

Our long-term interests with China require a carefully measured course of action. We cannot allow emotion to obscure our policy objectives. And we cannot determine China policy based on vague ideological images.

Like all Americans, I am outraged by the behavior of the Chinese Government in holding the crew of our reconnaissance plane and demanding an American apology, when the blame was so clearly with a reckless Chinese pilot following reckless orders.

I congratulate President Bush on his handling of the first foreign policy crisis of this administration. He kept emotions in check. He rejected the advice of those who wanted to take precipitous action. He secured the safe release of our crew without giving China the kowtowing apology they demanded.

President Bush's decision last week on which defense items to transfer to Taiwan was also responsible and correct. It will provide Taiwan with the hardware and the "humanware" it needs to defend itself, while avoiding actions that would have been unnecessarily provocative vis-a-vis China. Unfortunately, he followed this measured decision with a "shoot from the hip" comment on a possible U.S. response to Chinese military action against Taiwan. That remark has created unnecessary confusion, uncertainty, and potential instability across the Taiwan Strait.

We need to look at what is good for U.S. interests, not what is bad for China. There is no room for emotion as we defined the relationship we want with China and determine how to move them in the right direction.

Last year Congress approved, by a wide margin, legislation granting Permanent Normal Trade Relations status to China once they join the World Trade Organization. The benefits of incorporating China into the world trade community were clear.

American farmers, businesses, and workers would be well served by a growing and liberalized economy in China. Economic growth in China would, over the long term, lead to a larger middle class making its own demands on the government for greater accountability and personal choice, just as happened in South Korea and Taiwan. Membership in the WTO would bring international disciplines to the Chinese economy. And the reformers, led by Premier Zhu Rongji, would be strengthened.

The events of the last few weeks have not changed this calculation. If anything, nurturing growth in our economic and trade relationship with China is more important than ever. Let's be clear about what happened in China while our crew was detained on Hainan Island.

The delay in releasing our crew members was a reflection of a monumental struggle for China's future between reformers led by Premier Zhu Rongji and President Jian Zemin, on one side, and the old guard, including the People's Liberation Army, the managers of most state-owned enterprises, and many entrenched politicians, on the other side. That is, a battle between those who we hope will be China's future and those who should be made part of China's past.

One manifestation of this struggle is political and perhaps increasing military friction with the United States. Taiwan remains the No. 1 flashpoint. Add disputes over human rights, political prisoners, arrest of American citizens and permanent residents of Chinese origin, Tibet, regional policies, weapons transfer. These issues will remain with us for years, if not decades.

Our decisions must be measured through one optic: What are the core American strategic and economic interests vis-a-vis China?

First, we want stability in the Asian region. We must ensure that China does not threaten this stability. That means committing the United States to being a full participant in Asia—economically, politically, and militarily. This includes ensuring peace across the Taiwan Strait, and that means providing Taiwan with the tools necessary for its defense and assisting with the peaceful resolution of the China-Taiwan issue.

Second, we want to help in the transformation of China from a totalitarian state with a nonmarket economy toward a more liberalized political and economic regime. That means incorporating China into the world trade community while insisting on respect for basic human rights.

Third, we want full access for American goods and services to the largest country in the world with the fastest growing economy. That means completing China's accession to the WTO, granting them PNTR, and supporting our businesses' efforts to penetrate the Chinese economy. It does not mean revoking China's established normal trade status.

To isolate China and to seek retribution might feel good, but it would not do good. Even worse, it threatens our core long-term interests. We should responsibly protect our interests and confront China when situations warrant. But reason, not emotion, must guide our decisions.

Source: *Congressional Record,* May 1, 2001, S 4096–4097.

KYOTO CLIMATE PROTOCOL (JUNE 2001)

The Kyoto Protocol is an international treaty aimed at the limitation of greenhouse gas emissions that has created much stir within the U.S. political realm as well as the international arena. The climate treaty was negotiated in Kyoto, Japan, in 1997 and was presented for national signatures beginning in 1998. The agreement came into effect in 2005, and as of April 2006, a total of 163 countries have signed and ratified the agreement. The key exception continues to be the United States.

The United States has not ratified, nor has it withdrawn from, the Kyoto Protocol to this date. In July 1997, the U.S. Senate passed the Byrd-Hagel Resolution, which stated that the Senate felt the United States should not be a signatory to the Kyoto treaty. Though in 1998 Vice-President Gore signed the protocol, the Bush administration has indicated that it does not want to conform to the protocol stipulations. President Bush believes that the Kyoto Protocol would place a heavy strain on the

U.S. economy and has expressed many reservations about it. Though President Bush acknowledged the earth's rising temperature, he questioned the direct effect the rise had on the climate. Although he discussed the importance of decreased emissions, he also believed that the Kyoto Protocol was an unrealistic method. Citing the United States as the leader in innovation and technology, the president called upon the creation of another agency to further examine the correlation between global warming and greenhouse emissions.

Unlike President Bush, the majority of the world believes in the intrinsic value of decreased gas emissions. Supporters of the Kyoto treaty argue that the reduction of greenhouse gas emissions is vital for our planet's survival. Proponents such as the European Union, Russia, and even China believe that something needs to be done to slow down the effects of global warming. Furthermore, there is a grassroots movement in the United States that encourages the U.S. legislature to sign onto the Kyoto Protocol and begin to reduce greenhouse emissions.

BUSH'S REMARKS ON GLOBAL CLIMATE CHANGE
(JUNE 11, 2001)

The issue of climate change respects no border. Its effects cannot be reined in by an army nor advanced by any ideology. Climate change, with its potential to impact every corner of the world, is an issue that must be addressed by the world.

The Kyoto Protocol was fatally flawed in fundamental ways. But the process used to bring nations together to discuss our joint response to climate change is an important one. That is why I am today committing the United States of America to work within the United Nations framework and elsewhere to develop with our friends and allies and nations throughout the world an effective and science-based response to the issue of global warming.

First, we know the surface temperature of the Earth is warming. It has risen by .6 degrees Celsius over the past 100 years. There was a warming trend from the 1890s to the 1940s, cooling from the 1940s to the 1970s, and then sharply rising temperatures from the 1970s to today.

There is a natural greenhouse effect that contributes to warming. Greenhouse gases trap heat and thus warm the Earth because they prevent a significant proportion of infrared radiation from escaping into space. Concentration of greenhouse gases, especially CO_2, have increased substantially since the beginning of the industrial revolution. And the National Academy of Sciences indicates that the increase is due in large part to human activity.

Yet, the Academy's report tells us that we do not know how much effect natural fluctuations in climate may have had on warming. We do not know how much our climate could or will change in the future. We do not know how fast change will occur or even how some of our actions could impact it. For example, our useful efforts to reduce sulfur emissions may have actually increased warming, because sulfate particles reflect sunlight, bouncing it back into space. And finally, no one can say with any certainty what constitutes a dangerous level of warming and, therefore, what level must be avoided.

The policy challenge is to act in a serious and sensible way, given the limits of our knowledge. While scientific uncertainties remain, we can begin now to address the factors that contribute to climate change.

There are only two ways to stabilize concentration of greenhouse gases: One is to avoid emitting them in the first place; the other is to try to capture them after they're created. And there are problems with both approaches. We're making great progress through technology but have not yet developed cost-effective ways to capture carbon emissions at their source, although there is some promising work that is being done.

And a growing population requires more energy to heat and cool our homes, more gas to drive our cars. Even though we're making progress on conservation and energy efficiency and have significantly reduced the amount of carbon emissions per unit of GDP, our country, the United States, is the world's largest emitter of manmade greenhouse gases. We account for almost 20 percent of the world's manmade greenhouse emissions. We also account for about one-quarter of the world's economic output. We recognize the responsibility to reduce our emissions. We also recognize the other part of the story, that the rest of the world emits 80 percent of all greenhouse gases, and many of those emissions come from developing countries.

This is a challenge that requires a 100 percent effort, ours and the rest of the world's. The world's second largest emitter of greenhouse gases is China. Yet, China was entirely exempted from the requirements of the Kyoto Protocol. India and Germany are among the top emitters. Yet, India was also exempt from Kyoto. These and other developing countries that are experiencing rapid growth face challenges in reducing their emissions without harming their economies. We want to work cooperatively with these countries in their efforts to reduce greenhouse emissions and maintain economic growth.

Kyoto also failed to address two major pollutants that have an impact on warming: black soot and tropospheric ozone. Both are proven health hazards. Reducing both would not only address climate change but also dramatically improve people's health.

Kyoto is, in many ways, unrealistic. Many countries cannot meet their Kyoto targets. The targets themselves were arbitrary and not based upon science. For America, complying with those mandates would have a negative economic impact, with layoffs of workers and price increases for consumers. And when you evaluate all these flaws, most reasonable people will understand that it's not sound public policy. That's why 95 Members of the United States Senate expressed a reluctance to endorse such an approach.

Yet, America's unwillingness to embrace a flawed treaty should not be read by our friends and allies as any abdication of responsibility. To the contrary, my administration is committed to a leadership role on the issue of climate change. We recognize our responsibility and will meet it—at home, in our hemisphere, and in the world.

My Cabinet-level working group on climate change is recommending a number of initial steps and will continue to work on additional ideas. . . .

I also call on Congress to work with my administration to achieve the significant emission reductions made possible by implementing the clean energy technologies proposed in our energy plan. Our working group study has made it clear that we need to know a lot more.

America's the leader in technology and innovation. We all believe technology offers great promise to significantly reduce emissions, especially carbon capture, storage, and sequestration technologies. So we're creating the National Climate Change Technology Initiative to strengthen research at universities and national labs, to enhance partnerships in applied research, to develop improved technology for measuring and monitoring gross and net greenhouse gas emissions, and to fund demonstration projects for cutting-edge technologies, such as bioreactors and fuel cells.

Even with the best science, even with the best technology, we all know the United States cannot solve this global problem alone. We're building partnerships within the Western Hemisphere and with other like-minded countries. Last week Secretary Powell signed a new CONCAUSA Declaration with the countries of Central America, calling for cooperative efforts on science research, monitoring and measuring of emissions, technology development, and investment in forest conservation. We will work with the Inter-American Institute for Global Change Research and other institutions to better understand regional impacts of climate change. We will establish a partnership to monitor and mitigate emissions. And at home, I call on Congress to work with my administration on the initiatives to enhance conservation and energy efficiency outlined in my energy plan, to implement the increased use of renewables, natural gas, and hydropower that are outlined in the plan, and to increase the generation of safe and clean nuclear power.

By increasing conservation and energy efficiency and aggressively using these clean energy technologies, we can reduce our greenhouse gas emissions by significant amounts in the coming years. We can make great progress in reducing emissions, and we will. Yet, even that isn't enough.

Source: *Public Papers of the Presidents of the United States: George W. Bush* (Washington, DC: Government Printing Office), 876–879.

CRITICISM OF CAP AND TRADE APPROACH TO CLIMATE CHANGE (AUGUST 3, 2001)

Mr. Joseph I. Lieberman (D-CT).... I have been extremely troubled by the failure of our government to engage on this crucial issue. Last Monday, 180 nations agreed to take historic action against global warming by agreeing to the Kyoto Protocol. One did not. We are the one. I believe this failure abdicates the United States' position as a leader in environmental affairs and places U.S. industry at risk.

We now have general scientific agreement that climate change is a problem we must face. Early this year, the United Nation's Intergovernmental Panel on Climate Change released its Third Assessment Report on global warming. According to this panel of expert scientists, unless we find ways to stop global warming, the Earth's average temperature can be expected to rise between 2.5 and 10.4 degrees Fahrenheit during the next century. Such a large, rapid rise in temperature will profoundly alter the Earth's landscape in very practical terms. Sea levels could swell up to 35 feet, potentially submerging millions of homes and coastal property under our present-day oceans. Precipitation could become more erratic, leading to droughts that would aggravate the task of feeding the world's population. Diseases such as malaria and dengue fever could spread at an accelerated pace. Severe weather disturbances and storms triggered by climatic phenomena, such as El Nino, could become more routine.

As the IPCC report reminds us, this threat is being driven by our own behavior. Let me quote the scientists directly, "There is new and stronger evidence that most of the warming observed over the last 50 years is attributable to human activities." There is no doubt that human-induced emissions are warming the planet.

After receiving the IPCC's dire report, the White House requested and received a second opinion from the National Academy of Sciences. The NAS confirmed the findings of the IPCC. Let me quote:

"The IPCC's conclusion that most of the observed warming of the last 50 years is likely to have been due to the increase in greenhouse gas concentrations accurately reflects the current thinking of the scientific community on this issue. . . . Despite the uncertainties, there is general agreement that the observed warming is real and particularly strong within the past twenty years."

By going forward with the Kyoto Protocol even without the United States, the world has taken a giant stride forward in response to this pressing problem. That agreement will create a worldwide market in greenhouse gas reductions, using market forces to drive environmental gains. Unfortunately, because the United States did not participate, U.S. interests were virtually ignored in crafting the final deal. In the end, I believe that not just our environment but our economy will suffer as a result.

For example, let's say a multinational corporation is faced with the need to invest in new, more efficient technology, and has the choice of installing it in the United States or overseas. Under the Kyoto Protocol, the corporation will be able to receive valuable credits for making those efficiency gains—and therefore reducing its greenhouse gas emissions. Those credits will be worth cold, hard cash in the world market that will be established under the treaty. In contrast, the United States currently has no system by which the company will gain credit for the gains. The result will be that more efficient, more competitive technology will be driven overseas.

The agreement in Bonn also has probably made millions of dollars in U.S. investment worthless. A number of our large corporations have invested heavily in forest conservation on the assumption that they would receive credit for these forests' ability to pull carbon out of the atmosphere. In Bonn, however—without the U.S. at the table—credit for forest conservation was written out of the agreement.

After the agreement at Bonn, it will take a lot of work to convince the other nations of the world to reopen the negotiations to U.S. participation.

We can begin by creating a credible domestic system that can work in parallel with the Kyoto Protocol so the United States remains in tune with the remainder of the world as we move forward. Such an approach must move beyond our laudable but inadequate voluntary efforts. As we saw with the Rio Treaty, which former President Bush supported and the Senate ratified in 1992, voluntary programs unfortunately do not work. Instead, Senator McCain and I believe that we need a set of standards requiring action. We need an economy-wide cap and trade approach. In contrast to the current international agreement, such a system will take the interests of the United States into account.

I also believe having such a system in place will much better enable us to negotiate an acceptable international agreement with the Kyoto participants when the U.S. does come back to the table. If we do not have our own domestic cap and trade system, our companies will be years behind the rest of the world in operating within the system and therefore disadvantaged when we join an international agreement.

The bona-fides of a cap and trade approach are impressive. I was involved in the drafting of the cap and trade program in the Clean Air Act to reduce acid rain—one of the most successful environmental programs on the books. Recent reports from the CBO and the Resources for the Future espoused such an approach. Progressive companies such as British Petroleum have greatly reduced their greenhouse emissions by using their own internal cap and trade markets. And no less authority than the Wall Street Journal has endorsed such an approach to address our climate problems, stating that the Bush Administration should "propose a domestic cap and trade program for carbon dioxide that could, of course, be easily expanded to Canada and Mexico." It would be a giant step forward if the Bush Administration would make such a proposal to the next international meeting on climate change in Marrakesh, Morocco during October.

If we adopt a cap and trade system, we will create a market by which corporations will receive valuable credits for efficient investments. We also will create a market by which corporations can receive credit for the laudable investments they have made to date. And we will unleash the power of that market to drive the United States back into its leadership position in the international effort to avoid the worst effects of one of the most serious environmental problems the world community has ever faced.

Source: *Congressional Record*, August 3, 2001, S 8894–8896.

AFGHAN WOMEN AND CHILDREN RELIEF ACT OF 2001 (DECEMBER 2001)

In December 2001, the Afghan Women and Children Relief Act of 2001, was signed by President Bush. Before the attacks on September 11, 2001, many Americans had already heard of the Taliban from an e-mail being circulated that asked the world to save the women and children of Afghanistan from the Taliban. The Taliban were notorious for being extremely cruel to the women of their country. Almost every woman in Afghanistan would be able to recall one instance when they were abused by the Taliban. The Afghan Women and Children Relief Act of 2001 was a commitment from the United States to provide education and medical services to the women and children of the country. The two speeches given here are very similar in nature. The point where they differ is that the Democratic critic argues that the United States must commit itself to long-term assistance to the women and children of Afghanistan.

BUSH'S REMARKS ON SIGNING THE AFGHAN WOMEN AND CHILDREN RELIEF ACT OF 2001 (DECEMBER 12, 2001)

... We join those in the interim government who seek education and better health for every Afghan woman and child. And today, with the Afghan Women and Children Relief Act, we take an important step toward that goal.

Afghan women were banned from speaking or laughing loudly. They were banned from riding bicycles or attending school. They were denied basic health care and were killed on suspicion of adultery. One news magazine reports, "It's hard to find a woman in Kabul who does not remember a beating at the hands of the Taliban."

In Afghanistan, America not only fights for our security, but we fight for the values we hold dear. We strongly reject the Taliban way. We strongly reject their brutality toward women and children. They not only violate basic human rights; they're barbaric in their indefensible meting of justice. It's wrong. Their attitude is wrong for any culture. Their attitude is wrong for any religion.

You know, life in Afghanistan wasn't always this way. Before the Taliban came, women played an incredibly important part of that society. Seventy percent of the nation's teachers were women. Half of the government workers in Afghanistan were women, and 40 percent of the doctors in the capital of Kabul were women. The Taliban destroyed that progress. And in the process, they offered us a clear image of the world they and the terrorists would like to impose on the rest of us.

The central goal of the terrorists is the brutal oppression of women, and not only the women of Afghanistan. The terrorists who help rule Afghanistan are found in dozens and dozens of countries around the world. And that is the reason this great Nation, with our friends and allies, will not rest until we bring them all to justice.

This is an important achievement. Yet, a liberated Afghanistan must now be rebuilt so that it will never again practice terror at home or abroad. This work begins by ensuring the essential rights of all Afghans.

America and our allies will do our part in the rebuilding of Afghanistan. We learned our lessons from the past. We will not leave until the mission is complete. We will work with international institutions on long-term development—on the long-term development of Afghanistan. We will provide immediate humanitarian assistance to the people of Afghanistan.

After years of civil war and misrule by the Taliban, this is going to be an incredibly difficult winter in Afghanistan. We're doing what we can to help alleviate the suffering. In the month of November, the United Nations World Food Program, with our strong support, provided enough supplies to feed 4.3 million Afghans. And the Defense Department will continue to make sure that food is delivered in remote regions of that impoverished, poor, starving country.

The bill I sign today extends and strengthens our efforts. The Afghan Women and Children Relief Act commits the United States to providing education and medical assistance to Afghan women and children and to Afghan refugees in surrounding countries.

The overwhelming support for this legislation sends a clear message: As we drive out the Taliban and the terrorists, we are determined to lift up the people of Afghanistan. The women and children of Afghanistan have suffered enough. This great Nation will work hard to bring them hope and help. To the bill's sponsors, thank you from the bottom of our hearts. You show the true compassion of this great land.

Source: *Public Papers of the Presidents of the United States: George W. Bush* (Washington, DC: Government Printing Office), 1780–1782.

CRITICISM OF THE AFGHAN WOMEN AND CHILDREN ACT (NOVEMBER 19, 2003)

Mrs. Judy Bigger (R-IL). . . . Frankly, it is no secret that Afghan women had a very, very hard time under Taliban rule. Women were frequently beaten, raped, kidnapped and killed. They had no access to education or health care. For 5 years, they were told that the only place for them was at home with their husbands or in the grave. Women were systematically and routinely singled out for abuse simply because they were women. In short, they lived in nightmarish conditions that few of us could even imagine.

Two years after the fall of the Taliban, the women of Afghanistan are making tremendous progress in reclaiming their rightful place in society. Women are returning to positions they held in pre-Taliban times, working as doctors, lawyers, teachers, civil servants and in numerous other professions. Most girls are attending school, which was not true ever before in the history of this country. They are no longer forced to wear the burdensome burqa, although many of them do, and hopefully they are no longer living in fear of being brutalized simply because they are female.

These women have overcome unimaginable obstacles and they deserve our ongoing support as they work to build a new democracy. I have been involved in several meetings here in the United States and a video conference with women leaders in Afghanistan through the U.S.-Afghan Women's Council. It is encouraging to see that the country is transforming itself into a democracy and the Afghan women are participating, working towards elections, and some of these women will be candidates. All of this is good news, but there is still so much more that must be accomplished.

As part of the rebuilding process, the people of Afghanistan are drafting a constitution that will define the principles of their new democratic government. Under the Bonn agreement, the final draft will be finished in a few short months. As the drafters continue the hard work of crafting that important document, we must continue to encourage the inclusion of women and the protection of their most basic rights. The creation of a permanent Afghan government marks an important transition in the history of that country. It also provides a unique opportunity to commend the women of Afghanistan for overcoming the monumental challenges they have faced and to reiterate the U.S. commitment to protecting the human rights of all. This is what the resolution does.

The United States has a vested interest in promoting a democratic regime in Afghanistan. As President Bush put it, women will be the backbone of a new Afghanistan. It is critical, therefore, that women be assured of their right to participate in the civic life of their country. It is encouraging to note that women have been involved in the drafting of the constitution. However, in order for women to continue participating in public life, this right must be protected.

I am pleased that the U.S. has taken such an active role in aiding the women of Afghanistan. In the last Congress, we passed and the President signed into law the Afghan Women and Children's Relief Act. This much-needed legislation provided educational and health care assistance for women and children living in Afghanistan and as refugees in neighboring countries. This was an important first step that provided immediate assistance. Now, however, it is time to look beyond the short term and provide long-term assurance that the women of Afghanistan will never again be targeted for abuse by their government and forced to live under such horrific conditions. Mr. Speaker, this is an important and timely resolution. In order to promote true democracy in Afghanistan, we must do all we can to encourage the inclusion of women in the civic life of their country. I am honored to support this resolution, and I encourage my colleagues to do so as well.

Source: *Congressional Record,* November 19, 2003, H 11529–11533.

ROADMAP TO PEACE IN THE MIDDLE EAST (MARCH 2002)

The Roadmap to Peace is a plan that seeks to bring peace to the Middle East region by resolving the Israeli-Palestinian conflict. In 2002, President George W. Bush was the first American president to call for a two-state solution. By creating two states, Palestine and Israel, it was the hope of the United States and the international community that the violence in the region would cease. The Roadmap to Peace calls for the Palestinian authority led by Mahmoud Abbas to increase democratic reforms and discard the use of violence as a means of achieving political aims. In exchange for peaceful coexistence, Israel would have to accept the Palestinian authority's existence as well as the creation of a Palestinian State, and acknowledge the settlements in both the Gaza Strip and the West Bank.

When discussing the Roadmap to Peace, President Bush prognosticated an end of violence by 2003. Unfortunately, due to the increased violence after the Roadmap was signed, the plan had to be sidelined for a period of time. Increased violence from both sides caused the creation of a Palestinian state to be pushed back to the year 2005. President Bush has continuously encouraged an end to the violence in the Israeli-Palestinian conflict, mainly focusing on the violence against Israel. He reminded both sides that the United States was committed to seeing positive results in the region and creating a long-lasting, peaceful friendship.

Many of Bush's critics have voiced their opinion about the situation. Although congresswoman Capps encouraged solidarity between Israel and Palestine, she drew attention to the often forgotten violence perpetrated by Israel against the Palestinians. Due to the increasing number of deaths on both sides, she urged Congress and international leaders to take a further look at the enforceability of the Roadmap to Peace. She pointed out that the violence has had immense effect on both sides, and that it was time to end the violence and focus on the rebuilding of society.

In the summer of 2005, Israeli prime minister Ariel Sharon began the promised pullout of settlements from the Gaza Strip and handed over increased autonomy of the territory to the Palestinian authority. Many critics questioned Sharon's intentions as more settlements were being built in the West Bank, seemingly to compensate for those lost in the Gaza Strip. The Roadmap to Peace has been compromised recently yet again with the democratic election of Hamas to the Palestinian authority. Israel has refused to acknowledge the election, and the United States and the European Union have pulled foreign aid assistance from the Palestinian authority after Hamas' ascension to power. In the wake of the election, violence has increased in the region.

BUSH'S REMARKS FOLLOWING DISCUSSIONS WITH THE QUARTET PRINCIPALS AND AN EXCHANGE WITH REPORTERS (DECEMBER 20, 2002)

... I am strongly committed to the vision that I outlined on June the 24th. I believe it is in everybody's best interests that there be two states living side by side in peace. And this Government will work hard to achieve that. And I want [to] thank you all for joining us in working toward that important vision.

There are some keys to moving forward. All of us must work hard to fight against terror so that a few cannot deny the dreams of the many; that we must encourage the development of Palestinian institutions which are transparent, which promote freedom and democracy; that we must work together to ease the humanitarian situation. There's—too many Palestinian moms and dads grieve over the future for their children because of hunger and poverty, lack of health care.

I appreciate the fact that the Quartet is working on what we call a roadmap. I view the roadmap as a part of the vision that I described. It is a way forward. It sets conditions. It's a results-oriented document. It is a way to bring people together so that they share their responsibilities.

We're assuming our responsibilities. The people in the neighborhood must assume their responsibilities. All nations must be committed to peace in order for us to achieve peace, must be committed to the vision of two states side by side in order to achieve the vision of living side by side.

The roadmap is not complete yet, but the United States is committed to its completion. We are committed to its implementation in the name of peace.

Source: *Public Papers of the Presidents of the United States: George W. Bush* (Washington, DC: Government Printing Office), 2179–2181.

CRITICISM OF THE ROADMAP TO PEACE (JUNE 25, 2003)

Mrs. Lois Capps (D-CA). Mr. Speaker, I join my colleagues in expressing outrage at terrorism perpetrated by Palestinian extremists since the Aqaba Summit. The people of the United States continue to stand in solidarity with the people of Israel. But I regret this resolution is not as complete or constructive as it might be. We mourn the 22 innocent Israelis that have been killed since the summit, but over twice that number of innocent civilian Palestinians have also died as a result of military strikes from Israel. Their loss should also be explicitly recognized in such a resolution.

I sincerely wish the House had used this opportunity to offer its clear support for the President's road map to Middle East peace. This road map is not perfect, but it is currently the only legitimate way to stop terrorism and get the parties back to the path of peace. Under the road map the Palestinian Authority must crack down on terrorism, and Israel must dismantle illegal settlements and begin an end to occupation. Abandoning the road map in the wake of the recent terrorism would not help Israel. In contrast, it would reward the terrorists.

I object to the resolution's condemnation of the phrase "cycle of violence" because it is a fact for the past 2½ years we have witnessed a heartbreaking and endless cycle of terrorist attacks, assassinations, reprisals and retaliations. Since the peace process collapsed, 800 Israelis and 2,100 Palestinians have been killed. The Israeli economy has collapsed. The humanitarian crisis in the West Bank and in Gaza has intensified. Therefore, it is imperative that under the road map security cooperation would resume. This is critical because it is clear that neither prime minister Abu Mazen nor Sharon, neither of these can stop terrorism without the other. This conflict will never end without a comprehensive political solution; and we, the United States, must lead both parties to that agreement. Otherwise Israelis and Palestinians may be doomed to a life of violence and suffering forever. It is not what these people deserve, and it is surely not what America can afford.

Source: *Congressional Record,* June 25, 2003, H 5853–5866.

NUCLEAR ARMS REDUCTION WITH RUSSIA (MAY 2002)

In the past, nuclear weapons were seen as a sign of the strength and power of the world's two reigning super powers—the United States and the Soviet Union. In a joint press conference on May 24, 2004, U.S. president George W. Bush and Russian president Vladimir Putin announced the signing of a treaty that would significantly reduce the amount of nuclear warhead arsenals of both countries. The United States and Russia would decrease their arsenal of warheads from 6,000 to 1,700–2,200 warheads. Furthermore, the treaty included provisions to increase the relationship between the two countries and facilitated cooperation in the economic, political, and security realms.

The treaty marked a change of policy between the United States and Russia since the time when both countries fought for ideological domination in the cold war. Both presidents acknowledged the strained relations between their countries fueled by issues of trust and competition, and pledged to increase diplomatic relations through a common goal of nuclear nonproliferation.

Critics are less than pleased with the signing of the treaty. Although both countries would make significant reductions in their arsenals, they would still keep more than 1,700 nuclear warheads. Critics argue that if we are truly entering a new era of nonproliferation and open dialogue, there is no need for either country to possess this military technology. Furthermore, the term "nuclear warhead" has not been defined by either party and many are confused as to what the term precisely signifies. In addition, many claim that the treaty is not perfect and there are many outs for both sides to take. Due to the lackluster relationship between both countries in the past, the issue of trust and enforceability hangs in the air. When Senator Biden discussed the treaty, he described the process as that of two leaders working unilaterally. Furthermore, Biden questioned the timetable set for the treaty as both nations agreed to downsize their arsenals by 2012.

THE PRESIDENT'S NEWS CONFERENCE WITH PRESIDENT VLADIMIR V. PUTIN OF RUSSIA IN MOSCOW (MAY 24, 2002)

...President Putin and I have signed a treaty that will substantially reduce our nuclear—strategic nuclear warhead arsenals to the range of 1,700 to 2,200, the lowest level in decades. This treaty liquidates the cold war legacy of nuclear hostility between our countries.

We've also signed a joint declaration of new strategic relationship that charts a course toward greater security, political, and economic cooperation between Russia and the United States. Our nations will continue to cooperate closely in the war against global terror....

It's the statement of our countries to reduce our nuclear arsenals and the joint work for nonproliferation of weapons of mass destruction. It's the decision of two states which are particularly responsible for international security and strategic stability. We're on the level of adopting the declaration on [a] new strategic relationship which determines the basic directions in the security and international policy. It will have a positive impact for economic cooperation and development of our relations between the institutions of general public. And together with Mr. President, we discussed especially this aspect, the civil society between the people of our countries. The declaration formulates the principles of our dialog, antimissile dialog; that is, the transparency and openness and exclusion of potential threats. We confirmed the Genoa agreement on offensive and defensive systems in all their aspects.

Q. I have a question for both Presidents, please. If we've truly entered a new era, why do you each need 1,700 nuclear weapons? And President Putin, why does Russia need to continue producing nuclear warheads? And to President Bush, why does the United States need to keep some 2,000 of these weapons in storage, ready for deployment?

President Bush. Yes. First of all, remember where we've come from. We've come from 6,000 to 1,700 in a very quick—or to 1,700 to 2,200 in a very quick period of time. You know, friends really don't need weapons pointed at each other. We both understand that. But it's a realistic assessment of where we've been....

...I'm confident this sets the stage for incredible cooperation that we've never had before between our countries.

Q. Mayak Radio Station. To both Presidents, to what extent the treaty ensures real nuclear parity, and are there conditions that the treaty can be terminated by either side? And how true is the fact that Russia still remains as one of the nuclear targets for nuclear forces? And how does that relate to the announced new strategic relations between our two countries?

President Bush. Well, it is a treaty. This document is a treaty that will be confirmed by the United States Senate and the Duma, hopefully. Secondly, treaties have always had outs; there's nothing new about that. There are conditions of which things may change, and people get out of treaties. That's the way it's been. The Anti-Ballistic Missile Treaty had an out; there's nothing new about that. And thirdly, you know, we are going to work to end the—forever end the cold war. And that begins with the statement that Russia's our friend, not our enemy.

And you say "targeting"—I mean, the idea of our weaponry—our military has no aims at Russia. There may be old vestiges in place, but Russia's not an enemy. You don't think about how to deal with Russia the way they used to. Russia is a friend, and that's the new thinking. That's part of what's being codified today.

Source: *Public Papers of the Presidents of the United States: George W. Bush* (Washington, DC: Government Printing Office), 887–893.

CRITICISM OF NUCLEAR ARMS REDUCTION (MARCH 5, 2003)

Mr. Joseph R. Biden (D-DE). Mr. President, I am pleased to join our esteemed chairman, Senator Lugar, in presenting the Senate this resolution giving the Senate's advice and consent to ratification of the Treaty on Strategic Offensive Reductions, known in the vernacular as the Moscow Treaty. Let me state flatly at the outset, I urge my colleagues to support the treaty.

First, the Moscow Treaty should be ratified and implemented. It is true that there is much that the Moscow Treaty does not do, which I will discuss at some length. But virtually all of the witnesses at our hearing recommended the ratification of the treaty because its implementation would be a step toward a more secure world. Reducing each nation's deployed strategic warheads from approximately 6,000 to between 1,700 and 2,200, in my view, will move us further away from the cold war era and may—I emphasize may—and I hope promote a United States-Russian relationship based upon mutual cooperation.

Second, in my view, while the resolution does not include everything we may want, it does address many of our concerns. It requires significant annual reporting by the executive branch on implementation of the treaty so that the Senate can oversee and support that implementation. These are important gains from an administration that first opposed any treaty at all and then pressed for a clean resolution of ratification. The administration has agreed to support and implement this resolution before the Senate. I think the country will benefit from that.

But there is much the Moscow Treaty does not do. So in the spirit of not engaging in false advertisement, I think we should speak about that a little bit. It is very unusual, at least in my 30 years as a Senator working on many arms control agreements from the Senate perspective, that an arms control agreement by any standard be put forward the way in which this one has.

In our hearings, the Secretary of Defense proudly compared the three pages of this treaty to the roughly 300 pages of the START treaty signed by the first President Bush. But that is just the beginning. Traditional arms control agreements usually involve the negotiated level of arms to which the parties will be held. They usually require the destruction of some weapons. Often they specify milestones that must be achieved in reducing those arms and bar withdrawal from the treaty unless there is a good reason to withdraw and the President gives or the other side gives 6 months notice.

For decades, there has been emphasis on verifying that each party is complying with its obligations. We remember the famous phrase uttered by former President Reagan: Trust but verify.

According to the Secretary of State:

"We concluded before the Moscow Treaty was negotiated that we could and would safely reduce to 1,700 to 2,200 operationally deployed strategic nuclear warheads, regardless of what the Russians did."

Secretary Powell reports that President Bush then told President Putin:

"This is where we are going. We are going there unilaterally. Come with us or not, stay where you are or not."

In short, the Moscow Treaty does not codify an agreement. Rather, it codifies two unilateral decisions to reduce strategic forces. That is not a bad thing, but it is not such a significant thing.

Another way in which the Moscow Treaty differs from previous arms control agreements is that it does not require the elimination of any missiles, any bombers, any submarines, or any warheads. As a result, each party is free to stockpile its officially reduced weapons.

We used to fight with our conservative friends on this floor who said we could not support such-and-such arms control treaty proffered from President Nixon through to President Ford and President Reagan and President Bush—we could not do it unless we were certain that the missile was destroyed, the warhead was destroyed, the submarine was destroyed. We used to hear what is going to happen is they are going to take these missiles and they are going to hide them in barns and they are going to hide them in the woods and they are going to hide them in camouflaged areas.

Let's be clear what this treaty does. It says you have to get down to 1,700 to 2,200 of these within the next 10 years or so, but all you have to do is take them out of commission. You don't have to destroy them. You can stockpile them. You can put them in a warehouse. You can pile them up in a barn for ready reload. You can take them back out. You don't have to destroy anything. That is in fact what the United States plans to do with many of its reduced weapons. They are reduced, not destroyed.

Trident submarines that are taken off nuclear patrol will be converted to other purposes—and could presumably be reconverted to carry strategic nuclear weapons, although at some cost.

Bombers will also be converted; actually, their re-conversion to strategic nuclear uses might be rather difficult.

According to recent press stories, the United States might use ICBMs to deliver conventional payloads. That would leave the missiles still available for use with nuclear warheads instead.

An equal concern for me is the question of what the Russians will do with its reduced weapons. If it follows the lead of the United States, it will try to retain as many missiles and bombers as possible, and it will stockpile its downloaded nuclear weapons rather than dismantling them and disposing of the excess fissile material.

Under this treaty, Russia can do whatever it wants with its so-called reduced weapons. But we have a stake in Russia's decision on this. That is because of the risk that Russia will not adequately protect the weapons and nuclear materials it has stockpiled.

The Russians have incredibly, incredibly insecure facilities because they lack the money to be able to maintain these secure facilities. I worry that if Russia does not destroy them, that they will find themselves—and we will find ourselves—susceptible to the clandestine sale or the actual stealing of these materials, and they will fall into the hands of people who do not have our interests at heart.

The only threat to our very existence is the accidental launch of Russian missiles, and that is why I still worry about the MIRV'd ICBMs. But perhaps the worst other threat to America is that some Russian nuclear weapons, or material with which they make them, could be stolen or diverted to rogue states or terrorist groups. The more weapons Russia stockpiles, the greater the risk not all of them will be properly safeguarded.

U.S. assistance helps to improve the security of Russia's nuclear weapons by improving their physical protection (fencing, sensors, communications); accounting (improved hardware and software); personnel reliability (better screening); and guard force capabilities (more realistic training).

These improvements are particularly important because Russia faces a difficult threat environment—political instability, terrorist threats, and insider threats resulting from financial conditions in Russia.

The laissez-faire nature of the Moscow Treaty is also evident in the timing of its reduction requirement.

This is very unusual. Under Article I of the Treaty, the reductions must occur "by December 31, 2012." Until that date, there is no reduction requirement. Indeed, until that date, there is nothing barring each party from increasing its force levels.

To this day, the Russian Federation has yet to say how it defines the term "strategic nuclear warheads," or how its reductions will be made.

We can only hope that his laissez-faire approach to arms control obligations will not lead to misunderstandings down the road. With no agreed definitions and no benchmarks, I respectfully suggest that there is lots of room for quarrels over whether a party will really be in compliance by December 31, 2012.

Perhaps voluntary transparency by each party will assure the other that arms reductions are proceeding properly.

Let's pass it and then work together to make it a success and work together to take the next steps we have to take.

Source: *Congressional Record,* March 5, 2003, S 3128–3154.

WITHDRAWAL FROM THE 1972 ANTI-BALLISTIC MISSILE TREATY (JUNE 2002)

The Anti-Ballistic Missile (ABM) Treaty was a treaty between the United States of America and the Soviet Union for the limitation of anti-ballistic missile systems. Signed in 1972 by President Nixon and President Brezhnev, the treaty was in force for thirty years. In June 2002, six months after giving the required notice, President George W. Bush pulled the United States out of the treaty. This move marked the first time that the United States withdrew its support from a major international arms treaty. President Bush argued that the United States needed to exit the treaty in order to build the National Missile Defense system. Due to the increased violence throughout the world, as well as the threat of rogue states seeking nuclear weapons, Bush felt that the National Missile Defense System was vital to the nation's security.

The withdrawal from the treaty drew much criticism both domestically and internationally. Critics argued that pulling out of the treaty would jeopardize the effectiveness of other arms treaties including the Non-Proliferation Treaty (NPT). Furthermore, it would decrease restraints on other nations seeking to develop nuclear programs.

Initially, China and Russia were displeased by the actions taken by the United States; but even though the pullout signaled dangers to both nations, they were later convinced that it was more advantageous for them than originally anticipated. To Russia, President Bush promised a decrease in the number of nuclear warheads, which would in turn decrease Russia's own military spending. To China, Bush promised not to oppose the enhancement of their nuclear missile program.

BUSH'S STATEMENT ON FORMAL WITHDRAWAL FROM THE 1972 ANTI-BALLISTIC MISSILE TREATY (JUNE 13, 2002)

Six months ago, I announced that the United States was withdrawing from the 1972 Anti-Ballistic Missile (ABM) Treaty, and today that withdrawal formally takes effect. With the treaty now behind us, our task is to develop and deploy effective defenses against limited missile attacks. As the events of September 11 made clear, we no longer live in the cold war world for which the ABM Treaty was designed. We now face new threats, from terrorists who seek to destroy our civilization by any means available to rogue states armed with weapons of mass destruction and long-range missiles. Defending the American people against these threats is my highest priority as Commander in Chief.

The new strategic challenges of the 21st century require us to think differently. But they also require us to act. I call on the Congress to approve the full amount of the funding I have requested in my budget for missile defense. This will permit the United States to work closely with all nations committed to freedom to pursue the policies and capabilities needed to make the world a safer place for generations to come.

I am committed to deploying a missile defense system as soon as possible to protect the American people and our deployed forces against the growing missile threats we face. Because these threats also endanger our allies and friends around the world, it is essential that we work together to defend against them, an important task which the ABM Treaty prohibited. The United States will deepen our dialog and cooperation with other nations on missile defenses.

Last month, President Vladimir Putin and I agreed that Russia and the United States would look for ways to cooperate on missile defenses, including expanding military exercises, sharing early warning data, and exploring potential joint research and development of missile defense technologies. Over the past year, our countries have worked hard to overcome the legacy of the cold war and to dismantle its structures. The United States and Russia are building a new relationship based on common interests and, increasingly, common values. Under the Treaty of Moscow, the nuclear arsenals of our nations will be reduced to their lowest levels in decades. Cooperation on missile defense will also make an important contribution to furthering the relationship we both seek.

Source: *Public Papers of the Presidents of the United States: George W. Bush* (Washington, DC: Government Printing Office), 1011.

CRITICISM OF THE ANTI-BALLISTIC MISSILE TREATY WITHDRAWAL (JUNE 13, 2002)

Mr. Jack Reed (D-RI).... I rise to acknowledge the fact that today, 6 months after President Bush announced the U.S. intention to withdraw from the ABM Treaty, the Treaty lapses. The 30-year old treaty, which most consider to be the cornerstone of arms control, now no longer exists.

The significance of today has gone largely unnoticed. Press coverage has been minimal so most American[s] will likely not realize what happens today. The objections of Russia and China to the withdrawal have been muted. Our European allies have reluctantly accepted the withdrawal. Some would say that this lack of fanfare proves that the ABM Treaty was a relic of the cold war and needed to be renounced. I would argue that while today's withdrawal seems insignificant at this moment, it has profound implications for the future.

When President Bush announced his intention to withdraw from the treaty, he stated: "I have conclude[d] the ABM Treaty hinders our government's ability to develop ways to protect our people from future terrorist or rogue-state missile attacks." I would argue that this statement is incorrect. First, the greatest threat from terrorists is not from a long range missile but from methods we have witnessed and watched for since September 11—conventional transportation like planes and cargo ships, used as weapons.

Secondly, any testing of missile defenses that could be planned for the next several years would not violate the ABM Treaty. We simply do not have the technology yet to test a system in violation of the treaty. An article in today's New York Times states that on Saturday, ground will be broken for a missile test site in Fort Greely Alaska. The article states that this test site would violate the treaty. That is not correct. Under Article IV of the ABM treaty and paragraph 5 of a 1978 agreed statement, the U.S. simply has to notify Russia of U.S. intent to build another test range. As a matter fact, the fiscal year 2002 Defense authorization act authorized the funding for the Alaska test bed prior to the President's announcement to withdraw from the treaty.

As a supporter of the ABM Treaty and a member of the Senate Armed Services Committee, I can assure you that Congress clearly had no intent to authorize an action that would violate the treaty. The technologies which would indeed violate the ABM Treaty, sea-based and space-based systems, are mere concepts that are years away from constituting an action that would violate the treaty. In sum, despite the claims of the President, there was no compelling reason to withdraw at this time.

In addition, today, the United States becomes the first nation since World War II to withdraw from a major international security agreement. In the past 50 years only one other nation has attempted such an action. In 1993 North Korea announced its intention to withdraw from the Nuclear Nonproliferation Treaty which caused an international crisis until North Korea reconsidered. The U.S. withdrawal has not caused an international crisis, but it does send a subtle signal. If the U.S. can withdraw from a treaty at any time without compelling reasons, what is to stop Russia or China from withdrawing from an agreement? Furthermore, what basis would the U.S. have for objecting to such a withdrawal since our nation began the trend? This administration must keep in mind that other nations can also take unilateral actions, but we might not be as comfortable with those decisions. Indeed, as we seek to eliminate the threat of weapons of mass destruction, this withdrawal sends the opposite signal.

As I mentioned before, the ABM treaty was the cornerstone of arms control. With the cornerstone gone, there are worries about an increase in nuclear proliferation. As Joseph Cirincione said, "No matter what some people may tell you, each side's nuclear force is based primarily on the calculation of the other side's force." If China believes its force could be defeated by a U.S. missile shield, China may decide it is in its best interest to increase the number of weapons in its arsenal to overwhelm the shield. If China increases its nuclear missile production, neighboring rival India may find it necessary to recalculate the size of its force. Of course, Pakistan would then increase its inventory to match India. So, while there seems to be little consequence to cessation of the ABM Treaty today, if we are not careful it could be the spark of a new arms race.

Source: *Congressional Record*, June 13, 2002, S 5530–5531.

ZIMBABWE SANCTIONS (MARCH 2003)

On March 6, 2003, President Bush declared economic sanctions against Zimbabwe. The United States cited several clear undemocratic practices of the Mugabe regime, the lack of respect for human rights, and the rampant violence throughout the country as reasons for this step. By issuing this executive order, the president advanced his administration's stand on furthering the spread of democracy and the upholding of human rights in the region, both of which were seen as essential for achieving long-term stability. The European Union also decided to impose sanctions on the Zimbabwe government by freezing assets within the country.

Critics of the Bush administration questioned the United States' response. Senator Russell Feingold (D-WI) called to attention previous human rights violations committed by the Mugabe government and questioned the adequacy of the administration's response. Reports of the destruction of homes, evictions, food withholdings, and other repressive policies rightly called forth sanctions, but, according to Senator Feingold, more active assistance is also needed. Though Feingold supported the sanctions placed on the country, he urged his contemporaries to do more to stop the oppressive Zimbabwean government.

Some surrounding African neighbors were puzzled by the actions taken by the United States and the European Union. Leaders such as the Tanzanian president Benjamin Mkapa as well as the Nigerian president Olusegun Obasanjo questioned the alleged human rights violations and reminded both powers of the democratic ideals upheld in Zimbabwe. The Zimbabwean government strongly condemned the sanctions. Although the sanctions were put in place in 2003, they continue to be enforced today.

BUSH'S MESSAGE TO THE CONGRESS REPORTING ON THE NATIONAL EMERGENCY WITH RESPECT TO ZIMBABWE (MARCH 6, 2003)

... I hereby report that I have exercised my statutory authority to declare a national emergency with respect to the unusual and extraordinary threat to the foreign policy interests of the United States posed by the actions and policies of certain individuals who have formulated, implemented, or supported policies that have undermined Zimbabwe's democratic institutions.

Over the course of more than 2 years, the Government of Zimbabwe has systematically undermined that nation's democratic institutions, employing violence, intimidation, and repressive means including legislation to stifle opposition to its rule. This campaign to ensure the continued rule of Robert Mugabe and his associates was clearly revealed in the badly flawed presidential election held in March 2002. Subsequent to the election, the Mugabe government intensified its repression of opposition political parties and those voices in civil society and the independent press calling on the government to respect the nation's democratic values and the basic human rights of its citizens. To add to the desperation of the besieged

Zimbabwean people, the current government has engaged in a violent assault on the rule of law that has thrown the economy into chaos, devastated the nation's agricultural economy, and triggered a potentially catastrophic food crisis.

As a result of the unusual and extraordinary threat posed to the foreign policy of the United States by the deterioration of Zimbabwe's democracy and the resulting breakdown in the rule of law, politically motivated violence, and the political and economic instability in the southern African region, I have exercised my statutory authority and issued an Executive Order which, except to the extent provided for in regulations, orders, directives, or licenses that may be issued pursuant to this order, and notwithstanding any contract entered into or any license or permit granted prior to the effective date:

- blocks all property and interests in property of the individuals listed in the Annex to the order;
- prohibits any transaction or dealing by United States persons or within the United States in property or interests in property blocked pursuant to the order, including the making or receiving of any contribution of funds, goods, or services to or for the benefit of the persons designated pursuant to the order.

The Secretary of the Treasury is further authorized to designate any person determined, in consultation with the Secretary of State, to be owned or controlled by, or acting or purporting to act directly or indirectly for or on behalf of, any persons designated in or pursuant to the order. The Secretary of the Treasury is also authorized in the exercise of my authorities under the International Emergency Economic Powers Act to implement these measures in consultation with the Secretary of State. All Federal agencies are directed to take actions within their authority to carry out the provisions of the Executive Order.

This Executive Order further demonstrates the U.S. commitment to supporting Zimbabwe's democratic evolution, and strengthens our cooperation with the European Union in efforts to promote that evolution. The European Union has acted to freeze the assets of 79 individuals responsible for the political, economic, and social deterioration of Zimbabwe. With the exception of two individuals no longer associated with the Government of Zimbabwe, this order encompasses all those identified by the European Union.

Source: *Public Papers of the Presidents of the United States: George W. Bush* (Washington, DC: Government Printing Office), 306–307.

CRITICISM OF ZIMBABWE SANCTIONS (JULY 1, 2005)

Mr. Russell D. Feingold (D-WI). Mr. President, I rise to express my shock and alarm over the most recent turn taken in Zimbabwe's deepening political and economic crisis. As my colleagues know, the ruling regime in Harare recently launched a massive campaign to destroy the homes of hundreds of thousands of urban Zimbabweans, evicting men, women, and children—in at least one case reportedly evicting even AIDS orphans—under the auspices of "driving out the rubbish."

Many analysts believe that the Government is attempting to forcibly relocate the urban population—which tends to support the political opposition—to rural areas in order to diffuse resistance to its repressive policies. The ruling party may also be attempting to revitalize the agricultural sector, which has been devastated by its policies, through this campaign of forced relocation to rural areas. What is certain is that this kind of deliberate displacement of people in a country where 3 to 4 million already need food assistance is an absolute outrage.

Sadly, this is what we have come to expect from President Mugabe and his cronies. This same government has refused food assistance for hungry people; manipulated available food assistance for political purposes; systematically attacked the independence of the judiciary; silenced independent media voices; and created, often through coercion, brutally violent youth militias to terrorize civilians.

But we can and must do more to oppose this campaign of abuse. We must continue to speak plainly to Southern African leaders about the toll that their silence about this ongoing crisis takes on their credibility, and about the loss of investor and donor confidence in the region that is a consequence of Zimbabwe's ceaseless downward spiral over the past 5 years.

The administration has spoken out commendably regarding the Zimbabwe crisis, but more could be done to take action that would bolster their tough talk. Targeted sanctions could have more bite, and the U.S. and other key donors could more clearly link support for laudable initiatives such as the New Economic Partnership for Africa's Development to restoration of respect for civil and political rights and the rule of law in Zimbabwe.

Those of us who have followed the crisis in Zimbabwe often feel a sense of frustration as we watch so much of what was promising about that country be systematically dismantled by the current ruling party. But we must not give up on the people of Zimbabwe, many of whom continue to fight against repression despite considerable risk. Once Zimbabwe's corrupt leadership finally releases its grasp on power, the country will require substantial international assistance to rebuild the institutions of democracy and regain its economic footing.

I was pleased to work with the majority leader on the Zimbabwe Democracy and Economic Recovery Act, which became law in 2001. This law spells out Congress's commitment to come forward as a strong partner of a recovery in Zimbabwe when change finally does come and Zimbabwe's long, sad slide into authoritarianism and economic collapse has been halted. I still believe in the promise of that bill and look forward to the day conditions allow all of us to realize that promise, and to join with the people of Zimbabwe in rebuilding their country and safeguarding their democracy.

Source: *Congressional Record,* July 1, 2005, S 7904–7907.

AVIAN FLU (NOVEMBER 2005)

A potential pandemic and ensuing health crisis has been a major focus of the U.S. media outlets. It began with Mad Cow Disease (BSE), was followed by SARS, and, most recently, avian flu. Avian flu, commonly referred to as bird flu, first appeared in chickens and roosters in Southeastern Asia. The virus quickly spread through millions of chickens throughout Asia and, in some cases, was transmitted to human beings. Avian flu currently has no cure nor is there a vaccine available for this flu strain. Millions of birds across the world were destroyed in an effort to stop the spread of the virus since it was discovered. While the virus' main target has been birds, it has also been known to affect pigs and cats. The major focus of concern, however, continues to be birds, specifically chicken.

The H5N1 strain—the most lethal form of avian flu—has been reported throughout Asia, Europe, Eurasia, Africa, and the Near East. While no cases of the bird flu have appeared in the United States, the fear of its spread has been perpetuated by the media. According to President Bush, the virus is currently being controlled by the strict measures adopted in the various countries affected; and he has reassured the nation that the CDC is ready. Still, some senators have expressed their doubts. Fueling their concerns is the high mortality rate for this disease: there have already been 205 cases of the avian flu in humans throughout the world and 113 of these cases resulted in death.

BUSH'S REMARKS ON THE NATIONAL STRATEGY FOR PANDEMIC INFLUENZA PREPAREDNESS AND RESPONSE IN BETHESDA, MARYLAND (NOVEMBER 1, 2005)

... At this moment, the men and women of the NIH are working to protect the American people from another danger, the risk of avian and pandemic influenza. Today, I have come to talk about our Nation's efforts to address this vital issue to the health and the safety of all Americans. I'm here to discuss our strategy to prevent and protect the American people from a possible outbreak.

Pandemic flu is another matter. Pandemic flu occurs when a new strain of influenza emerges that can be transmitted easily from person to person and for which there is little or no natural immunity. Unlike seasonal flu, most people have not built up resistance to it. And unlike seasonal flu, it can kill those who are young and healthy as well as those who are frail and sick.

At this moment, there is no pandemic influenza in the United States or the world. But if history is our guide, there is reason to be concerned. In the last century, our country and the world have been hit by three influenza pandemics, and viruses from birds contributed to all of them....

Scientists and doctors cannot tell us where or when the next pandemic will strike or how severe it will be, but most agree, at some point, we are likely to face another pandemic. And the scientific community is increasingly concerned by a new influenza virus known as H5N1 or avian flu that is now spreading through bird populations across Asia and has recently reached Europe.

At this point, we do not have evidence that a pandemic is imminent. Most of the people in Southeast Asia who got sick were handling infected birds. And while the avian flu virus has spread from Asia to Europe, there are no reports of infected birds, animals, or people in the United States. Even if the virus does eventually appear on our shores in birds, that does not mean people in our country will be infected. Avian flu is still primarily an animal disease. And as of now, unless people come into direct, sustained contact with infected birds, it is unlikely they will come down with avian flu.

While avian flu has not yet acquired the ability to spread easily from human to human, there is still cause for vigilance. The virus has developed some characteristics needed to cause a pandemic. It has demonstrated the ability to infect human beings, and it has produced a fatal illness in humans. If the virus were to develop the capacity for sustained human-to-human transmission, it could spread quickly across the globe.

Our country has been given fair warning of this danger to our homeland and time to prepare. My responsibility as the President [is] to take measures now to protect the American people from the possibility that human-to-human transmission may occur. So several months ago, I directed all relevant departments and agencies in the Federal Government to take steps to address the threat of avian and pandemic flu. Since that time, my administration has developed a comprehensive national strategy, with concrete measures we can take to prepare for an influenza pandemic.

Today, I am announcing key elements of that strategy. Our strategy is designed to meet three critical goals: First, we must detect outbreaks that occur anywhere in the world; second, we must protect the American people by stockpiling vaccines and antiviral drugs and improve our ability to rapidly produce new vaccines against a pandemic strain; and third, we must be ready to respond at the Federal, State, and local levels in the event that a pandemic reaches our shores.

To meet these three goals, our strategy will require the combined efforts of government officials in public health, medical, veterinary, and law enforcement communities and the private sector. It will require the active participation of the American people. And it will require the immediate attention of the United States Congress so we can have the resources in place to begin implementing this strategy right away.

The first part of our strategy is to detect outbreaks before they spread across the world. In the fight against avian and pandemic flu, early detection is our first line of defense....

In September at the United Nations, I announced a new International Partnership on Avian and Pandemic Influenza, a global network of surveillance and preparedness that will help us to detect and respond quickly to any outbreaks of the disease. The partnership requires participating countries that face an outbreak to immediately share information and provide samples to the World Health Organization. By requiring transparency, we can respond more rapidly to dangerous outbreaks.

...I've requested $251 million from Congress to help our foreign partners train local medical personnel, expand their surveillance and testing capacity, draw up preparedness plans, and take other vital actions to detect and contain outbreaks.

A flu pandemic would have global consequences, so no nation can afford to ignore this threat, and every nation has responsibilities to detect and stop its spread.

Here in the United States, we're doing our part. To strengthen domestic surveillance, my administration is launching the National Bio-Surveillance Initiative. This initiative will help us rapidly detect, quantify, and respond to outbreaks of disease in humans and animals and deliver information quickly to State and local and national and international public health officials. By creating systems that provide continuous situational awareness, we're more likely to be able to stop, slow, or limit the spread of the pandemic and save American lives.

The second part of our strategy is to protect the American people by stockpiling vaccines and antiviral drugs and accelerating development of new vaccine technologies. One of the challenges presented by a pandemic is that scientists need a sample of the new strain before they can produce a vaccine against it. This means it is difficult to produce a pandemic vaccine before the pandemic actually appears, and so there may not be a vaccine capable of fully immunizing our citizens from the new influenza virus during the first several months of a pandemic.

To help protect our citizens during these early months when a fully effective vaccine would not be available, we're taking a number of immediate steps. Researchers here at the NIH have developed a vaccine based on the current strain of the avian flu virus. The vaccine is already in clinical trials. And I'm asking that the Congress fund $1.2 billion for the Department of Health and Human Services to purchase enough doses of this vaccine from manufacturers to vaccinate 20 million people.

We're also increasing stockpiles of antiviral drugs such as Tamiflu and Relenza. Antiviral drugs cannot prevent people from contracting the flu. It can [sic]—but they can reduce the severity of the illness when taken within 48 hours of getting sick. . . .

To protect the greatest possible number of Americans during a pandemic, the cornerstone of our strategy is to develop new technologies that will allow us to produce new vaccines rapidly. If a pandemic strikes, our country must have a surge capacity in place that will allow us to bring a new vaccine on line quickly and manufacture enough to immunize every American against the pandemic strain.

. . . Today, the NIH is working with vaccine makers to develop new cell-culture techniques that will help us bring a pandemic flu vaccine to the American people faster in the event of an outbreak.

. . . I'm asking Congress for $2.8 billion to accelerate development of cell-culture technology. By bringing cell-culture technology from the research laboratory into the production line, we should be able to produce enough vaccine for every American within 6 months of the start of a pandemic.

I'm also asking Congress to remove one of the greatest obstacles to domestic vaccine production, the growing burden of litigation. In the past three decades, the number of vaccine manufacturers in America has plummeted as the industry has been flooded with lawsuits. Today, there is only one manufacturer in the United States that can produce influenza vaccine. . . .

The third part of our strategy is to ensure that we are ready to respond to a pandemic outbreak. . . .

To respond to a pandemic, we must have emergency plans in place in all 50 States and every local community. We must ensure that all levels of government are ready to act to contain an outbreak. We must be able to deliver vaccines and other treatments to frontline responders and at-risk populations.

So my administration is working with public health officials in the medical community to develop effective pandemic emergency plans. We're working at the

Federal level. We're looking at ways and options to coordinate our response with State and local leaders....

To respond to a pandemic, we need medical personnel and adequate supplies of equipment. In a pandemic, everything from syringes to hospital beds, respirators, masks, and protective equipment would be in short supply. So the Federal Government is stockpiling critical supplies in locations across America as part of the Strategic National Stockpile. The Department of Health and Human Services is helping States create rosters of medical personnel who are willing to help alleviate local shortfalls during a pandemic. And every Federal department involved in health care is expanding plans to ensure that all Federal medical facilities, personnel, and response capabilities are available to support local communities in the event of a pandemic crisis.

... To provide Americans with more information about pandemics, we're launching a new web site, pandemicflu.gov. That ought to be easy for people to remember: pandemicflu.gov. The web site will keep our citizens informed about the preparations underway, steps they can take now to prepare for a pandemic, and what every American can do to decrease their risk of contracting and spreading the disease in the event of an outbreak.

Now, all the steps I've outlined today require immediate resources. Because a pandemic could strike at any time, we can't waste time in preparing. So to meet all our goals, I'm requesting a total of $7.1 billion in emergency funding from the United States Congress. By making critical investments today, we'll strengthen our ability to safeguard the American people in the awful event of a devastating global pandemic and, at the same time, will bring our Nation's public health and medical infrastructure more squarely in the 21st century.

Source: *Public Papers of the Presidents of the United States: George W. Bush* (Washington, DC: Government Printing Office), 1627–1632.

AVIAN FLU PANDEMIC (SEPTEMBER 29, 2005)

Mr. Tom Harkin (D-IA). ... Mr. President, I come to the floor at this time to discuss a matter of grave national security. If recent Hurricane Katrina and Hurricane Rita have taught us anything, it is that we have to do a dramatically better job of preparing for diseases before they strike so we are not left picking up the pieces afterward.

I am very gravely concerned that the United States is totally unprepared for an outbreak—and a subsequent international pandemic—of avian flu. We have had two disasters in the last 4 years—9/11 and Katrina followed by Rita. And the Federal Government was totally unprepared for both, despite clear warnings. Similarly, we have been warned in no uncertain terms about avian flu, but our preparations so far have been grossly inadequate.

I think I got my first briefing on this about a year ago from CDC in Atlanta. I have been following it closely in our Labor, Health and Human Services, Education and Related Agencies Appropriations Subcommittee.

As it has unfolded over the last several months, it is clear that it is not a question of if avian flu is going to reach us, it is a question of when—not if, just when.

As many of my colleagues know, avian flu—or as it is called in the technical jargon, H5N1—has been known to pass first in bird species. It was passed from bird to bird, chicken to chicken, and that type of thing. It has then gotten into migratory waterfowl, which has spread from countries such as Thailand, Cambodia, Vietnam, and Hong Kong. And they have now found it as far away as Kazakhstan and as far north as the northern regions of Russia. It is just a matter of time before it gets here.... Where do our efforts stand, and what can we be doing better?

First, where do we stand?

The Centers for Disease Control, under the great leadership of Dr. Gerberding, is doing a fine job working in cooperation with the World Health Organization and governments in affected regions to detect the disease and to help to stop its spread. Surveillance can alert us to an outbreak and governments can then take measures to isolate the disease so that widespread infection does not occur.

Again, we know how to do this. The CDC knows how to do this. They had great success with surveillance, isolation, and quarantine during the SARS outbreak, and they managed to control its spread. We never got SARS in the United States because we were able to isolate it and quarantine it in other countries.

We also learned valuable lessons from this SARS episode. We need to be doing a better job of surveillance. We have had some problems with some countries which do not have a very good public health infrastructure. They may not report illnesses and deaths as do we or some other places.

But we have CDC personnel on the ground in these countries. They know what to do. But they are woefully inadequate in funds. They don't have the funds needed to conduct adequate surveillance in these countries such as Cambodia, Thailand, Vietnam, Russia, and places such as that. They need some more support for surveillance. I will get into that in a little bit.

In order for us to get the necessary vaccines for this drug, it is going to take a few months.

The best thing we can be about in the initial stages is surveillance, finding out where it is outbreaking, control it, isolate it, and quarantine it.

As I said, the Centers for Disease Control and Prevention know how [to] do that. There are other things we can be doing better. The World Health Organization is encouraging the purchase of antiviruses, medicines that help mitigate the infectious disease once you have already gotten it. Unfortunately, the United States only has enough antiviral medication for 1 percent of our population. That is not enough. We need to invest approximately $3 billion to build an adequate stockpile of antiviral medications. That would get us enough for about 50 percent of the population.

The experts tell us that we ought to be prepared for that kind of an infectious rate in the United States; that it could be up to 50 percent or more of our people in the United States affected by this—140 million people.

If we stay where we are, and we only have 1 percent or 10 percent, then you raise the question: Who gets it? How is it distributed?

We need to reassure our people that we have enough of these antivirals. These antivirals have a long shelf life—7 to 10 years, and maybe even more.

It is not as if we are buying something that is going to disintegrate right away. These antivirals have a long shelf life.

In addition, the President's budget cut $120 million from State and public health agencies. These are the agencies that will be on the front lines of both surveillance and disease prevention should an outbreak occur. We have to restore this funding. But that is not adequate.

In the future, our public health infrastructure would be stretched to the limits by an outbreak of avian influenza.

We need to invest in more public health professionals, epidemiologists, physicians, laboratory technicians, and others.

As I said, if we have an outbreak and it gets to the United States, the first thing we want to do is have good surveillance, isolation, and quarantine. That costs money.

Lastly, we also must take measures to increase our Nation's vaccine capacity. Currently, there is only one flu vaccine manufacturing facility in the United States.

I have wondered about that. Why is that so?

In meetings with the drug industry and others, I have learned that vaccine production is not very profitable compared to other types of drug development and manufacturing. Plus, they do not know if there is going to be a market for it.

This is a classic point of market failure—where the market really can't respond to a future need.

This is where the Government must step in to provide incentives for more manufacturers to build facilities in the United States.

Source: *Congressional Record*, September 29, 2005, S 10652–10656.

FOREIGN POLICY WEB SITES

ABC News. "Avian Flu: Is the Government Ready for an Epidemic." September 15, 2005. http://abcnews.go.com/Primetime/Investigation/story?id=1130392&page=1

Arms Control Association. "Bush Announces U.S. Intent to Withdraw from ABM Treaty." January/February 2002. http://www.armscontrol.org/act/2002_01-02/abmjanfeb02.asp

BBC News. "Analysis: Bush's Foreign Policy." April 7, 2001. http://news.bbc.co.uk/1/hi/world/americas/1265039.stm

———. "Bush Outlines Foreign Policy." November 20, 1999. http://newswww.bbc.net.uk/1/hi/world/americas/529018.stm

Bolton, John R. "U.S.-Russian Arms Reduction Talks." March 22, 2002. http://www.state.gov/t/us/rm/8889.htm

"Bush and Putin Sign Historic Arms Reduction Treaty." *Newsmax.com*, May 25, 2002. http://www.newsmax.com/archives/articles/2002/5/24/125852.shtml

CNN. "Bush Nominates Bolton as U.N. Ambassador." March 8, 2005. http://www.cnn.com/2005/US/03/07/bolton/

———. "Former Officials to Condemn Bush Foreign Policy." June 14, 2004. http://www.cnn.com/2004/ALLPOLITICS/06/13/bush.criticism/

———. "Retired General: Bush Foreign Policy a National Disaster." July 31, 2004. http://www.cnn.com/2004/ALLPOLITICS/07/31/dems.radio/

———. "Sidestepping Senate, Bush Sends Bolton to U.N." August 2, 2005. http://www.cnn.com/2005/POLITICS/08/01/bolton.appointment/

———. "U.S. Quits: ABM Treaty." December 14, 2001. http://archives.cnn.com/2001/ALLPOLITICS/12/13/rec.bush.abm/

———. "U.S. Surveillance Plane Lands in China after Collision with Fighter." April 1, 2001. http://archives.cnn.com/2001/US/04/01/us.china.plane/

Daalder, Ivan, and James M. Lindsay. "A New Agenda for Nuclear Weapons: On Nuclear Weapons, Destroy and Codify." *Brookings Institute*, February 2002. http://www.brookings.edu/comm/policybriefs/pb94.htm

Issues 2000. "George W. Bush on Foreign Policy." http://www.issues2000.org/George_W_Bush_Foreign_Policy.htm
Karon, Tony. "When It Comes to Kyoto, U.S. Is the Rogue Nation." *Time.com*, July 21, 2001. http://www.time.com/time/world/article/0,8599,168701,00.html
Kay, Joseph. "Withdrawal from ABM Treaty Signals Escalation of U.S. Militarism." World Socialist Website, December 27, 2001. http://www.wsws.org/articles/2001/dec2001/abm-d27.shtml
Marshall, Joshua Micah. "Remaking the World: Bush and the Neoconservatives." *Foreign Affairs*, November/December 2003. http://www.foreignaffairs.org/20031101fareview essay82614/joshua-micah-marshall/remaking-the-world-bush-and-the-neoconservatives.html
Middle East History and Resources. "Middle East Historical and Peace Process Documents." http://www.mideastweb.org/history.htm
Milbank, Dana. "Bush Outlines Foreign Policy." *Washington Post*, December 2, 2004. http://www.washingtonpost.com/wp-dyn/articles/A25380-2004Dec1.html
Military.com. "U.S. Protests Access to Spy Plane." http://www.military.com/Content/MoreContent/1,12044,FL_planeaccess_040201.htm,00.html
Morehead, Melissa. "Bush Attacks Zimbabwe with Sanctions." *Workers World*. http://www.workers.org/ww/2003/zimbabwe0320.php
Natural Resource Defense Council. "Bush Administration Errs on Kyoto Global Warming Protocol." March 2001. http://www.nrdc.org/globalWarming/akyotoqa.asp
Phillips, James A. "A Middle East Roadmap to Gridlock." *The Heritage Foundation*, June 2003: http://www.heritage.org/Research/MiddleEast/wm287.cfm
Shanker, Tom. "Spy-Plane Papers Survived." *New York Times*, May 20, 2001. http://query.nytimes.com/gst/fullpage.html?res=9E00E0DE173DF933A15756C0A9679C8B63&n=Top%2fReference%2fTimes%20Topics%2fPeople%2fS%2fShanker%2c%20Thom
U.S. Department of State. "Afghan Women and Child Relief Act of 2001." http://www.state.gov/g/wi/7186.htm
———. "Roadmap for Peace in the Middle East: Israeli/Palestinian Reciprocal Action, Quartet Support." July 16, 2003. http://www.state.gov/r/pa/ei/rls/22520.htm
U.S. Treasury. "What You Need to Know about Zimbabwe Sanctions." http://www.ustreas.gov/offices/enforcement/ofac/programs/zimbabwe/zimb.pdf
The White House. "President Outlines Pandemic Influenza Preparations and Response." November 2005. http://www.whitehouse.gov/news/releases/2005/11/20051101-1.html
———. "President Signs Afghan Women and Child Relief Act." December 2001. http://www.whitehouse.gov/news/releases/2001/12/20011212-9.html
World Wildlife Federation. "Bush Abandons Kyoto Protocol." March 29, 2001. http://www.wwf.org.uk/News/n_0000000268.asp

FOREIGN POLICY REFERENCE ARTICLES AND BOOKS

Adler, David Gray. "The Law: Termination of the ABM Treaty and the Political Question Doctrine: Judicial Succor for Presidential Power." *Presidential Studies Quarterly* 34, no. 1 (March 2004): 156.
Benard, Cheryl. *Veiled Courage: Inside the Afghan Women's Resistance*. New York: Broadway Books, 2002.
Bleek, Phillip. "Bush Reviews Threat Reduction Programs, Contemplates Cuts." *Arms Control Today* 31, no. 3 (April 2001): 26.
Bolton, M. Kent. *U.S. Foreign Policy and International Politics: George W. Bush, 9/11, and the Global Terrorist Hydra*. Upper Saddle River, NJ: Pearson/Prentice Hall, 2005.
Cimbala, Stephen, and James Scouras. *Nuclear Deterrence and Arms Control: A New Century*." Westport, CT: Praeger Publishers, 2002.

Coon, Charli. "Why Bush Is Right to Abandon the Kyoto Protocol." *Heritage Foundation*, May 11, 2001.

Coyle, Philip E., and John Rhinelander. "National Missile Defense and the ABM Treaty: No Need to Wreck the Accord." *World Policy Journal* 18, no. 3 (Fall 2001): 15.

Daalder, Ivo H. *America Unbound: The Bush Revolution in Foreign Policy*. Hoboken, NJ: Wiley, 2005.

Deller, Nicole. "Arms Control Abandoned: The Case of Biological Weapons." *World Policy Journal* 20, no. 2 (Summer 2003): 37.

"Four Views: Bush's Speech—What Next?" *Washington Report on Middle East Affairs* 21, no. 6 (August 2002): 6.

Glad, Betty, and Chris Dolan, eds. *Striking First: The Preventive War Doctrine and the Reshaping of U.S. Foreign Policy*. New York: Palgrave Macmillan, 2004.

Grigg, William Norman. "Bird Flu." *The New American* 21, no. 25 (December 12, 2005): 18.

Haney, Patrick Jude. *The Cuban Embargo: The Domestic Politics of an American Foreign Policy*. Pittsburgh, PA: University of Pittsburgh Press, 2005.

Hayes, Stephen. "I Don't Do Carrots: The Big Stick Diplomacy of Bush's Nominee for U.N. Ambassador." *The Weekly Standard* 10, no. 25 (March 21, 2005): 11.

Jervis, Robert. *American Foreign Policy in a New Era*. New York: Routledge, 2005.

Judis, John. *The Folly of Empire: What George W. Bush Could Learn from Theodore Roosevelt and Woodrow Wilson*. New York: Scribner, 2004.

Leverett, Flynt Lawrence, and Martin Indyk, eds. *The Road Ahead: Middle East Policy in the Bush Administration's Second Term*. Washington, DC: Brookings Institute, 2005.

Marshall, Rachel. "Bush's Flight from Reality." *Washington Report on Middle East Affairs* 24, no. 8 (November 2005): 7.

Melanson, Richard. *American Foreign Policy since the Vietnam War: The Search for Consensus from Richard Nixon to George W. Bush*. Armonk, NY: M.E. Sharpe, 2005.

Moens, Alexander. *The Foreign Policy of George W. Bush*. Brookfield, VT: Ashgate, 2004.

Pauly, Robert. *U.S. Foreign Policy and the Persian Gulf: Safeguarding American Interests through Selective Multilateralism*. Brookfield, VT: Ashgate, 2005.

Pomper, Miles. "Bush Gives Bolton Recess Appointment." *Arms Control Today* 35, no. 7 (September 2005): 37.

Siegel, Marc. *Bird Flu: Everything You Need to Know about the Next Pandemic*. New York: Wiley, 2006.

U.S. Government. *2005 Federal Pandemic Influenza Plan: Bush Administration Health and Human Services Department Strategic Plan for Potential Avian Flu-Bird Flu Outbreaks*.

"A Welcome Arms Pact." *The Register Guardian*, May 15, 2002, A12.

TERRORISM AND MILITARY ACTIONS

INTRODUCTION

By most accounts, the terrorist attacks on September 11, 2001, defined the Bush presidency. Not only did George W. Bush become a war president overnight, but the direction of his administration and the balance of power in Washington, D.C., shifted sharply. But the September 11 attacks hardly began the United States' struggle against terrorist organizations, nor do most experts believe that 9/11 will be the last attack of its kind on American soil. Having recently ended the old and mostly "cold" war against the Soviet Union, American defense policy had to shift its focus to a new long-term war against terrorist organizations. The primary focus of the Bush administration and its strategy for fighting international terrorism is highly controversial, with many arguing that the war in Iraq was unnecessary or poorly executed, or that the administration's handling of homeland security falls far short of what Americans need to remain safe.

AMERICA'S FIGHT AGAINST TERRORISM

Modern terrorism is a strategy of opposition groups with the intention of striking fear into a population. The main tactic of terrorist groups is to inflict unexpected violence on civilians. While a guerrilla operation is more likely to attack a military instillation or a bridge needed by an occupying army, terrorists are more likely to bomb a subway station during rush hour. Similarly, while both guerrillas and terrorists use surprise, their purpose is somewhat different. For the guerrilla, surprise is a tactic of a weaker military. For terrorists, surprise is used to provoke fear because it instills the sense that an attack can happen at any time. Moreover, in the current use of the term, a terrorist group is an opposition group, not a government. Saddam Hussein had gassed and murdered civilians with the intention of terrorizing them, and while the Bush administration alleged that Hussein supported terrorist groups, they did not accuse him of being a terrorist.

Terrorism as a political or military strategy has been used in one form or another over the past few centuries, but the current form of international terrorism is often traced back to the late 1960s. After the Six-Day War, when Israel swiftly defeated its neighbors, a strong sense of despair emerged among Palestinians, and terrorists groups began to emerge. This approach developed gradually, but from the American standpoint, 1979 was a critical turning point. In Iran, the American-backed Shah fell from power; the Ayatollah Khomeini took control and made Iran into an Islamic theocracy. Backed by Khomeini, militant students stormed the U.S. embassy in Tehran and took its occupants hostage. Also in 1979, the Soviet Union attacked Afghanistan. Backed with American money and weapons, Islamic extremists swarmed into Afghanistan to fight the Russian occupiers. After the Russians withdrew from Afghanistan in 1989, these groups shifted their focus to other enemies, including the United States.

Throughout the 1980s, the number of terrorist attacks affecting Americans directly increased steadily. In 1983, for example, U.S. embassies in Kuwait and Iran were attacked by suicide bombers, and in 1984 a U.S. embassy annex was bombed in Beirut. In 1988, Pan Am Flight 103, en route from London to New York City, exploded suddenly over Lockerbie, Scotland, killing 270 people in the plane and on the ground, including 243 Americans.

A problem for American presidents before the second Bush administration was what had been commonly referred to as the "Vietnam syndrome." Following the defeat in Vietnam, Americans in general showed significant opposition to any form of military involvement with significant casualties. Both Democratic and Republican presidents believed that they could not commit U.S. troops unless American casualties would be very low. So, in 1979, the Carter administration took any military response off the table after American hostages were taken in Iran. In 1983, a marine barracks in Beirut, Lebanon, was attacked by a suicide bomber, killing a large number of Americans. The Reagan administration aborted any attempt to counterattack, and a few months later the Marines were withdrawn.

A second critical turning point was the first terrorist attack on the World Trade Center in 1993, soon after Bill Clinton took office. Hoping to cause both towers to collapse, the terrorists drove a Ryder truck filled with explosives into the parking deck under the North Tower. The bombs killed six people, and the perpetrators were soon arrested and incarcerated. For President Clinton, the bombing acted as a wake-up call. But, with Americans still squeamish about any military action that might lead to significant casualties, the Clinton administration's response to the rising terrorist threat during its eight years in office remained limited.

Around this time, a new and especially dangerous group was emerging. After the Soviet Union withdrew from Afghanistan, a civil war broke out among various groups, and eventually the Taliban gained power over much of the country. This government made Afghanistan a safe haven for terrorist groups, including al Qaeda. Al Qaeda was largely composed of those who had fought the Russians in Afghanistan and had been funded by the United States during the Soviet occupation. Leading this group was Osama bin Laden, who was not only a charismatic figure but also, as a member of a prominent Saudi oil family, a source of significant funds. Quite unlike the far less ambitious terrorists of the early 1970s, al Qaeda was determined to cause significant pain to the United States and its allies.

THE BUSH ADMINISTRATION

When the Bush administration took over the White House in January, 2001, it showed little indication that terrorism was a primary concern in its defense policy. Instead, the new administration had several other items in the agenda. It wanted to finish building a version of the missile defense system that Ronald Reagan had proposed nearly twenty years before. Known at the time as the Strategic Defense Initiative, and called "Star Wars" by its critics, the plan was to create a system that could shoot nuclear missiles from the sky before they reached American soil. The

Bush administration claimed that it was promoting a less ambitious version of the much-criticized plan, which would help defend the United States if a rogue nation attempted a missile attack. The administration also withdrew from the 1972 Anti-Ballistic Missile (ABM) Treaty, which set strict limits on anti-ballistic missiles, or missiles designed to shoot down other missiles.

The Bush administration also promoted two other key changes to military policy. First, it wanted to produce a leaner and faster military. For example, the administration wanted to significantly reduce the number of nuclear missiles and create a military that could successfully attack another country with fewer troops. This was a dramatic change from the Powell Doctrine, named after its author, Colin Powell, George W. Bush's first secretary of state. This doctrine stated that if the United States enters armed combat, it should attack with overwhelming force and always have an exit strategy from the conflict. The second key change was the administration's desire to end "nation building" missions, like those in the Balkans, where U.S. troops were stationed by the Clinton administration to stabilize governments and deter further genocide.

This all changed on September 11, 2001. The terrorist attacks on civilian and government targets in New York City and Washington, D.C., provoked a fundamental shift in both American politics and the White House. The Vietnam syndrome disappeared; angry and scared Americans were prepared to go to war to prevent another attack. At the same time, the president's public support, which had been weakening, suddenly jumped to over 90 percent.

The Bush administration's immediate response to the terrorist attacks was not controversial. A few weeks after September 11, the American and British military began air attacks against key targets in Afghanistan. This was soon followed by a ground attack. By the end of 2001, the Taliban regime collapsed, a new government was put in its place, and the army began its hunt for bin Laden. While there were some antiwar protests against this invasion, most Americans supported it as a necessary response to a nation harboring a dangerous terrorist organization.

However, most of the other responses of the Bush administration were controversial. In his 2002 State of the Union address, President Bush dubbed Iran, Iraq, and North Korea the "Axis of Evil," an obvious twist on the Axis Powers in World War II (i.e., Germany, Italy, and Japan) and the Evil Empire speech of Ronald Reagan against the Soviet Union. After the address, the focus quickly became Iraq and Saddam Hussein. With little resistance from congressional Democrats, the White House made a case for war on two main grounds. First, Iraq was argued to have weapons of mass destruction and the intention to gather more. Central to this claim was that Iraq was quickly developing nuclear weapons, including that Hussein had sought uranium from Africa to produce these bombs. Second, the administration argued that Hussein was actively helping al Qaeda and its terrorist activities.

Congress gave President Bush the authority to go to war against Iraq in a joint resolution. The resolution passed both the House and the Senate with significant support. Nonetheless, soon after the war began, critics began to loudly challenge its justification. The first issue raised was the supposed connection between Iraq and Niger regarding Hussein's attempt to gather uranium to build nuclear weapons. A former diplomat, Ambassador Joseph Wilson, insisted that the reports were false, and, moreover, that the CIA had warned President Bush that they were questionable, but that the administration kept the claim in the president's State of the Union speech to bolster the case for war. Then, after Baghdad fell, the American military made a concerted search for weapons of mass destruction and found none. Eventually, even the Bush administration admitted that there were no such weapons hidden by the former regime.

IRAQ WAR CONTROVERSIES

As the United States moved toward war with Iraq in 2002 and 2003, the American public was divided over whether there should be an invasion. While President Bush had many supporters, there were also significant antiwar demonstrations. However, these opponents of the war had little voice in Washington. While the Republicans were solidly behind the president, the Democrats were deeply divided. Most of the candidates for the Democratic presidential nomination in 2004 had voted in favor of the war, including both John Kerry and John Edwards. The opposition did not seem to gain momentum until the campaign for the presidential nomination developed, and the most vocal antiwar candidate, Governor Howard Dean, began gaining widespread support among Democratic voters. By the summer of 2004, opposition began to express itself as anger, and Americans, unified a few years earlier by the September 11 attacks, were now polarizing.

The first major controversy to develop after the war began grew directly out of the inability to find weapons of mass destruction in Iraq. The controversy centered around the question of why the administration had been so wrong about these weapons, and whether the country was justified going to war. The White House claimed that the problem was faulty intelligence and blamed the CIA. Critics like Wilson claimed that the CIA had warned the White House that the information was incomplete and uncertain, but that the administration pressed the agency to make the case for war as strong as possible. The same argument was made about Saddam Hussein's alleged relationship with al Qaeda. Critics point out that bin Laden and his organization had a long history of opposition against the Hussein regime. Bin Laden had even argued against American troops liberating Kuwait during the Gulf War and instead argued that Muslims themselves should defeat the Iraqi leader.

A second controversy was over why the mission in Iraq seemed to be failing. After Baghdad and the Hussein regime quickly fell, and after Bush took a victory trip to the USS *Abraham Lincoln*, where he was greeted with a banner reading "Mission Accomplished," a violent insurgency broke out in Iraq. American military deaths continued to rise while Iraqi civilian deaths skyrocketed, and despite significant work by the American military to stop it, the country slipped toward civil war. Critics of the war fell into two groups, neither of them positive toward the Bush administration. The first argued that a civil war was unavoidable and that removing Saddam Hussein by force inevitably led to this crisis. In other words, it was foolhardy to enter Iraq in the first place. The second group, largely conservatives, argued that the war was being lost because of repeated mistakes by the administration. Some of these critics argued that the problem was that the administration had abandoned the Powell Doctrine and invaded Iraq with too few soldiers. The American military was strong enough to topple the regime, they argued, but a much stronger force was needed to stabilize the country.

Another controversy was related to the Abu Ghraib Prison torture crisis. The prison at Abu Ghraib had been one used by the Hussein regime to torture and execute political prisoners. After the American-led coalition defeated the Hussein regime, it made the prison into a detention center for insurgents and criminals. Rumors began soon afterward that American guards were mistreating Iraqi detainees.

Within a year, photographs surfaced showing U.S. soldiers gleefully abusing prisoners. Some argued that these were simply "bad apples" who needed to be punished. But critics made another argument: soon after the September 11 attacks, the Bush administration began to make the claim that the Geneva Convention, which outlawed the torture of enemy soldiers, did not apply to enemy combatants, since they did not represent an actual army. These critics argued that loose torture standards by the civilian leadership opened the door to the Abu Ghraib crisis, which significantly damaged the legitimacy of the United States in the region.

Finally, there is significant debate over whether the war in Iraq benefits or hinders the War on Terror. Proponents argue that eliminating Hussein has eliminated a significant source of support to terrorists, and some argue further that the battle in Iraq has attracted terrorists, thereby placing the battle far from North America. Critics argue that the Iraq War actually helps international terrorists in two ways. First, it fuels the hatred against the United States and has created a basis of recruitment for more terrorists. Second, they argue that the war against Iraqi insurgents has taken significant resources away from the fight against international terrorists. They argue that the administration has done too little to build homeland security, and they cite the poor response by the new Office of Homeland Security to Hurricane Katrina as evidence that America is not prepared for another terrorist attack.

During his first term in office, it was assumed that President Bush would likely be judged more by his response to the September 11 attacks than any other aspect of his administration. In the year after the attacks, he was hailed as a decisive leader. But after several years of war in Iraq, President Bush's public support dropped markedly, and even his former supporters are questioning his decisions. It remains to be seen how he will be viewed in another decade.

SEPTEMBER 11 AND OSAMA BIN LADEN (SEPTEMBER 2001)

September 11, 2001, will forever be a black mark in U.S. history. The first attacks occurred in New York City against the two towers of the World Trade Center—the largest and the most prominent points in the New York skyline. When the Twin Towers fell, estimates of the death toll ranged from 7,000 to 11,000 people. America was shocked and appalled. The second attack, just minutes later, unfolded at the Pentagon. Following this, a fourth plane, United flight 93, crashed in a remote part of Pennsylvania. In total, four planes were hijacked by nineteen terrorists.

The great majority of the terrorists were of Saudi descent. The nation called upon the president to take swift action, and many called for retaliation. On September 15, 2001, the president declared that the mastermind behind the attacks was Osama bin Laden, a prominent, wealthy Saudi. Bin Laden had been a Muhjahadeen soldier in the Afghan fight against Soviet aggression. After the defeat of the Soviet Union in

Afghanistan, bin Laden turned his sights back to the Middle East, and in so doing found stark objections to the actions of the U.S. government and its military forces in the area.

Following the terrorist attacks, America was united and very few questions were asked of the administration and the military, but after emotions had settled down, questions began to arise as to why more was not done to stop this. Later it was revealed that intelligence reports claiming Osama bin Laden had imminent plans to attack the United States had been overlooked. But it was not until much later that the July 2001 sanctioning of Afghanistan was revealed to be an indication that the president himself had seen bin Laden as an imminent danger to Americans both at home and abroad.

BUSH'S RESPONSE TO OSAMA BIN LADEN AND THE TERRORIST ATTACKS OF SEPTEMBER 11, 2001 (JUNE 30, 2001)

On July 4, 1999, the President issued Executive Order 13129, "Blocking Property and Prohibiting Transactions with the Taliban," to deal with the unusual and extraordinary threat to the national security and foreign policy of the United States posed by the actions and policies of the Taliban in Afghanistan. The order blocks all property and interests in property of the Taliban and prohibits trade-related transactions by United States persons involving the territory of Afghanistan controlled by the Taliban. The last notice of continuation was signed on June 30, 2000.

The Taliban continues to allow territory under its control in Afghanistan to be used as a safe haven and base of operations for Osama bin Laden and the al Qaeda organization who have committed and threaten to continue to commit acts of violence against the United States and its nationals. For these reasons, I have determined that it is necessary to maintain in force these emergency authorities beyond July 4, 2001. Therefore, . . . I am continuing the national emergency declared on July 4, 1999, with respect to the Taliban . . .

Public Papers of the Presidents of the United States: George W. Bush (Washington, DC: Government Printing Office), 1003.

SEPTEMBER 11, 2001

Good evening. Today our fellow citizens, our way of life, our very freedom came under attack in a series of deliberate and deadly terrorist acts. The victims were in airplanes or in their offices: secretaries, business men and women, military and Federal workers, moms and dads, friends and neighbors. Thousands of lives were suddenly ended by evil, despicable acts of terror.

The pictures of airplanes flying into buildings, fires burning, huge structures collapsing, have filled us with disbelief, terrible sadness, and a quiet, unyielding anger. These acts of mass murder were intended to frighten our Nation into chaos and retreat, but they have failed. Our country is strong.

A great people has been moved to defend a great nation. Terrorist attacks can shake the foundations of our biggest buildings, but they cannot touch the foundation of America. These acts shattered steel, but they cannot dent the steel of American resolve. America was targeted for attack because we're the brightest beacon for freedom and opportunity in the world. And no one will keep that light from shining.

Today our Nation saw evil, the very worst of human nature. And we responded with the best of America, with the daring of our rescue workers, with the caring for strangers and neighbors who came to give blood and help in any way they could.

Immediately following the first attack, I implemented our Government's emergency response plans. Our military is powerful, and it's prepared. Our emergency teams are working in New York City and Washington, DC, to help with local rescue efforts.

Our first priority is to get help to those who have been injured and to take every precaution to protect our citizens at home and around the world from further attacks.

The functions of our Government continue without interruption. Federal agencies in Washington which had to be evacuated today are reopening for essential personnel tonight and will be open for business tomorrow. Our financial institutions remain strong, and the American economy will be open for business, as well.

The search is underway for those who are behind these evil acts. I've directed the full resources of our intelligence and law enforcement communities to find those responsible and to bring them to justice. We will make no distinction between the terrorists who committed these acts and those who harbor them.

I appreciate so very much the Members of Congress who have joined me in strongly condemning these attacks. And on behalf of the American people, I thank the many world leaders who have called to offer their condolences and assistance.

America and our friends and allies join with all those who want peace and security in the world, and we stand together to win the war against terrorism. Tonight I ask for your prayers for all those who grieve, for the children whose worlds have been shattered, for all whose sense of safety and security has been threatened. And I pray they will be comforted by a power greater than any of us, spoken through the ages in Psalm 23: "Even though I walk through the valley of the shadow of death, I fear no evil, for You are with me."

This is a day when all Americans from every walk of life unite in our resolve for justice and peace. America has stood down enemies before, and we will do so this time. None of us will ever forget this day. Yet, we go forward to defend freedom and all that is good and just in our world.

Thank you. Good night, and God bless America.

Source: *Public Papers of the Presidents of the United States: George W. Bush* (Washington, DC: Government Printing Office), 1301–1302.

SEPTEMBER 15, 2001

The President. I've asked the highest levels of our Government to come to discuss the current tragedy that has so deeply affected our Nation. Our country mourns for the loss of life and for those whose lives have been so deeply affected by this despicable act of terror.

I am going to describe to our leadership what I saw: the wreckage of New York City, the signs of the first battle of war.

We're going to meet and deliberate and discuss, but there's no question about it, this act will not stand. We will find those who did it; we will smoke them out of their holes; we will get them running; and we'll bring them to justice. We will not only deal with those who dare attack America; we will deal with those who harbor them and feed them and house them.

Q. Sir, are you satisfied that Osama bin Laden is at least a kingpin of this operation?

The President. There is no question he is what we would call a prime suspect. And if he thinks he can hide and run from the United States and our allies, he will be sorely mistaken.

Source: *Public Papers of the Presidents of the United States: George W. Bush* (Washington, DC: Government Printing Office), 1319–1321.

CRITICISM OF BUSH'S RESPONSE TO OSAMA BIN LADEN AND SEPTEMBER 11 (OCTOBER 20, 2003)

Mr. Kent Conrad (D-ND). Mr. President, over the weekend, Osama bin Laden was again seen vowing that al Qaeda would launch suicide attacks against Americans and our allies. Frankly, it angered me to see these taped reports that again Osama bin Laden is threatening Americans.

It has now been 771 days since al Qaeda launched terrorist attacks on American targets on September 11, 2001. For me, this report raised the question of why is Osama bin Laden still able to threaten this country? Why have we not been able to find him and bring him to account?

I was reminded, in seeing these tapes, that just several weeks ago *Newsweek* magazine did a detailed analysis on where Osama bin Laden might be. They narrowed it down to Kunar province on the border between Afghanistan and Pakistan. They had detailed reports in that article of Osama bin Laden being seen in this area.

It struck me at the time, if we have a pretty good idea of where Osama bin Laden is, why are we not flooding that area with American forces to take him out? *Newsweek* went on to report that

> [B]in Laden appears to be not only alive, but thriving. And with America distracted in Iraq and Pakistani President Pervez Musharraf leery of stirring up an Islamist backlash, there is no large-scale military force currently pursuing the chief culprit in the 9/11 attacks, U.S. officials concede.

I find that alarming. Osama bin Laden led the attacks on this country. We know that. There is no doubt about it. If we are being distracted by Iraq, in my view, that is a serious mistake. I must say it is one that I very much feared one year ago when we were considering whether to attack Iraq. I voted against attacking Iraq at that time because I believed our top priority ought to be going after al Qaeda and Osama bin Laden.

There has just recently been a report in the *Boston Globe* that says: "As the hunt for Saddam Hussein grows more urgent, and the guerilla war in Iraq shows no signs of abating, the Bush administration is continuing to shift highly specialized intelligence officers from the hunt for Osama bin Laden in Afghanistan to the Iraq crisis."

I believe that is the wrong priority. I believe the priority ought to be al Qaeda and Osama bin Laden, and we ought to be going into this area that has been identified in seeking to find him and holding him to account.

When I reflect on the decision to go into Iraq, I am reminded that many in the public believe that Iraqis were part of the 9/11 operation. In fact, 69 percent of the American people believe Saddam was involved in the September 11 attacks. Half of Americans believe that Iraqis were among the 9/11 hijackers.

We know that is not the case. There were no Iraqis, none, zero, involved in the 19 who hijacked the planes in our country that turned them into flying bombs that attacked the World Trade Center and the Pentagon. Of the 19 hijackers, 15 were from Saudi Arabia, two were from the United Arab Emirates, one was from Egypt, and one was from Lebanon. Not a single one was from Iraq. Yet even now many Americans believe it was in fact Iraqis who attacked this country. In fact, more Americans believe most of the hijackers were Iraqis—21 percent—than the 17 percent who correctly stated none of the hijackers was Iraqi.

We are making decisions here, and the American people are supporting decisions, and apparently they do not have the accurate information.

Unfortunately, it is not hard to figure out why. In speech after speech, the President and his top officials have juxtaposed 9/11 with Saddam and Iraq, strongly implying there is a clear and direct link between Saddam and 9/11. To take only one of dozens of examples, as recently as last month Vice President Cheney again linked 9/11 with Iraq, describing Iraq as the geographic base of the terrorists who have had us under assault for many years, but most especially on 9/11.

This is the Vice President of the United States suggesting that Iraq was at the center of the attack on America on 9/11.

The President himself was forced to correct the record just a few days later, when he said we have had no evidence Saddam Hussein was involved on September 11; no evidence.

The record is overwhelmingly clear. We know who attacked us on September 11. It was not Iraq. There were no Iraqis. The people who attacked us on September 11 were al Qaeda, led by Osama bin Laden. In 770 days, we have not yet held him to account. That has to be our priority.

The President and his top officials have sought to link Saddam, not just with 9/11 specifically but with al Qaeda more generally. They have cited three pieces of evidence to back that claim.

First, the administration stated that one of the 9/11 hijackers, Mohamed Atta, met with an Iraqi agent in Prague in the spring of 2001. For example, last year the Vice President asserted: "We have reporting that places him [Atta] in Prague with a senior Iraqi intelligence officer a few months before the attacks on the World Trade Center."

That is what the Vice President said then. But what do we know now? The fact is, the CIA and FBI have concluded this report was simply not accurate because Mohammed Atta was in this country, in Virginia Beach, VA, at the time the Vice President had asserted he was in Prague. As the Washington Post reported on September 29:

"In making the case for war against Iraq, Vice President Cheney has continued to suggest that an Iraqi intelligence agent met with a September 11, 2001, hijacker months before the attacks, even as the story was falling apart under scrutiny by the FBI, the CIA, and the foreign government that first made the allegation."

Second, the administration has argued a senior al Qaeda operative, Al-Zarqawi, was seen in Baghdad. He may very well have been in Baghdad, but that doesn't prove anything about a formal link between Iraq and al Qaeda. We know senior operatives spent months in our own country prior to 9/11. That doesn't make the United States an ally of al Qaeda any more than the presence of an al Qaeda operative in Baghdad makes Saddam Hussein an ally of al Qaeda.

Third, the administration said al Qaeda maintained a training camp in northern Iraq. Again, this sounds convincing, but as the former director of the Strategic Proliferation and Military Affairs Office at the State Department's intelligence bureau points out, one finds this is not a very honest explanation: "... I mean, you had terrorist activity described that was taking place in Iraq, without the mention that it was taking place in an area under the control of the Kurds rather than an area under the control of Saddam Hussein."

On this map, this is the camp they were talking about. This is the Ansar al-Islam area. There was a terrorist camp here.

This is a map of Iraq that shows very clearly that is an area controlled by the Kurds. The Kurds are our allies. This is an area that was not under the control of Saddam Hussein.

If the American people are going to make sound judgments about who is responsible for what, and who we ought to hold responsible, and who we ought to prioritize for attack, it seems very clear to me the ones we ought to be attacking are al Qaeda. The ones we ought to be going after first and foremost are Osama bin Laden and his allies. Over and over, I believe the American people have been led to believe there is this strong link between al Qaeda and Saddam Hussein. I do not think the facts bear out that connection.

The President himself has now said Saddam Hussein has not been linked to September 11. Yet the majority of the American people believe that he was. That mistaken understanding is right at the core of what has been to me a serious mistake in the strategy in fighting this war on terror. Our first priority, our top priority, one we should not be distracted from, is going after Osama bin Laden and al Qaeda. I don't think we should be distracted, chasing the mirage of terrorism being fundamentally a product of Iraq. I don't think the record bears that out.

If there is not a strong connection between Iraq and al Qaeda, why have we repeatedly had that linkage made? I think there has been very little credible evidence of a direct connection between al Qaeda and Saddam Hussein. As a former State Department intelligence official said in the same Front Line interview, "His [Secretary Powell's] own intelligence officials and virtually everyone else in the terrorist community said there is no significant connection between al Qaeda and Saddam Hussein."

If there is not a strong connection, why have we heard so many references linking the two? That is a question we all need to ask and try to answer.

In addition to the link to al Qaeda, the President and his administration have also repeatedly indicated that Iraq had weapons of mass destruction. First, the President suggested over and over there were close links between Saddam and al Qaeda, implying Saddam had something to do with the September 11 terrorist attack on this country. We now see that is a very weak case.

The point is simply this: We have not found biological and chemical weapons. We have not found evidence of a reconstituted nuclear program. We have not found any serious links between al Qaeda and Iraq. Those were the fundamental reasons we went to war with Iraq. I believe it was a mistake to attack Iraq at the time we did. I believe it was a priority that simply did not make sense given the threat to this country.

The imminent threat to this country is in the form of al Qaeda. The imminent threat to this country is the forces led by Osama bin Laden. It has now been 771 days since they attacked this country. Newsweek magazine reports they have a pretty good idea where Osama bin Laden is—right on the border between Pakistan and Afghanistan. Yet there is no large-scale military operation underway to take out Osama bin Laden. I think the American people deserve to know why not. Why not? Why aren't we launching massive forces into the area identified as the place where Osama bin Laden is hiding? Have we been distracted by Iraq? I hope not. But the evidence I see is that the resources and the attention, which I believe should have been first directed at taking out Osama bin Laden and al Qaeda, are going to Iraq.

I very much hope we will have answers to these questions in the coming days.

The Senator in the Chair, whom I count as a friend in this body, is the chairman of the Intelligence Committee. Obviously he has knowledge none of the rest of us possess. As one Senator, I saw Osama bin Laden on these tapes again over the weekend and read the stories in the news magazines that said we have a pretty good idea where Osama bin Laden is. But we have not found him, leading to the suggestion that we have been distracted by Iraq. That disturbs me a great deal. I believe the overriding priority for this country and the national security of America is in holding Osama bin Laden to account, finding him, and stopping him.

Source: *Congressional Record*, October 20, 2003, S 12864–12866.

ATTACK ON AFGHANISTAN (OCTOBER 2001)

A month after the attacks on the World Trade Center towers, the United States attacked Afghanistan. As the United States embarked on their fight in the "War on Terror," the administration wanted to oust the oppressive Taliban regime and bring democracy into the Middle Eastern country. In addition to democratizing Afghanistan, the United States had its mind set on capturing Osama bin Laden who was believed to be behind the attacks on New York City and the Pentagon. Countries such as the United Kingdom, Germany, France, and Canada joined the United States in "Operation Enduring Freedom" as the United States attempted to make Afghanistan safer, and at the same time attempted to dismantle the terrorist organization of al Qaeda.

Prior to the invasion, President Bush issued several demands to the Taliban government in Afghanistan, which where ignored. These demands included the closure of terrorist training camps, the extradition of al Qaeda leaders, and arranging the safe return of foreign nationals. As a result, the United States staged an invasion that has claimed thousands of civilian lives, as well as the lives of U.S. troops.

Nonviolent protests occurred throughout the country against the invasion, claiming that diplomatic means had not been exhausted. The opposition cited that this unjustified invasion had the potential for massive loss of civilian life and it would send the country into further chaos.

Even though the Taliban regime has fallen, the country of Afghanistan has not enjoyed the stability that the United States desired. There are reports from organizations such as the Human Rights Watch that are questioning the behavior of the U.S. armed forces, especially in the Afghani prisons.

BUSH'S ADDRESS TO THE NATION ANNOUNCING STRIKES AGAINST AL QAEDA TRAINING CAMPS AND TALIBAN MILITARY INSTALLATIONS IN AFGHANISTAN (OCTOBER 7, 2001)

Good afternoon. On my orders, the United States military has begun strikes against al Qaeda terrorist training camps and military installations of the Taliban regime in Afghanistan. These carefully targeted actions are designed to disrupt the use of Afghanistan as a terrorist base of operations and to attack the military capability of the Taliban regime.

We are joined in this operation by our staunch friend, Great Britain. Other close friends, including Canada, Australia, Germany, and France, have pledged forces as the operation unfolds. More than 40 countries in the Middle East, Africa, Europe, and across Asia have granted air transit or landing rights. Many more have shared intelligence. We are supported by the collective will of the world.

More than 2 weeks ago, I gave Taliban leaders a series of clear and specific demands: Close terrorist training camps; hand over leaders of the al Qaeda network; and return all foreign nationals, including American citizens, unjustly detained in your country. None of these demands were met. And now the Taliban will pay a price. By destroying camps and disrupting communications, we will make it more difficult for the terror network to train new recruits and coordinate their evil plans.

Initially, the terrorists may burrow deeper into caves and other entrenched hiding places. Our military action is also designed to clear the way for sustained, comprehensive, and relentless operations to drive them out and bring them to justice.

At the same time, the oppressed people of Afghanistan will know the generosity of America and our allies. As we strike military targets, we'll also drop food, medicine, and supplies to the starving and suffering men and women and children of Afghanistan.

The United States of America is a friend to the Afghan people, and we are the friends of almost a billion worldwide who practice the Islamic faith. The United States of America is an enemy of those who aid terrorists and of the barbaric criminals who profane a great religion by committing murder in its name.

This military action is a part of our campaign against terrorism, another front in a war that has already been joined through diplomacy, intelligence, the freezing of financial assets, and the arrests of known terrorists by law enforcement agents in 38 countries. Given the nature and reach of our enemies, we will win this conflict by the patient accumulation of successes, by meeting a series of challenges with determination and will and purpose.

Today we focus on Afghanistan, but the battle is broader. Every nation has a choice to make. In this conflict, there is no neutral ground. If any government sponsors the outlaws and killers of innocents, they have become outlaws and murderers, themselves. And they will take that lonely path at their own peril.

Source: *Public Papers of the Presidents of the United States: George W. Bush* (Washington, DC: Government Printing Office), 1432–1433.

CRITICISM OF THE ATTACK ON AFGHANISTAN (OCTOBER 17, 2001)

Mr. Dana Rohrabacher (R-CA). Mr. Speaker, America should be in favor of the people of Afghanistan running their own government, and we have an alternative. Let us all remember, America's greatest allies in this are the Afghan people themselves. The desire to dominate Afghanistan by Pakistan is what created the evil force, the Taliban, in the first place.

So what is our alternative? We have an alternative, and we should not be undermining it. First of all, we need to support those people who will fight to liberate their country from the Taliban. But there is another alternative in terms of government. It was a golden age which almost all Afghans remember; it was a moment like Camelot when there was peace and prosperity for decades in Afghanistan. That is when the old King, Zahir Shah, ruled Afghan. He ruled for almost 4 decades.

As I say, he was overthrown in 1972 and that is what began that cycle of horror that they have not even finished yet. But millions of Afghans remember the King and they have told their children, that was a good time for our country.

Well, King Zahir Shah still lives. He is 86 years old. He lives in exile in Rome. The old King is the most beloved person in Afghanistan. The people love him there, but our government under Bill Clinton and right now even our government with CIA officials and State Department officials in our government, they have done everything they can to suppress even the consideration of bringing back the King as an alternative. As I say, the people of Afghanistan love the King.

There was a very famous meeting that took place among Taliban leaders and one that they were badmouthing the King, this good-hearted person everyone loves, and one Taliban leader says, "Now, wait a minute, you can say anything you want about the King, but when I was a boy my mother asked me to pick berries along the river and the King was fishing at the river. I had a basketful of berries and when the King's guard tried to take it from me, I wouldn't give him the berries. The King walked over and said, 'What's the confusion?' The guard explained to the King that I refused to give him the berries and I told the King that my mother sent me here to bring these berries back for my family. The King kissed me on my forehead and said, 'Always obey your parents. Your mother is very wise. Bring these berries back for your family.'"

Then the Taliban leader turned to his other Taliban leaders and said, "And there's not one of us in this meeting that wouldn't have taken those berries for ourselves and eaten them." That shows you even how much those people know that the King of Afghanistan is a very good-hearted person. Do not let anybody in our government try to undermine this alternative saying that the leaders of the opposition, the so-called Northern Alliance, which is now an alliance of commanders from all over the country—they call themselves the United Front now—those people have sworn their allegiance to the King because the King has said that he wants to go back to Afghanistan, he will do it for 2 years or 3 years as head of a transition government, and during that time period people with education will come back, they will lay the foundation for a civil government and they will have some sort of democratic process, and then the people of Afghanistan will then proceed to elect their leaders, instead of having our faith in some strong guy to come in and take control of Afghanistan who happens to be a friend of Pakistan.

During the Cold War, we backed many tinhorn dictators, we backed despots and strong guys, and in the Muslim world we had a series of alliances with corrupt and repressive regimes, many of them just based, as I say, on a royal family or some tough guy who was willing to do our bidding. That is not what America is supposed to be about. It would be a better world if we would not be that way and we need not to continue that past mistake.

The exiled King of Afghanistan wants to help in a transition for his country into a more peaceful and democratic nation, like the King of Spain did for his people after his people were plagued by a dictatorship for decades. The United States, in fact, should be working with other monarchies who are willing to do this, too, monarchies to evolve into a democratic process. The royal family in Qatar, for example, is establishing an electoral process in which the rights of women to vote are being respected. In Kuwait they are going somewhat in the same direction. But by and large America's dealings in the Arab world have not furthered the cause of liberty and justice. If we just stick with our ideals, stick with people who want to make a difference in this world, who have good hearts and want and believe in treating people decently and believe in democratic government, we will win. We will affect the entire world. We must make allies with those people in the Islamic world, for example, who want to live in freedom, want to have a democratic government and want to have a more peaceful and prosperous life for their children. Even in Afghanistan, these people would be on our side and they would throw away any relationship with blood-thirsty fanatics.

We do not need to use our troops to invade Afghanistan. Let me make this clear. We are going to hear stories of dissension in the ranks of the anti-Taliban forces. No, there is no dissension. They know that they support the King, but they are going to be told by our own government that there is dissension. These people will do the job. The anti-Taliban coalition is ready to overthrow the rule of the Taliban. They might need some help from Special Forces teams or Rangers who can help them with logistics or with some ammunition, let us say, but the Afghans do not need us to fight. They know how to fight and they are willing to liberate their land from these fanatics and terrorists who have held them hostage. With our help they can free themselves and we can join with them after they free themselves from the Taliban in hunting down and killing every member in bin Laden's terrorist gang and bringing them to ultimate justice. I am saying this not as revenge, because that would be inconsistent with our own values, but killing bin Laden and his gang of fanatics and by joining in an effort to stamp out the scourge of terrorism, we are setting a new moral standard and we are deterring in future such terrorism.

The United States has led the world in the defeat of the totalitarianisms of the 20th century. We can now defeat the evil of terrorism by elevating the commitment of civilized nations not to make war on unarmed people. Perhaps it will be called the George W. Doctrine. But what our President is suggesting is that targeting noncombatants anywhere in the world for whatever reason will no longer be tolerated.

This can truly be a step forward for the forces of civilization if this becomes a new standard. We are indeed building a better world on the ashes of the World Trade Center. If it is to be a new standard and not just a justification for our retaliation for the September 11 massacre of our people, if it is to be a new standard, it will help us build a new world. If we are to build on the ashes, we have to start, however, by seeing to it that the bin Ladens of this planet are never again given safe haven. So it not only means hunting down the terrorists but a commitment by all governments of the world not to give safe haven, not to themselves make war on noncombatants but not to give safe haven to terrorists who make war on noncombatants.

Those countries, Afghanistan, Pakistan and Saudi Arabia, have a price to pay. To be fair, the Pakistanis and the Saudis now understand the horrible things that they have done and are trying to work with us, but they have got to make up for the colossal mistakes they have made and we have got to make sure that we are the ones making the decision, not them making the decisions for us.

Source: *Congressional Record*, October 17, 2001, H 7112–7119.

ANTHRAX (NOVEMBER 2001)

Beginning on September 18, 2001, the United States experienced a series of anthrax attacks. Letters containing the anthrax bacteria were mailed to several media outlets as well as two congressmen. Five postal workers died of the bacteria exposure. In addition, buildings were evacuated due to the anthrax threats and more than $1 million was spent to fund efforts to avoid anthrax exposure.

The anthrax incident placed biological warfare at the center of media attention. The federal response included interviews and several antibiotic regimes. President Bush commended the work of the United States Postal Service employees and urged the public to stay calm and come forward with information. The response by the federal government sparked a series of criticisms from Congress, particularly relating to the response time. While Congresswoman Watson commended the authorities handling the evacuation plans in D.C., she questioned why the same protocol was not followed across the country. Though the perpetrators were never discovered, the anthrax incident sparked several hoaxes that continued in the aftermath of the attacks.

BUSH'S RESPONSE TO THE ANTHRAX ATTACKS
(NOVEMBER 3, 2001)

Good morning. As all Americans know, recent weeks have brought a second wave of terrorist attacks upon our country, deadly anthrax spores sent through the U.S. mail. There's no precedent for this type of biological attack, and I'm proud of the way our law enforcement officers, our health care and postal workers, and the American people are responding in the face of this new threat.

At this point in our investigation, we have identified several different letters that contained anthrax spores. Among them were the letters mailed to Senate Majority Leader Tom Daschle on Capitol Hill, NBC News in New York, and the *New York Post* newspaper. Four Americans have died as a result of these acts of terrorism. At least 13 others have developed forms of anthrax disease, either in the lungs or, less severely, on the skin.

Public health officials have acted quickly to distribute antibiotics to people who may have been exposed to anthrax. When anthrax exposure is caught early, preventative treatment is effective. Anthrax can be treated with many antibiotics, and several pharmaceutical companies have offered medicine at reduced prices. The Government is swiftly testing post offices and other sites for anthrax spores and is closing them where potential threats to health are detected. We are working to protect people based on the best information available.

And as we deal with this new threat, we are learning new information every day.

Originally, experts believed the anthrax spores could not escape from sealed envelopes. We now know differently, because of cases where postal workers were exposed even though the envelopes they processed were not open.

Anthrax apparently can be transferred from one letter to another, or from a letter to mail sorting equipment. But anthrax is not contagious, so it does not spread from human to human the way a cold or a flu can. Anthrax can be killed by sterilization, and the Postal Service is purchasing sterilizing equipment to be installed across the country.

More than 30 billion pieces of mail have moved through the Postal Service since September the 11th, so we believe the odds of any one piece of mail being tainted are very low. But still, people should take appropriate precautions: look carefully at your mail before opening it; tell your doctor if you believe you may have been exposed to anthrax. An excellent summary of the symptoms of this disease can be found on the web site of the Centers for Disease Control and Prevention, www.cdc.gov.

If you see anything suspicious or have useful information, please contact law enforcement authorities. The Postal Service and the FBI have offered a reward of up to $1 million for information leading to the arrest and the conviction of the anthrax terrorists.

And those who believe this is an opportunity for a prank should know that sending false alarms is a serious criminal offense. At least 20 individuals have already been arrested for anthrax hoaxes, and we will pursue anyone who tries to frighten their fellow Americans in this cruel way.

We do not yet know who sent the anthrax, whether it was the same terrorists who committed the attacks on September the 11th or whether it was the—other international or domestic terrorists. We do know that anyone who would try to infect other people with anthrax is guilty of an act of terror. We will solve these crimes, and we will punish those responsible. As we learn more about these anthrax attacks, the Government will share the confirmed and credible information we have with you. I'm proud of our citizens' calm and reasoned response to this ongoing terrorist attack.

Source: *Public Papers of the Presidents of the United States: George W. Bush* (Washington, DC: Government Printing Office), 1600–1601.

CRITICISM OF THE ANTHRAX ATTACKS (NOVEMBER 13, 2001)

Ms. Diane Watson (D-CA). Mr. Speaker, I am proud to be one of the 47 cosponsors of this resolution honoring our Nation's postal workers.

My mother worked hard for the post office, as do all the other postal workers who each day labor to keep millions of letters, checks, cards, packages, and even bills moving around our country. These hard-working Americans provide a vital link for each and every community across our country, across our world, no matter how remote. One irony of the Information Age is that it has made us more dependent on the mail. There has to be some way to get packages we order over the World Wide Web; and the Postal Service has seen their duties expanded with the expansion of the Internet. It should come as no surprise then that postal workers would be on the front lines, exposed to a bioterrorist threat that tried to exploit our society's infrastructure for the free exchange of information.

What is surprising and galling is that it took so long for the authorities to respond to the threat that anthrax posed to our postal workers. When anthrax was discovered on Capitol Hill, Congress moved quickly to seal off the impacted buildings and protect ourselves and our staff. It pains me that the authorities failed to act in a similar manner to protect the postal workers who faced an even greater threat of exposure. It took the death of postal worker Thomas Morris, Jr. for postal officials and law enforcement to acknowledge that they had failed to respond in time to the threat anthrax posed to Postal Service employees.

I hope that with our greater awareness of their roles comes a renewed commitment to provide for their safety.

Source: *Congressional Record*, November 13, 2001, H 8048–8053.

AXIS OF EVIL (JANUARY 2002)

In President Bush's 2002 State of the Union address, he emphasized the need for greater international security for the prevention of terrorism, specifically acts such as 9/11. The United States was at war with Afghanistan and at war with terror. A central theme of the president's speech was the need to stop dangerous regimes worldwide. It was during the State of the Union address that Bush coined the term "axis of evil." Three nations made up the president's axis of evil: Iran, Iraq, and North Korea; and in connection with these three countries, the president began the rhetoric of preemption. He said that it would be in the best interests of the United States to protect ourselves from the terrorist groups aided by or given safe haven in these three nations. After the State of the Union address, the media quickly turned axis of evil into a term of common usage in American political discourse.

Diplomats around the world found the president's discourse to be inflammatory and dangerous to American foreign policy and national security. Many believed that a unilateral preemptive strike on any one of these nations was being planned, while the United States quickly found itself talking about a possible war with Iraq and the dangers of Iran and North Korea. The leaders of all three nations were labeled as notorious dictators by the Bush administration and constantly referred to as the axis of evil. After the U.S. invasion of Iraq in 2003, it was removed from the Axis of Evil list and replaced by Syria.

BUSH'S ADDRESS BEFORE A JOINT SESSION OF THE CONGRESS ON THE STATE OF THE UNION (JANUARY 29, 2002)

...Our second goal is to prevent regimes that sponsor terror from threatening America or our friends and allies with weapons of mass destruction. Some of these regimes have been pretty quiet since September the 11th, but we know their true nature.

North Korea is a regime arming with missiles and weapons of mass destruction, while starving its citizens.

Iran aggressively pursues these weapons and exports terror, while an unelected few repress the Iranian people's hope for freedom.

Iraq continues to flaunt its hostility toward America and to support terror. The Iraqi regime has plotted to develop anthrax and nerve gas and nuclear weapons for over a decade. This is a regime that has already used poison gas to murder thousands of its own citizens, leaving the bodies of mothers huddled over their dead children. This is a regime that agreed to international inspections, then kicked out the inspectors. This is a regime that has something to hide from the civilized world.

States like these and their terrorist allies constitute an axis of evil, arming to threaten the peace of the world. By seeking weapons of mass destruction, these regimes pose a grave and growing danger. They could provide these arms to terrorists, giving them the means to match their hatred. They could attack our allies or attempt to blackmail the United States. In any of these cases, the price of indifference would be catastrophic.

We will work closely with our coalition to deny terrorists and their state sponsors the materials, technology, and expertise to make and deliver weapons of mass destruction. We will develop and deploy effective missile defenses to protect America and our allies from sudden attack. And all nations should know: America will do what is necessary to ensure our Nation's security.

We'll be deliberate; yet, time is not on our side. I will not wait on events while dangers gather. I will not stand by as peril draws closer and closer. The United

States of America will not permit the world's most dangerous regimes to threaten us with the world's most destructive weapons.

Our war on terror is well begun, but it is only begun. This campaign may not be finished on our watch; yet, it must be and it will be waged on our watch. We can't stop short. If we stop now, leaving terror camps intact and terrorist states unchecked, our sense of security would be false and temporary. History has called America and our allies to action, and it is both our responsibility and our privilege to fight freedom's fight.

Our first priority must always be the security of our Nation, and that will be reflected in the budget I send to Congress. My budget supports three great goals for America: We will win this war; we will protect our homeland; and we will revive our economy.

Source: *Public Papers of the Presidents of the United States: George W. Bush* (Washington, DC: Government Printing Office), 133–139.

CRITICISM OF BUSH'S DECLARATION OF AXIS OF EVIL (MARCH 11, 2003)

Mr. Chris Van Hollen (D-MD). Mr. Speaker, tonight I want to take some time to address one of the most serious questions facing our Nation today, whether we go to war against Iraq in the next few weeks.

...Polls show that anti-American sentiment is rising around the world, and some 70 percent of the world's citizens believe that the United States presents the greatest threat to world peace today, ahead of Iraq and North Korea.

U.S. relations with many of our traditional allies in the North Atlantic Alliance are more strained than at any point in that organization's history. Moderates in the Muslim world feel isolated and have begun to question their relationship with the United States. Our credibility has been damaged, and our moral authority eroded. Many serious threats to our security are not receiving the attention they deserve.

How did we get to this state of affairs just 18 months after the world community united behind U.S. leadership in the war on terrorism? How did we so quickly squander the reservoir of goodwill that we had immediately after September 11?

The answer lies squarely with the Bush administration's defense and foreign policies and the arrogance with which they have conducted those policies. Following the successful military campaign against the Taliban in Afghanistan, the administration began to redirect its energies toward Iraq and the removal of Saddam Hussein from power. In his 2002 State of the Union Address, his speech delivered just 4 months after the terrible al Qaeda attacks on our country, the President identified Iraq, Iran and North Korea as the Axis of Evil; but very quickly thereafter it became clear that the administration would focus its attention narrowly on just one of these, Iraq. And even while bin Laden, the architect of the September 11 attacks, was still at large, Saddam Hussein took his place as the symbol of the new threat facing America.

Let me make something crystal clear here. Saddam Hussein is a brutal dictator and his quest for weapons of mass destruction does pose a threat. The question for our country is what is the nature and extent of that threat, and what is the best way for us to address it.

Following the President's 2002 Axis of Evil speech, the administration's goal of regime change in Iraq began to take shape quickly. As columnist William Safire observed, regime change is a diplomatic euphemism for overthrow of government or the toppling of Hussein.

On February 5, 2002, testifying before the Senate Committee on Foreign Relations, Secretary of State Colin Powell stated, "We still believe strongly in regime change in Iraq, and we are looking at a variety of options that would bring that about."

By March of that year the debate in Washington over the pros and cons of military action against Iraq was fully engaged in the newspapers, the talk shows and the backrooms. Kenneth Adelman, President Reagan's arms control czar and a close ally of the hawks in the administration, wrote in the *Washington Post* that military action to remove Saddam Hussein and bring democracy to Iraq would be "a cake walk." Others, including former National Security Advisers to the President's father, Brent Scowcroft and James Baker, III, argued openly at that time against unilateral U.S. action to deal with Saddam.

Even the super hawks within the administration recognized that providing a legal rationale for regime change outside the context of the United Nations could prove tricky. While we may have the power, the power to go around knocking off nasty dictators, nothing under international law gives one country the right to invade another simply to change the regime. So what to do?

The Bush administration needed an argument, an argument that would provide the legal underpinning for unilateral American military action against Iraq or other nations that we determine to be a similar threat, and the answer devised by the administration was laid out in September 2002 in the national security strategy document, the so-called Doctrine of Preventive War. That theory is simple. It is also tempting. It goes like this: If we believe that a country will use weapons of mass destruction or arm terrorists with weapons of mass destruction against us, then we would "not hesitate to act alone if necessary to exercise our right of self-defense by acting preemptively."

In other words, the United States has the right to strike militarily, even if we have no evidence that such activities are occurring. We do not have to know that an attack is imminent, we can act on our belief that such action may occur at some point. It may sound good, but it does not take much to see that this doctrine is a recipe for international chaos.

Mr. Speaker, just imagine if India and Pakistan adopted this approach, South Asia would be decimated. The Preventive War Doctrine violates every principle of international law that the United States has fought to uphold.

The Bush administration was in fact asserting that the United States would be exempt from the very rules we expect all other nations in the international community to obey, because under international law we, and any other country, already have the right to take military action to defend ourselves against an imminent attack upon ourselves or our citizens. If we know another country is about to launch missiles against us, we do not have to wait for the missiles to land, we can act preemptively. If we know a foreign government is arming terrorists with weapons of any kind, including weapons of mass destruction, we do not have to wait in order to strike. We can take preemptive action under Article 51 of the U.N. Charter in the face of that kind of imminent threat.

But Iraq does not fit into that framework. The administration has never claimed that Iraq was behind the September 11 attacks. It is not an imminent threat. It is not poised to attack us. We have no evidence that it has transferred or is going to transfer weapons of mass destruction to any terrorist group. It has never possessed missiles capable of delivering weapons onto U.S. soils, and it is currently in the process under the U.N. regime of destroying its missiles with a range of over 93 miles. Not even this administration has claimed that an Iraqi attack is imminent.

Now as the administration rolled out its new theory of preventive war, and molded its approach to Iraq it did not want to go to the United Nations originally, and it also wanted to cut Congress out of the process in the early days. Administration lawyers claimed that the January 12, 1991 Congressional resolution authorizing the first President Bush to use force in the Persian Gulf War gave President Bush, the son, the right to send American troops into Iraq without further Congressional action.

The American people back then sensed that things were not going the right way. Polls showed that Americans might support military action against Iraq, but were not comfortable with America going it alone. And while the administration never conceded the legal point about having to go to Congress, it recognized the practical and political importance of requesting Congressional support, and it got it.

In the U.N. context, the context we took ourselves in November of last year, regime change is the last-ditch option. It only becomes a choice after it is determined that disarmament has failed. How and when you reach that point and what efforts must be taken before you get to that point is not clearly spelled out in the resolution. In this process that we set up, the findings and judgment of the international inspectors headed by Hans Blix and the head of the International Atomic Energy Agency, Mohammed ElBaradei, hold enormous weight. And Iraq through its actions or inactions can influence the process and its outcome. The cost of going to the Security Council was clearly going to be over control of the timetable as we move forward.

But while the administration took the decision to go to the United Nations, it did not slow or adjust its military timetable. The deployment of U.S. forces went forward at an accelerated pace. The deadline for full deployment was mid-February or early March. We now have over 250,000 troops in the Gulf; and according to news reports, they are ready to attack whenever a decision is made. But the only deadline spelled out in Security Council Resolution 1441, passed unanimously by the Council on November 8, was that inspectors were to report to the Council on progress of disarmament, quote, "60 days after inspections resume," which turned out to be January 27, 2003. Resolution 1441 did not provide any guidance as to what would happen if Saddam Hussein was found to be at least in partial compliance with the inspections by this deadline, or if there was not a decision in the council to take military action by then. It did not foresee the situation we are in today; a U.N. process focused on the goal of disarmament with one timetable and the U.S. goal of regime change with its own military timetable.

Source: *Congressional Record*, March 11, 2003, H 1735–1739.

TERROR ALERT SYSTEM (MARCH 2002)

Following the atrocities of September 11, 2001, the United States endeavored to better its homeland security. Following the creation of the Department of Homeland Security, President Bush endorsed the Terror System Alert. The system began in January 2003 and continues to be used today. It consists of five colors that predict the level of a threat for a particular day: Red signifies severe risk and it places the nation on the highest possible alert. Orange signifies a high risk of a terror attack followed by yellow for elevated risk, blue for guarded risk and finally green for a low level risk day. In its brief existence, the threat level has never reached red nor has it been lowered to blue or green.

Since there are no set criteria for the risk levels, the level findings remain ambiguous and their accuracy has been subject to ridicule. Furthermore, some critics accuse the Bush administration of using the Terror System Alert to better their election standings and place fear into the minds of the American citizens. Opposition to the system questions its effectiveness and its ability to keep people safe. Critics also argue that the system created by the Department of Homeland Security is an expensive undertaking not worth the annual expenditures. Even if a threat is issued, no uniform action is organized by those needing to respond. The system has drawn many criticisms from domestic politicians, and it continues to be on the receiving end of many jokes by American comedians.

BUSH'S DIRECTIVE ON THE HOMELAND SECURITY ADVISORY SYSTEM (MARCH 11, 2002)

Homeland Security Presidential Directive-3

Purpose

The Nation requires a Homeland Security Advisory System to provide a comprehensive and effective means to disseminate information regarding the risk of terrorist acts to Federal, State, and local authorities and to the American people. Such a system would provide warnings in the form of a set of graduated "Threat Conditions" that would increase as the risk of the threat increases. At each Threat Condition, Federal departments and agencies would implement a corresponding set of "Protective Measures" to further reduce vulnerability or increase response capability during a period of heightened alert.

This system is intended to create a common vocabulary, context, and structure for an ongoing national discussion about the nature of the threats that confront the homeland and the appropriate measures that should be taken in response. It seeks to inform and facilitate decisions appropriate to different levels of government and to private citizens at home and at work.

Homeland Security Advisory System

The Homeland Security Advisory System shall be binding on the executive branch and suggested, although voluntary, to other levels of government and the private sector. There are five Threat Conditions, each identified by a description and corresponding color. From lowest to highest, the levels and colors are:

Low = Green;
Guarded = Blue;
Elevated = Yellow;
High = Orange;
Severe = Red.

The higher the Threat Condition, the greater the risk of a terrorist attack. Risk includes both the probability of an attack occurring and its potential gravity. Threat Conditions shall be assigned by the Attorney General in consultation with the Assistant to the President for Homeland Security. Except in exigent circumstances, the Attorney General shall seek the views of the appropriate Homeland Security Principals or their subordinates, and other parties as appropriate, on the Threat Condition to be assigned. Threat Conditions may be assigned for the entire Nation, or they may be set for a particular geographic area or industrial sector. Assigned Threat Conditions shall be reviewed at regular intervals to determine whether adjustments are warranted.

The assignment of a Threat Condition shall prompt the implementation of an appropriate set of Protective Measures. Protective Measures are the specific steps an organization shall take to reduce its vulnerability or increase its ability to respond during a period of heightened alert. The authority to craft and implement Protective Measures rests with the Federal departments and agencies....

Protective Measures

The decision whether to publicly announce Threat Conditions shall be made on a case-by-case basis by the Attorney General in consultation with the Assistant to the President for Homeland Security. Every effort shall be made to share as much information regarding the threat as possible, consistent with the safety of the Nation....

The Director of Central Intelligence and the Attorney General shall ensure that a continuous and timely flow of integrated threat assessments and reports is provided to the President, the Vice President, Assistant to the President and Chief of Staff, the Assistant to the President for Homeland Security, and the Assistant to the President for National Security Affairs. Whenever possible and practicable, these integrated threat assessments and reports shall be reviewed and commented upon by the wider interagency community.

A decision on which Threat Condition to assign shall integrate a variety of considerations. This integration will rely on qualitative assessment, not quantitative calculation. Higher Threat Conditions indicate greater risk of a terrorist act, with risk including both probability and gravity. Despite best efforts, there can be no guarantee that, at any given Threat Condition, a terrorist attack will not occur. An initial and important factor is the quality of the threat information itself. The evaluation of this threat information shall include, but not be limited to, the following factors:

1. To what degree is the threat information credible?
2. To what degree is the threat information corroborated?
3. To what degree is the threat specific and/or imminent?
4. How grave are the potential consequences of the threat?

Threat Conditions and Associated Protective Measures

The world has changed since September 11, 2001. We remain a Nation at risk to terrorist attacks and will remain at risk for the foreseeable future. At all Threat Conditions, we must remain vigilant, prepared, and ready to deter terrorist attacks....

1. Low Condition (Green). This condition is declared when there is a low risk of terrorist attacks....
2. Guarded Condition (Blue). This condition is declared when there is a general risk of terrorist attacks....
3. Elevated Condition (Yellow). An Elevated Condition is declared when there is a significant risk of terrorist attacks....
4. High Condition (Orange). A High Condition is declared when there is a high risk of terrorist attacks....
5. Severe Condition (Red). A Severe Condition reflects a severe risk of terrorist attacks....

Source: *Public Papers of the Presidents of the United States: George W. Bush* (Washington, DC: Government Printing Office), 394–397.

CRITICISM OF THE DEPARTMENT OF HOMELAND SECURITY APPROPRIATIONS ACT, 2004 (JULY 23, 2003)

Mr. Frank Lautenberg (D-NJ). Mr. President, with this amendment to the Homeland Security appropriations bill, I want to see if we can improve in some measure the terrorist threat warning system that we have in place and make sure that it is working as it is intended.

I believe the current homeland security advisory system—the colorful tiered alert system—does little to reassure the public they are safer as a result of these warnings. Based on reports I get from first responders in my State and experts throughout the country, I believe this advisory system must be reevaluated and improved.

The amendment simply calls for a report from the Department of Homeland Security within 90 days of the passage of this bill evaluating how effective the terror advisory system is in meeting its goals. We are all familiar with this program. There are five levels, ranging from low risk to severe risk. You can see on the chart this color-coordinated presentation. The Department has color coded each risk level to make it easy to understand.

However, I don't believe this color war against terrorists is working. On four instances over the past year, Secretary Ridge has raised the threat level from yellow, elevated risk, to orange, high risk of terror attacks, based on increased terrorist chatter or other intelligence information. Aside from these instances in which the threat level was at orange, the system has been evaluated at the elevated yellow status since its inception in March 2002.

What I want to do now is discuss a series of concerns I have about the color-coded system and its repercussions.

First, the system evokes confusion and fear among Americans who want to respond to the elevated risk levels, but the question they raise is, Should they be changing their daily patterns without advanced knowledge about where or when they vacate their homes, offices, schools, factories, et cetera? Some Americans have stopped going to malls, some avoid public transportation, and many cancel trips. These arbitrary behavioral changes can have a serious impact on our already weak economy.

These are questions we have to ask: Does work stop? Do classrooms close? Does shopping halt, no matter how essential the goods? Should Americans take precautions?

The Department of Homeland Security doesn't tell us. I am not faulting the work they are doing, honestly, at the Department of Homeland Security. This is all still in its formative stages. We don't know quite where it is going to come to rest yet or where it is most effective.

DHS tells us to be vigilant. I don't know what that means. I am sure most of the American public doesn't know exactly what being vigilant means. The system presents high costs to local communities. When the threat level is elevated, local first responders are forced to respond by deploying already overworked police and firefighting people and by bolstering other first response systems without added Federal financial assistance.

When the DHS raises the alert, they provide almost no specific guidance to State and local governments. It requires State and local authorities to make many of their own decisions, or perhaps all of them, on how they should respond. In my State, like the rest of the country, when the alert is elevated to orange, or high, local officials tighten security on highways, railroads, bridges, bus terminals, Federal buildings, and densely populated areas. And this is an extremely expensive undertaking for State and local governments. Cost alone, while important, is not the only factor. Disruption of normal life is a victory for terrorists without any demonstrable benefit to our society.

The U.S. Conference of Mayors recently released new data compiled from a survey of nearly 150 cities nationwide. They estimate that cities throughout the country are spending, on average, nearly $70 million each and every week in additional homeland security costs due to the heightened threat alert level.

These costs come in addition to the existing homeland security spending since 9/11, which the mayors estimated to be around $2.6 billion in the first 15 months after the tragedy. However, this only asks the cities about direct costs. There are also indirect economic ramifications of code orange alerts that diminish tourism and other lucrative industries. The mayor of Atlanta, for example, has said the city's hotel occupancy is down 8 percent and 16,000 hotel jobs have been lost.

There are also innumerable indirect nonfinancial costs of the current terror alert system. For example, when a police officer who is normally assigned to antigang work, or some other assignment, is reassigned to guard a public building, that is a real serious cost to a city. And also it damages the law and order structure that must be contended with at the same time.

My third concern is that the system is not tailored to give warnings on a regional basis. Increased terrorist chatter may suggest that a major New England city is subject to a possible threat. But small towns in the Southwest are also now asked to respond.

Other nations that face terrorist threats have a more sophisticated localized system. Experts continue to recommend that the United States establish a threat alert system similar to that in Israel, where intelligence or terrorist chatter is translated into specific warnings about geographical areas that might be more susceptible to a terrorist attack. For example, in Israel, threat warnings are easier to understand. For example, the Israeli Government would issue a terror alert for an area of the country such as Galilee. If we have reference to a targeted region in the U.S., we ought to provide specific information. Is it New Jersey? Is it Los Angeles? Is it Des Moines, IA? Where is it? Is it the port that we were discussing before? We have so many port assets in our country that need to be protected against terrorist attack. So where do you apply the pressure? Where do you spend the money?

Four, when the threat level is issued, there is no description of the nature of the threat that can help those expected to respond. We are not going to be naive about this. We are not saying we have information that such-and-such shopping mall is going to be attacked and, therefore, avoid that mall. We cannot be that specific. But we ought to be able to narrow it down from just a general alert across this great country of ours to something that gives people a direction for their actions when they hear the call.

Should the Governors call out their National Guard troops to protect every chemical plant in the country—and there are hundreds of those—or transportation centers, or do they bolster rail security in every place? I do not think so. Again, this is not criticism of a system that is developing against a very serious threat to our society.

Finally—and I believe this is a key point—the system does not provide adequate instructions for the American people or local authorities. When I talk to the police in my area—and before I came to the Senate, I was a commissioner of the Port Authority of New York and New Jersey. They may get a call about something they ought to be on the lookout for, but the New York State capital is in Albany and the New Jersey State capital is in Trenton.

Do they call out their State troopers to cover all of those areas, all those police departments? In New Jersey, we have 567,000 municipalities. Some of them only have two or three policemen. What do they do? We need direction from those who have the knowledge and have the resources to research this.

The Homeland Security Department requires Federal agencies to respond to an elevated threat at the Department's own discretion, but does not issue specific guidance to Americans in State and local governments.

This lack of guidance can cause a lot of confusion and, in some cases, real panic. I have, through the process of these alerts, had calls–less now than I had in months past: Should I go to New York? My children have to travel to school on the turnpike. Should they be on the turnpike? Should we do this and should we do that? In many cases, people want to know whether they should stay home and guard their household and their families.

Lord knows we hope not, and we should take that kind of action. We cannot let the terrorists win by immobilizing our activities. We need to do better. The system has problems that at least ought to be reviewed, and I believe that improvements must be made.

I am not saying we should not spend the necessary money to deploy more police officers to malls, nuclear plants, chemical manufacturing or distribution facilities, train stations, or Federal buildings. I am a firm believer in spending whatever we have to spend to protect our security at home. But I am not convinced the homeland security advisory system is the most efficient way of assessing threat and organizing local response.

On June 6, shortly after the threat level returned to yellow from a Memorial Day elevation to orange, Secretary Ridge himself acknowledged the color-coded alert system needed readjustment. He said to the Washington Post:

"We worry about the credibility of the system. We want to continue to refine it because we understand it has caused a kind of anxiety."

Anxiety is an understatement. The system causes financial hardships, fear, panic, confusion among Americans and people who want to be conscientious about protecting their families, sometimes exaggerating what they ought to be doing and creating a lot of tension within a family, within a household.

Experts warn that with the continuing volleying between orange and yellow alerts there will be a new threat level that we might call fatigue. Secretary Ridge has not offered a time line for revising the system. My amendment will make reviewing this system an important priority for the Department of Homeland Security.

I urge my colleagues to support the amendment. It will send a message to the Department that the alert system needs to be enhanced to increase its efficiency, its specificity, its overall usefulness to first responders, police, fire, and other emergency personnel.

I wish to point out this entails no further expense. A review is common in a situation such as this where such a big change is taking place. I hope everybody will take a serious look at this and think about their constituents back home who have called them, who have written them letters, who asked for advice. Let them ask the mayors in their communities or the Governors in their States what they think.

I want to make sure it is understood. I am not leveling broadside criticism at the Department of Homeland Security or Secretary Ridge. I think he is a very capable executive. We all want to do our best with this issue, spend our money most efficiently, but disrupt life as little as possible.

Source: *Congressional Record*, July 23, 2003, S 9748–9788.

AUTHORIZATION OF THE USE OF FORCE AGAINST IRAQ (OCTOBER 2002)

The invasion of Iraq in 2002 was highly debated by the American public, but not very much by Congress. In March 2002, the president called upon Congress to authorize the use of force in Iraq. He called for a swift vote on the preemptive defense of the nation and indicated that this was an opportunity for Congress to unite in opposition against terrorism. The president claimed that the weapons of mass destruction that Iraqi president Saddam Hussein was allegedly hiding were intended for deployment against the United States. He also claimed that congressional support of the use of force in Iraq was necessary for the War on Terror and would serve to unite Americans behind this action. The authorization of force was passed in October with only twenty-three senators voting against it, and gave the president the ability to declare war against Iraq at will. Those who opposed the use of force claimed that diplomatic means had not been exhausted and that the diplomatic path should be continued. Senator Donald Payne (D-NJ) rose in opposition to the authorization of force arguing that, under the War Powers Act, the president already had this ability. He claimed that the president asked for authorization from Congress in order to obtain unquestionable authority in all military actions in Iraq.

BUSH'S REMARKS ON SIGNING THE AUTHORIZATION FOR USE OF MILITARY FORCE AGAINST IRAQ RESOLUTION OF 2002 (OCTOBER 16, 2002)

The resolution I'm about to sign symbolizes the united purpose of our Nation, expresses the considered judgment of the Congress, and marks an important event in the life of America. The 107th Congress is one of the few called by history to authorize military action to defend our country and the cause of peace.

With this resolution, Congress has now authorized the use of force. I have not ordered the use of force. I hope the use of force will not become necessary. Yet, confronting the threat posed by Iraq is necessary, by whatever means that requires. Either the Iraqi regime will give up its weapons of mass destruction, or for the sake of peace, the United States will lead a global coalition to disarm that regime. If any doubt our Nation's resolve, our determination, they would be unwise to test it.

The Iraqi regime is a serious and growing threat to peace. On the commands of a dictator, the regime is armed with biological and chemical weapons, possesses ballistic missiles, promotes international terror, and seeks nuclear weapons. The same dictator has a history of mass murder, of striking other nations without warning, of intense hatred for America, and of contempt for the demands of the civilized world.

If Iraq gains even greater destructive power, nations in the Middle East would face blackmail, intimidation, or attack. Chaos in that region would be felt in Europe and beyond. And Iraq's combination of weapons of mass destruction and ties to terrorist groups and ballistic missiles would threaten the peace and security of many nations. Those who choose to live in denial may eventually be forced to live in fear.

Every nation that shares in the benefits of peace also shares in the duty of defending the peace. The time has arrived once again for the United Nations to live up to the purposes of its founding to protect our common security. The time has arrived once again for free nations to face up to our global responsibilities and confront a gathering danger.

In 1991, Iraq was given 15 days to fully disclose all weapons of mass destruction. The dictator has successfully defied that obligation for 4,199 days. The dictator has—and during this 11-year period of his dictatorship, the regime has become highly skilled in the techniques of deception. It has blocked effective inspections of so-called Presidential sites—actually 12 square miles with hundreds of structures where sensitive materials could be hidden. The regime has forged documents, disabled surveillance cameras, and developed mobile weapons facilities to keep ahead of any inspector.

The Iraqi regime has frustrated the work of international inspectors by firing warning shots, by tapping their telephones, confiscating their documents, blocking aerial inspection flights, and barring access to sites for hours while evidence is carried away. At one location, inspectors actually witnessed Iraqi guards moving files, burning documents, and then dumping the ashes in a river. Aboard U.N. helicopters, Iraqi escorts have physically struggled with inspectors to keep them from approaching certain areas.

For Iraq, the old weapons inspection process was little more than a game in which cheating was never punished. And that game is over. The ploys and promises of the Iraqi regime no longer matter. The regime is free to continue saying whatever it chooses. Its fate depends entirely on what it actually does.

Our goal is not merely to limit Iraq's violations of Security Council resolutions or to slow down its weapons program. Our goal is to fully and finally remove a real threat to world peace and to America. Hopefully, this can be done peacefully. Hopefully, we can do this without any military action. Yet, if Iraq is to avoid military action by the international community, it has the obligation to prove compliance with all the world's demands. It's the obligation of Iraq.

Compliance will begin with an accurate and full and complete accounting for all chemical, biological, and nuclear weapons materials, as well as missiles and other means of delivery anywhere in Iraq. Failure to make such an accounting would be a further indication of the regime's bad faith and aggressive intent. Inspectors must have access to any site in Iraq at any time, without preclearance, without delay, without exceptions. Inspectors must be permitted to operate under new, effective rules. And the Iraqi regime must accept those rules without qualification or negotiation.

To ensure that we learn the truth, the regime must allow witnesses to its illegal activities to be interviewed outside of the country. These witnesses must be free to bring their entire families with them, so they're beyond the reach of Saddam Hussein's terror, Saddam Hussein's torture, Saddam Hussein's murder.

In addition to declaring and destroying all of its weapons of mass destruction, Iraq, in accordance with U.N. Security Council demands, must end its support for terrorism. As the U.N. demands, Iraq must cease the persecution of its civilian population. As the U.N. demands, Iraq must stop all illicit trade outside the oil-for-food program. Iraq must also release or account for all Gulf war personnel, including an American pilot whose fate is still unknown.

The United States takes the resolutions of the Security Council seriously. We urge other nations to do the same. We're working to build the broadest possible coalition to enforce the demands of the world on the Iraqi regime. I've told all the members of the United Nations, America will play its historic role in defeating aggressive tyranny.

I hope the good people of Iraq will remember our history and not pay attention to the hateful propaganda of their Government. America has never sought to dominate, has never sought to conquer. We've always sought to liberate and to free. Our desire is to help Iraqi citizens find the blessings of liberty within their own culture and their own traditions. The Iraqi people cannot flourish under a dictator that oppresses them and threatens them. Gifted people of Iraq will flourish if and when oppression is lifted.

When Iraq has a government committed to the freedom and well-being of its people, America, along with many other nations, will share a responsibility to help

Iraq reform and prosper. And we will meet our responsibilities. That's our pledge to the Iraqi people.

Like the Members of Congress here today, I've carefully weighed the human cost of every option before us. If we go into battle, as a last resort, we will confront an enemy capable of irrational miscalculations, capable of terrible deeds. As the Commander in Chief, I know the risks to our country. I'm fully responsible to the young men and women in uniform who may face these risks. Yet those risks only increase with time, and the costs could be immeasurably higher in years to come. To shrink from this threat would bring a false sense of temporary peace, leading to a future in which millions live or die at the discretion of a brutal dictator. That's not true peace, and we won't accept it.

The terrorist attacks of last year put our country on notice. We're not immune from the dangers and hatreds of the world. In the events of September the 11th, we resolved as a nation to oppose every threat from any source that could bring sudden tragedy to the American people. This Nation will not live at the mercy of any foreign power or plot. Confronting grave dangers is the surest path to peace and security. This is the expectation of the American people and the decision of their elected representatives....

Source: *Public Papers of the Presidents of the United States: George W. Bush* (Washington, DC: Government Printing Office), 1777–1779.

CRITICISM OF THE AUTHORIZATION OF FORCE IN IRAQ (OCTOBER 8, 2002)

Mr. Donald M. Payne (D- NJ). Mr. Speaker, we have a very difficult decision to make here. We will be watched by the world. I think that the strength of America is that people can have different opinions. In my opinion, that does not weaken our cause.... We are the most diverse Nation in the world, and we are the strongest; so I think that it is important that dissenting voices be heard.

First of all, let me say from the outset that I oppose a unilateral first-strike attack by the United States without a clearly demonstrated and imminent threat of attack on our soil. The President's resolution does not prove that the United States is in imminent danger of attack, and we in Congress have received no evidence of such an imminent and immediate threat.

If the United States is in fact in danger of immediate attack, the President already has the authority under the Constitution, the War Powers Act, the United Nations Charter, and international law to defend our Nation.

A unilateral first strike would be codified in this resolution. The fact that it could set an example for potential conflicts between India and Pakistan, between Russia and Georgia, between China and Taiwan, and many other corners of the world is something that we have to be concerned about.

Only Congress has the authority to declare war. House Joint Resolution 114 is not a declaration of war, but it is a blank check to use force without moral or political authority of the declaration of war that, for example, Franklin Delano Roosevelt did [sic] on December 8 to begin World War II.

Every diplomatic option must be exhausted. This resolution authorizes the potential use of force immediately, long before diplomatic options can be exhausted or even fully explored.

Other governments, including France and Russia, have proposed a two-step process in which the world community renews vigorous and unfettered inspections. This resolution, however, is a one-step process. Rather than letting the United Nations do its work to seek out and destroy weapons through inspections, it places immediate force on the table.

A unilateral first strike would undermine the moral authority of the United States, result in substantial loss of life, destabilize the Middle East region, and undermine the ability of our Nation to address unmet domestic priorities. The President's resolution authorizes all of these outcomes by authorizing and codifying the doctrine of preemption.

This resolution can unleash all these consequences: destabilization of the Middle East; casualties among U.S. troops and Iraqi citizens; a huge cost, estimated at between $100 and $200 billion; and a question about our own domestic priorities, with such a cost looming over our heads.

Further, any post-strike plan for maintaining stability in the region would be costly and would require a long-term commitment. Experts tell us that the United States might have to remain in Iraq for a decade. Such a commitment would drain resources for critical domestic and international priorities. Failure to make such a commitment would leave another post-intervention disaster scene.

We still have the commitment that we were making to Afghanistan, where we said we would rebuild schools and we would repair roads and we would build water treatment plants to bring water out for the people there. We have been unable to do that in Afghanistan; however, now we are moving to Iraq.

Many have even suggested that Iran is more of a threat to us than Iraq. They are more advanced in their weapons of mass destruction. Therefore, is our next attack on Iran; after Afghanistan, Iraq and then Iran?

So many people have spoken recently, and we have heard many calls from our constituents. There has been a tremendous amount of discussion. Vice President Al Gore began it several weeks ago when he raised a question on the first resolution that was proposed by the President.

We heard Senator Kennedy state that al Qaeda offers a threat he believes more imminent than Iraq. The Senator also underscored that our first objectives should be to get U.N. inspectors back to the task without conditions. Only when all responsible alternatives are exhausted should we discuss military action, which poses the risk of spurring a larger conflict in the Middle East. Furthermore, Senator Kennedy correctly observed[,] one's view on how to handle the situation in Iraq is not a reflection of one's loyalty to the United States.

Senator Dodd noted that international cooperation is necessary to counter terrorism. This cooperation should not be diminished by our unwillingness to address Iraq through multinational channels.

Senator Feinstein questioned the immediacy of the threat posed by Iraq and argued that there was time to build support within the international community.

Our own Representatives, the gentleman from Washington (Mr. McDermott) and the gentleman from Michigan (Mr. Bonior), went to Iraq to see firsthand. They support unfettered, unrestricted weapons restrictions and said, let us give that an opportunity.

Senator Breaux observed that "with America so divided on this issue, a strong burden remains on the administration to demonstrate the need for military action to address the threat posed by Iraq."

Last night, Senator Byrd had strong observations about this and questioned whether at this time it is a time for us to move into the Iraq situation possibly unilaterally.

All of these opinions and observations bear testimony to the belief that the United States should confront the evidence on Iraq directly and should make decisions based from a broad base. I concur with many others who believe that we must work cooperatively with the United Nations, both to foster collective action and to reinforce the strength and sanctity of the United Nations Security Council.

I strongly believe that unfettered inspections must resume promptly in Iraq and that Iraq must allow the U.N. weapons inspectors to carry out their responsibilities. This and a full range of diplomatic efforts need to take place before we can conclude that military action is warranted.

Therefore, in conclusion, we must keep our eyes on the main objective, that of countering terrorism and working with others to ensure that this world will be a better place tomorrow for our children than it is today. This calls for cooperation, communication, consensus, and careful calculation.

Source: *Congressional Record,* October 8, 2002, H 7189–7247.

NATIONAL MISSILE DEFENSE (DECEMBER 2002)

After President Bush's election in 2001, he began ambitious plans to revamp U.S. security. He began talking to foreign leaders about the Anti-Ballistic Missile (ABM) Treaty and the development of a national missile system. Many Democrats were outraged over talks to pull out of the ABM Treaty, but despite the outrage, the president continued to make plans for a national missile defense system. After the terrorist attacks on September 11, 2001, the president had his justification for such a system. He has since pulled out of the ABM Treaty and begun work on the missile defense system.

The system has undergone many tests but none have been successful, despite the billions of dollars that have already been poured into the program. Opponents of the missile defense system claim that it is not a necessary, or even a very useful, means of national defense, citing that it was not a missile that attacked the United States on September 11, but rather a series of planes. There was an international outcry over both the pulling out of the ABM Treaty and the development of the ballistic missile system.

BUSH'S STATEMENT ANNOUNCING A NATIONAL MISSILE DEFENSE INITIATIVE (DECEMBER 17, 2002)

When I came to office, I made a commitment to transform America's national security strategy and defense capabilities to meet the threats of the 21st century. Today I am pleased to announce that we will take another important step in countering these threats by beginning to field missile defense capabilities to protect the United States as well as our friends and allies. These initial capabilities emerge from our research and development program and build on the test bed that we have been constructing. While modest, these capabilities will add to America's security and serve as a starting point for improved and expanded capabilities later, as further progress is made in researching and developing missile defense technologies and in light of changes in the threat.

September 11, 2001, underscored that our Nation faces unprecedented threats, in a world that has changed greatly since the cold war. To better protect our country against the threats of today and tomorrow, my administration has developed a new national security strategy and new supporting strategies for making our homeland more secure and for combating weapons of mass destruction. Throughout my administration, I have made clear that the United States will take every necessary measure to protect our citizens against what is perhaps the gravest danger of all: the catastrophic harm that may result from hostile states or terrorist groups armed with weapons of mass destruction and the means to deliver them.

Missile defenses have an important role to play in this effort. The United States has moved beyond the doctrine of cold war deterrence reflected in the 1972 ABM Treaty. At the same time, we have established a positive relationship with Russia that includes partnership in counterterrorism and in other key areas of mutual concern. We have adopted a new concept of deterrence that recognizes that missile defenses will add to our ability to deter those who may contemplate attacking us with missiles. Our withdrawal from the ABM Treaty has made it possible to develop and test the full range of missile defense technologies and to deploy defenses capable of protecting our territory and our cities.

I have directed the Secretary of Defense to proceed with fielding an initial set of missile defense capabilities. We plan to begin operating these initial capabilities in 2004 and 2005, and they will include ground-based interceptors, sea-based interceptors, additional Patriot (PAC-3) units, and sensors based on land, at sea, and in space.

Because the threats of the 21st century also endanger our friends and allies around the world, it is essential that we work together to defend against them. The Defense Department will develop and deploy missile defenses capable of protecting not only the United States and our deployed forces but also our friends and allies. The United States will also structure our missile defense program in a manner that encourages industrial participation by other nations. Demonstrating the important role played by our friends and allies, as part of our initial missile defense capabilities, the United States will seek agreement from the United Kingdom and Denmark to upgrade early-warning radars on their territory.

The new strategic challenges of the 21st century require us to think differently, but they also require us to act. The deployment of missile defenses is an essential element of our broader efforts to transform our defense and deterrence policies and capabilities to meet the new threats we face. Defending the American people against these new threats is my highest priority as Commander in Chief and the highest priority of my administration.

Source: *Public Papers of the Presidents of the United States: George W. Bush* (Washington, DC: Government Printing Office), 2172–2173.

CRITICISM OF THE MISSILE DEFENSE SYSTEM (MAY 20, 2003)

Mr. Jack Reed (D-RI).... Ballistic missile programs used to have performance criteria, such as how many incoming missiles they should be able to engage, and how much area a system should defend. This enabled Congress to understand the characteristics of missile defense programs that were being funded and why they were necessary. Such criteria have been removed, and Congress does not know, for example, how many incoming missiles each missile defense system is being designed to defend against or how much area the system is being designed to defend.

Without such information, Congress is essentially writing an $8 billion to $9 billion blank check each year to the administration for missile defense.

Over the previous 2 years, Congress has tried and tried again to get the administration to provide the most basic information on its missile defense programs. Time and again, the administration has refused to provide it.

In fiscal year 2002, Congress directed the Department of Defense to provide its most basic cost, schedule and performance goals for missile defense.

We also asked the General Accounting Office to assess the progress being made towards achieving these goals.

As late as the end of fiscal year 2002, when the first GAO assessment was due, the Department had still not established a single meaningful goal for its missile defense programs. GAO was forced to write to Congress saying that it could not complete its assess because there were no goals to measure missile defense programs.

Lately, in response to continued Congressional pressure, the administration has begun to establish a few very broad, very near-term goals. But even these goals are misleading.

Secretary Aldridge, the Pentagon's acquisition chief, recently testified before the Senate Armed Services Committee that he thought the administration's 2004 missile defense would have a 90 percent chance of hitting an incoming warhead from North Korea.

Whether this is a firmly established goal or simply the individual opinion of a very sophisticated observer but nevertheless an individual opinion, it is hard to tell. Indeed, one can raise many questions about whether this 90-percent figure as a goal is being achieved and can be achieved by 2004. Secretary Rumsfeld has said in public that the 2004 system is rudimentary. Does that mean a 90-percent goal will be achieved or does it mean something less?

Indeed, if we look at the system closely, there are many issues that emerge which would suggest that this is such a situation in which there are no goals. For example, the booster for the system that is designed to be deployed in 2004 has yet to be flown in an actual intercept. So there is the question of making it work with the actual kill vehicle in an operationally feasible mode. That is a pretty significant issue when it comes to whether this system will have a certain degree of reliability.

The radar for the system was never designed for missile defense and can never be actually tested in an actual intercept attempt. The Pentagon's chief tester has told the Senate Armed Services Committee that the 2004 missile defense, in his words, has not yet demonstrated operational capability. Yet it seems clear that, regardless, there is an intention to field this system in 2004.

All of these issues raise real questions as to the capability of this system. If we accept, in fact, that it might be 90 percent, is it 90 percent of hitting a missile with defense decoys or 90 percent of hitting a missile without a decoy? These are important points that I think can be answered and should be answered by the Department of Defense as we go forward to invest something on the order of $9 billion a year in missile defense.

The administration also claims that the missile defense system it plans to field in 2004 will protect all 50 States, but if we look at the details such a defense is only possible if we have Navy ships constantly patrolling the waters of North Korea using their radars to pick up any ICBM launches headed towards Hawaii.

Initially, in the Clinton proposal there was a plan to build a very large radar designed particularly for ballistic missile defense that was intended to and had established criteria that would include protecting and covering all 50 States.

This new approach may in fact be effective, but, once again, we are not sure—the Congress is not officially on record in either an unclassified or a classified sense—of what is the standard. Is it all 50 States? Is it 50 States assuming that the Navy will have ships constantly patrolling the waters off North Korea? Indeed, it is not quite sure whether those ships can constantly be patrolling the waters off of North Korea given the numerous missions in the war on terror, given the numerous military operations. That, too, has to be looked at and examined based upon some clear criteria.

Another point is that the radar on these ships is being adapted, but it was not originally designed to identify and track ICBM-type targets. There is a question of whether the radar would be accurate enough to perform this mission.

If the Navy ships are not there, if the radar truly does not work as they hope it works or it is not modified quickly enough, there is a real question about the coverage of the system.

All of these points are being made to say in order to assess what we are buying, it helps to have these performance goals, to have them clearly delineated, to have the assumption laid out, and to have all of this operationally tested, so when we deploy a system we can say with great confidence to the American people that it will provide this level of protection. I do not think we can say that at this point.

This amendment in no way inhibits the administration from fielding a system, any type of system, in 2004, but what it will give us is an opportunity to measure that system. How effective is that system? What threats will this system engage? That type of knowledge is very important for us as we make our decisions. It is also incumbent upon the administration to provide such knowledge. Again, I emphasize it can be done either on a classified or unclassified basis because I understand there is a utility sometimes to have a system which our adversaries might assume is 100-percent effective. But at least the Congress must know this information.

The other fact of this lack of clarity and goals is it inhibits operational testing. Administrative witnesses have testified as to the need for operational testing. We have passed laws establishing operational testing. This is the traditional routine way in which we verify whether a system works and also, as we improve the system, how effective the modifications and improvements are.

Every major defense program I can think of, except missile defense, has established plans for operational testing. Without these criteria for performance and operational testing, I do not know if we can, in fact, create and deploy a system of which we can be confident.

As we reestablish these performance criteria for missile defense programs and require a plan for operational testing, Congress will regain an important tool to understand how well our missile defense program is succeeding, how our money is being spent—not our money, frankly, but the American people's money. Without such criteria and operational testing, none of that clarity will be available to us.

I think something else will be very important. It will require the Department of Defense to face squarely these tough issues: What type of threats can we defeat? How wide is the coverage of our system? What additional resources must we bring to bear to make it effective? Is this investment cost effective and cost efficient in terms of protecting the American people?

Right now all of that is very amorphous, very nebulous because there is no standard to measure it, even a general standard, these general goals I talked about. I hope this amendment could be accepted because it builds on provisions in the law that were adopted by the committee.

Source: *Congressional Record,* May 20, 2003, S 6644–S6657.

ATTACK ON IRAQ (MARCH 2003)

On March 2003, the United States began its attack on Iraq. Despite little international support and no United Nations resolution for military intervention, the United States embarked on this highly contested military operation alongside of a "Coalition of the Willing." This coalition included Afghanistan, Albania, Australia, Azerbaijan, Bulgaria, Colombia, the Czech Republic, Denmark, El Salvador, Eritrea, Estonia, Ethiopia, Georgia, Hungary, Italy, Japan, South Korea, Latvia, Lithuania, Macedonia, the Netherlands, Nicaragua, the Philippines, Poland, Romania, Slovakia, Spain, Turkey, United Kingdom, and Uzbekistan.

The greatest opposition to the war in Iraq came from France and Germany. Nations opposed to the U.S. military action argued that the UN weapons inspectors led by Hans Blix were not given enough time to search for weapons of mass destruction in Iraq. Senator Richard Durbin (D-IL) stated that the president had alternative motives for going to Iraq, mainly oil. He also stated that the intelligence being used to justify an invasion of Iraq was unreliable. The Bush administration's decision to invade Iraq continues to be a hotly contested issue that is losing support even amongst Americans who initially supported it.

BUSH'S ADDRESS TO THE NATION ON IRAQ
(MARCH 19, 2003)

My fellow citizens, at this hour, American and coalition forces are in the early stages of military operations to disarm Iraq, to free its people, and to defend the world from grave danger.

On my orders, coalition forces have begun striking selected targets of military importance to undermine Saddam Hussein's ability to wage war. These are opening stages of what will be a broad and concerted campaign. More than 35 countries are giving crucial support, from the use of naval and air bases, to help with intelligence and logistics, to the deployment of combat units. Every nation in this coalition has chosen to bear the duty and share the honor of serving in our common defense.

To all the men and women of the United States Armed Forces now in the Middle East, the peace of a troubled world and the hopes of an oppressed people now depend on you. That trust is well-placed. The enemies you confront will come to know your skill and bravery. The people you liberate will witness the honorable and decent spirit of the American military.

In this conflict, America faces an enemy who has no regard for conventions of war or rules of morality. Saddam Hussein has placed Iraqi troops and equipment in civilian areas, attempting to use innocent men, women, and children as shields for his own military, a final atrocity against his people.

I want Americans and all the world to know that coalition forces will make every effort to spare innocent civilians from harm. A campaign on the harsh terrain of a nation as large as California could be longer and more difficult than some predict. And helping Iraqis achieve a united, stable, and free country will require our sustained commitment.

We come to Iraq with respect for its citizens, for their great civilization, and for the religious faiths they practice. We have no ambition in Iraq, except to remove a threat and restore control of that country to its own people.

I know that the families of our military are praying that all those who serve will return safely and soon. Millions of Americans are praying with you for the safety of your loved ones and for the protection of the innocent. For your sacrifice, you have the gratitude and respect of the American people. And you can know that our forces will be coming home as soon as their work is done.

Our Nation enters this conflict reluctantly. Yet our purpose is sure. The people of the United States and our friends and allies will not live at the mercy of an outlaw regime that threatens the peace with weapons of mass murder. We will meet that threat now, with our Army, Air Force, Navy, Coast Guard and Marines, so that we do not have to meet it later with armies of firefighters and police and doctors on the streets of our cities.

Now that conflict has come, the only way to limit its duration is to apply decisive force. And I assure you, this will not be a campaign of half measures, and we will accept no outcome but victory.

My fellow citizens, the dangers to our country and the world will be overcome. We will pass through this time of peril and carry on the work of peace. We will defend our freedom. We will bring freedom to others, and we will prevail....

Source: *Public Papers of the Presidents of the United States: George W. Bush* (Washington, DC: Government Printing Office), 342–343.

CRITICISM OF THE ATTACK ON IRAQ (MARCH 13, 2003)

Mr. Richard J. Durbin (D-IL). Mr. President, there is an interesting turn of events. Those who were looking for a debate on the war in Iraq had best turn to C-SPAN and witness the question period in London before the British House of Commons. I have been watching it. It is a fascinating debate.

Tony Blair is defending his position in support of the United States. His own party is divided. The conservatives support him. The questioning is very tough. In the course of defending his position, some important questions are being asked and answered in the British House of Commons.

If you would expect the same thing here in the U.S. Congress, you might be surprised or disappointed to learn it is not taking place. What is taking place is speeches on the floor by individual Senators. Today, I have seen Senator Byrd of West Virginia, Senator Dayton of Minnesota, Senator Kennedy of Massachusetts. Others have come to the floor to speak about the war in Iraq. But there has literally been no active debate on this issue on Capitol Hill, in the United States of America, since last October.

The reason, of course, is that last October we enacted a use of force resolution which virtually gave to the President of the United States the authority to declare war and execute it against Iraq at the time and place of his choosing. I was one of 23 Senators who voted against that resolution, believing that there were better ways to achieve our goals, and that if Congress did that, we would be giving to this President the greatest delegation of authority to wage war ever given to a President.

The time that has intervened since the passage of that resolution has proven me right. Congress has had no voice. Oh, we have had moments of criticism, moments of comment, but we are not a serious part of this national concern and national conversation over what will happen in Iraq. That is indeed unfortunate.

There are several facts I think everyone concedes, virtually everyone, on either side of the issue. The first and most obvious is that Saddam Hussein is a ruthless dictator. His continued domination over the nation of Iraq will continue to pose a threat to the region and a concern for peace-loving nations around the world. The sooner his regime changes, the better. The sooner we control his weapons of mass destruction, the better for the region and for the whole world. No one argues that point, not even the nations in the U.N. Security Council that are arguing with the United States about the best approach.

The second thing I think should be said at the outset is no one questions the fact that the U.S. military, the men and women who make it the best military in the world, deserve our support and our praise. They deserve our continued devotion to their success, whatever our debate about the policy in the Middle East or even in Iraq. As far as those 250,000 American servicemen now stationed around Iraq, and many others on the way, whatever our position on the President's policy, that is irrelevant. We are totally committed to their safety and their safe return. That is exactly the way it should be.

Having said that, though, I think it is still important for us to step back and ask how we have possibly reached this state that we are in today. The United States finds itself in a period of anti-Americanism around the world that is almost unprecedented. I traveled abroad a few weeks ago. I was stunned to find in countries that have traditionally been our friends and allies that, although they are saying little, in private they are very critical of the United States and what we have done.

I want to enter into the Record a letter sent to Secretary of State Colin Powell from John Brady Kiesling, who is with the United States Embassy in Athens, Greece....

Hon. Colin Powell,
Secretary of State,
Washington, DC.

Dear Mr. Secretary: I am writing you to submit my resignation from the Foreign Service of the United States and from my position as Political Counselor in U.S. Embassy Athens, effective March 7. I do so with a heavy heart. The baggage of my upbringing included a felt obligation to give something back to my country. Service as a U.S. diplomat was a dream job. I was paid to understand foreign languages and, to seek out diplomats, politicians, scholars and journalists, and to persuade them that U.S. interests and theirs fundamentally coincided. My faith in my country and its values was the most powerful weapon in my diplomatic arsenal.

It is inevitable that during twenty years with the State Department I would become more sophisticated and cynical about the narrow and selfish bureaucratic motives that sometimes shaped our policies. Human nature is what it is, and I was rewarded and promoted for understanding human nature. But until this Administration it had been possible to believe that by upholding the policies of my president I was also upholding the interests of the American people and the world. I believe it no longer.

The policies we are now asked to advance are incompatible not only with American values but also with American interests. Our fervent pursuit of war with Iraq is driving us to squander the international legitimacy that has been America's most potent weapon of both offense and defense since the days of Woodrow Wilson. We have begun to dismantle the largest and most effective web of international relationships the world has ever known. Our current course will bring instability and danger, not security.

The sacrifice of global interests to domestic politics and to bureaucratic self-interest is nothing new, and it is certainly not a uniquely American problem. Still, we have not seen such systematic distortion of intelligence, such systematic manipulation of American opinion, since the war in Vietnam. The September 11 tragedy left us stronger than before, rallying around us a vast international coalition to cooperate for the first time in a systematic way against the threat of terrorism. But rather than take credit for those successes and build on them, this Administration has chosen to make terrorism a domestic political tool, enlisting a scattered and largely defeated al Qaeda as its bureaucratic ally. We spread disproportionate terror and confusion in the public mind, arbitrarily linking the unrelated problems of terrorism and Iraq. The result, and perhaps the motive, is to justify a vast misallocation of shrinking public wealth to the military and to weaken the safeguards that protect American citizens from the heavy hand of government. September 11 did not do as much damage to the fabric of American society as we seem determined to do to ourselves. Is the Russia of the late Romanovs really our model, a selfish, superstitious empire thrashing toward self-destruction in the name of a doomed status quo?

We should ask ourselves why we have failed to persuade more of the world that a war with Iraq is necessary. We have over the past two years done too much to assert to our world partners that narrow and mercenary U.S. interests override the cherished values of our partners. Even where our aims were not in question, our consistency is at issue. The model of Afghanistan is little comfort to allies wondering on what basis we plan to rebuild the Middle East, and in whose image and interests. Have we indeed become blind, as Russia is blind in Chechnya, as Israel is blind in the Occupied Territories, to our own advice, that overwhelming military power is not the answer to terrorism? After the shambles of post-war Iraq joins the shambles in Grozny and Ramallah, it will be a brave foreigner who forms ranks with Micronesia to follow where we lead.

We have a coalition still, a good one. The loyalty of many of our friends is impressive, a tribute to American moral capital built up over a century. But our closest allies are persuaded less that war is justified than that it would be perilous to allow the U.S. to drift into complete solipsism. Loyalty should be reciprocal. Why does our President condone the swaggering and contemptuous approach to our friends and allies this Administration is fostering, including among its most senior officials. Has "oderint dum metuant" really become our motto?

I urge you to listen to America's friends around the world. Even here in Greece, purported hotbed of European anti-Americanism, we have more and closer friends than the American newspaper reader can possibly imagine. Even when they complain about American arrogance, Greeks know that the world is a difficult and dangerous place, and they want a strong international system, with the U.S. and EU in close partnership. When our friends are afraid of us rather than for us, it is time to worry. And now they are afraid. Who will tell them convincingly that the United States is as it was, a beacon of liberty, security, and justice for the planet?

Mr. Secretary, I have enormous respect for your character and ability. You have preserved more international credibility for us than our policy deserves, and salvaged something positive from the excesses of an ideological and self-serving Administration. But your loyalty to the President goes too far. We are straining beyond its limits an international system we built with such toil and treasure, a web of laws, treaties, organizations, and shared values that sets limits on our foes far more effectively than it ever constrained America's ability to defend its interests.

I am resigning because I have tried and failed to reconcile my conscience with my ability to represent the current U.S. Administration. I have confidence that our democratic process is ultimately self-correcting, and hope that in a small way I can contribute from outside to shaping policies that better serve the security and prosperity of the American people and the world we share.

Sincerely,

John Brady Kiesling,
U.S. Embassy Athens.

Mr. Durbin. . . . Those are the words of a man who was a career diplomat serving the United States with principle and convictions and who resigned from the diplomatic corps over our policy in Iraq. That is a sad commentary, but it is a reality.

The reality is that we are following a course of foreign policy that is a dramatic departure from what we have followed for almost 50 years. We are making decisions relative to this war in Iraq which are changing the rules the United States has not only lived by but preached for decades. We are confronting the world that has most recently been our allies in the war on terrorism and telling them that, with or without their cooperation and approval, we are going forward with an invasion of Iraq. We are saying to the rest of the world that the United States has the power and will to use it. It is certain that we have the power and the strength. The question is whether or not we have the wisdom—the wisdom to understand that simply having the strength is not enough.

Mr. President, I close by saying, I return now, in just a few moments, to my home State of Illinois. As I walk the streets of Springfield, of Chicago, and of other cities, people come up to me and say: "Why don't I hear a debate in the U.S. Congress about Iraq?"

Source: *Congressional Record*, March 13, 2003, S 3704–3708.

WAR IS OVER IN IRAQ (MAY 2003)

Less than two months after the invasion of Iraq in 2003, President Bush landed on the USS *Abraham Lincoln* to address a jubilant military and declared that major combat operations in Iraq had ended. While President Bush did not claim that the war was over, he gave his press conference standing in front of a sign that read "Mission Accomplished." At this time, the city of Baghdad had fallen and the republican guard had surrendered or disbanded.

Criticism of the president's jubilant press conference came immediately, many pointing out that Iraq had yet to be stabilized and that three years later the war is still ongoing. Since the claim "mission accomplished," the death toll has risen and the attacks by insurgents have grown exponentially. A year after Bush's speech onboard the USS *Lincoln*, Senator Robert C. Byrd (D-VA) reminded his fellow members of Congress of the event. In his speech, Senator Byrd pointed out that although only a year had passed since the president's bombastic press conference, the number of U.S. servicemen and women who had died in the conflict increased five-fold. As of this publication date, more than 2,000 servicemen and women have been killed in Iraq. The war has been ongoing for over three years, with the latest estimates for the withdrawal of U.S. troops being 2008. Politicians on both sides of the aisle have asked for a withdrawal plan, as well as more support for our nation's military. Debate continues as to when the United States could reasonably withdraw its troops.

BUSH'S ADDRESS TO THE NATION ON IRAQ FROM THE USS *ABRAHAM LINCOLN* (MAY 1, 2003)

Thank you all very much. Admiral Kelly, Captain Card, officers and sailors of the USS *Abraham Lincoln*, my fellow Americans: Major combat operations in Iraq have ended. In the battle of Iraq, the United States and our allies have prevailed. And now our coalition is engaged in securing and reconstructing that country.

In this battle, we have fought for the cause of liberty and for the peace of the world. Our Nation and our coalition are proud of this accomplishment; yet it is you, the members of the United States military, who achieved it. Your courage, your willingness to face danger for your country and for each other, made this day possible. Because of you, our Nation is more secure. Because of you, the tyrant has fallen, and Iraq is free.

Operation Iraqi Freedom was carried out with a combination of precision and speed and boldness the enemy did not expect and the world had not seen before. From distant bases or ships at sea, we sent planes and missiles that could destroy an enemy division or strike a single bunker. Marines and soldiers charged to Baghdad across 350 miles of hostile ground, in one of the swiftest advances of heavy arms in history. You have shown the world the skill and the might of the American Armed Forces.

This Nation thanks all the members of our coalition who joined in a noble cause. We thank the Armed Forces of the United Kingdom, Australia, and Poland, who shared in the hardships of war. We thank all the citizens of Iraq who welcomed our troops and joined in the liberation of their own country. And tonight I have a special word for Secretary Rumsfeld, for General Franks, and for all the men and women who wear the uniform of the United States: America is grateful for a job well done.

... When Iraqi civilians looked into the faces of our service men and women, they saw strength and kindness and good will. When I look at the members of the United States military, I see the best of our country, and I'm honored to be your Commander in Chief.

In the images of falling statues, we have witnessed the arrival of a new era. For a hundred years of war, culminating in the nuclear age, military technology was designed and deployed to inflict casualties on an ever-growing scale. In defeating Nazi Germany and Imperial Japan, Allied forces destroyed entire cities, while enemy leaders who started the conflict were safe until the final days. Military power was used to end a regime by breaking a nation.

Today, we have the greater power to free a nation by breaking a dangerous and aggressive regime. With new tactics and precision weapons, we can achieve military objectives without directing violence against civilians. No device of man can remove the tragedy from war; yet it is a great moral advance when the guilty have far more to fear from war than the innocent.

In the images of celebrating Iraqis, we have also seen the ageless appeal of human freedom. Decades of lies and intimidation could not make the Iraqi people love their oppressors or desire their own enslavement. Men and women in every culture need liberty like they need food and water and air. Everywhere that freedom arrives, humanity rejoices, and everywhere that freedom stirs, let tyrants fear.

We have difficult work to do in Iraq. We're bringing order to parts of that country that remain dangerous. We're pursuing and finding leaders of the old regime, who will be held to account for their crimes. We've begun the search for hidden chemical and biological weapons and already know of hundreds of sites that will be investigated. We're helping to rebuild Iraq, where the dictator built palaces for himself instead of hospitals and schools. And we will stand with the new leaders of Iraq as they establish a government of, by, and for the Iraqi people.

The transition from dictatorship to democracy will take time, but it is worth every effort. Our coalition will stay until our work is done. Then we will leave, and we will leave behind a free Iraq.

The battle of Iraq is one victory in a war on terror that began on September the 11th, 2001, and still goes on. That terrible morning, 19 evil men, the shock troops of a hateful ideology, gave America and the civilized world a glimpse of their ambitions. They imagined, in the words of one terrorist, that September the 11th would be the "beginning of the end of America." By seeking to turn our cities into killing fields, terrorists and their allies believed that they could destroy this Nation's resolve and force our retreat from the world. They have failed.

In the battle of Afghanistan, we destroyed the Taliban, many terrorists, and the camps where they trained. We continue to help the Afghan people lay roads, restore hospitals, and educate all of their children. Yet we also have dangerous work to complete. As I speak, a Special Operations task force, led by the 82d Airborne, is on the trail of the terrorists and those who seek to undermine the free Government of Afghanistan. America and our coalition will finish what we have begun.

The liberation of Iraq is a crucial advance in the campaign against terror. We've removed an ally of al Qaeda and cut off a source of terrorist funding. And this much is certain: No terrorist network will gain weapons of mass destruction from the Iraqi regime, because the regime is no more.

Our war against terror is proceeding according to the principles that I have made clear to all: Any person involved in committing or planning terrorist attacks against the American people becomes an enemy of this country and a target of American justice; any person, organization, or government that supports, protects, or harbors terrorists is complicit in the murder of the innocent and equally guilty of terrorist crimes; any outlaw regime that has ties to terrorist groups and seeks or possesses weapons of mass destruction is a grave danger to the civilized world and will be confronted; and anyone in the world, including the Arab world, who works and sacrifices for freedom has a loyal friend in the United States of America.

Our commitment to liberty is America's tradition...We are committed to freedom in Afghanistan, in Iraq, and in a peaceful Palestine. The advance of freedom is the surest strategy to undermine the appeal of terror in the world. Where freedom takes hold, hatred gives way to hope. When freedom takes hold, men and women turn to the peaceful pursuit of a better life. American values and American interests lead in the same direction: We stand for human liberty.

The United States upholds these principles of security and freedom in many ways, with all the tools of diplomacy, law enforcement, intelligence, and finance. We're working with a broad coalition of nations that understand the threat and our shared responsibility to meet it. The use of force has been and remains our last resort. Yet all can know, friend and foe alike, that our Nation has a mission: We will answer threats to our security, and we will defend the peace.

Our mission continues. Al Qaeda is wounded, not destroyed. The scattered cells of the terrorist network still operate in many nations, and we know from daily intelligence that they continue to plot against free people. The proliferation of deadly weapons remains a serious danger. The enemies of freedom are not idle, and neither are we. Our Government has taken unprecedented measures to defend the homeland, and we will continue to hunt down the enemy before he can strike.

The war on terror is not over, yet it is not endless. We do not know the day of final victory, but we have seen the turning of the tide. No act of the terrorists will change our purpose or weaken our resolve or alter their fate. Their cause is lost. Free nations will press on to victory.

Those we lost were last seen on duty. Their final act on this Earth was to fight a great evil and bring liberty to others. All of you—all in this generation of our military have taken up the highest calling of history. You're defending your country and protecting the innocent from harm. And wherever you go, you carry a message of hope, a message that is ancient and ever new. In the words of the prophet Isaiah, "To the captives, 'come out,' and to those in darkness, 'be free.'" ...

Source: *Public Papers of the Presidents of the United States: George W. Bush* (Washington, DC: Government Printing Office), 516–518.

MISSION NOT ACCOMPLISHED (APRIL 29, 2004)

Mr. Robert C. Byrd (D-WV). Mr. President, a year ago the President of the United States harkened back to his days as an aviator for the Texas Air National Guard to deliver a dramatic made-for-television speech. Eager to experience the thrill of a carrier landing, the President donned a flight suit, strapped into a jet, and rocketed off into the wild blue yonder for a 30-mile journey.

This flight of fancy concluded with the dramatic landing of that speeding plane onto the deck of an aircraft carrier, the USS *Abraham Lincoln*—so named for the stoic leader who guided our country through one of its most troubled times.

Such was the scene on May 1, 2003, under the warming rays of the California sun. The President delivered to the sailors on that ship a welcome and long overdue message: He commended the men and women on their outstanding service to our country during the trials of the war in Iraq, and welcomed them back to the United States of America.

While the President delivered those words of appreciation, every television viewer in the country—and, indeed, the world—could see in the background a banner with the words "Mission Accomplished"—"Mission Accomplished"—superimposed upon the Stars and Stripes.

In contrast to the simple humility of President Lincoln's Gettysburg Address, President Bush's speech was designed from the outset to be remembered right up until November 2, 2004.

The President announced unequivocally that "major combat operations in Iraq have ended," and that "in the battle of Iraq, the United States and our allies have prevailed." Now, 1 year later, combat deaths are more than five times that of a year ago when our President celebrated "mission accomplished."

Since that time, Iraq has become a veritable shooting gallery. This April has been the bloodiest month of the entire war, with more than 120 Americans killed. Young lives cut short in pointless conflict, and all the President can say is that it "has been a tough couple of weeks"—a tough couple of weeks, indeed.

Plans have obviously gone tragically awry. But the President has, so far, only managed to mutter that we must "stay the course." But what course is there to keep when our ship of state is being tossed like a dinghy in a storm of Middle East politics? If the course is to end in the liberation of Iraq and bring a definitive end to the war against Saddam Hussein, one must conclude, mission not accomplished, Mr. President.

The White House argues time and again that Iraq is the "central front" on the war on terrorism. But instead of keeping murderous al Qaeda terrorists on the run, the invasion of Iraq has stoked the fires of terrorism against the United States and our allies. Najaf is smoldering. Fallujah is burning. And there is no exit in sight. What has been accomplished, Mr. President?

Al Qaeda has morphed into a hydra-headed beast, no longer dependent on Osama bin Laden. The administration has flippantly claimed that it is better to tie down terrorists in Iraq than to battle them in our homeland. Mr. President, with hundreds of thousands of American troops in Iraq for the foreseeable future, and a worldwide campaign of terrorism gathering steam, who is tying down whom?

Indeed, our attack on Iraq has given Islamic militants a common cause and has fertilized the field for new recruits. The failures by the United States to secure the peace in Iraq has virtually guaranteed al Qaeda a fertile field of new recruits ready to sacrifice their lives to fight the American infidels. These extremists openly call for "jihad," swear allegiance to bin Laden, and refer to the September 11 murderers as the "magnificent 19." According to intelligence sources, hundreds of young Muslims are answering recruitment calls with a resounding "yes."

Amidst all this, the American people are asking themselves one central question: Have we been made more safe by the President's war in Iraq? Do we sleep more soundly in our beds now that Saddam Hussein has been captured? Or, instead, are we starting to fully comprehend and regret the fury which has been unleashed by the unprovoked attack on Iraq?

Deaths and casualties of Iraqi citizens are in the thousands—their blood is on our hands—but an actual number cannot be obtained. Is it any wonder that Iraqis see us, not as liberators, but as crusaders and conquerors? A growing number of Iraqis see us as we would see foreign troops on the streets of Chicago or New York or Washington, or any small town in America. Surely one can understand the hatred brewing in Iraq in the hearts of the men and women and children—the boys and girls—in Iraq when we see the agony—the agony—of an Iraqi family that has lost a loved one due to an errant bomb or bullet.

One year after President Bush proclaimed the conclusion of major combat operations in Iraq, is the world any safer from terrorism? Iraq has become a breeding ground for terrorists of all stripes. The Middle East seethes in deepening violence and the culture of revenge. Our war on terror appears to many as a war against Islam. A one-sided policy on the Arab-Israeli conflict drives both sides away from the peace table, and hundreds of millions more to hatred of our country. No, the world is not safer.

One year after the "mission accomplished" speech, is America safer? We have not secured our homeland from terrifying threats of destruction. This President has sown divisions in our longstanding alliances. He has squandered our treasure in Iraq and put us deep in debt. Our brave soldiers are pinned down in Iraq while our enemies see the invincible American armor as penetrable by the sword of urban guerrilla warfare. No, America is not safer.

One year ago, the President announced an end to major combat operations in Iraq. And yet our troops are having their deployments extended in Iraq while our lines are stretched thin everywhere else. Billions upon billions of taxpayer dollars are being poured into Iraq. Seven hundred and twenty-two American lives have been lost before today. And we hear that 8 to 10 additional lives have been lost today. Unknown thousands of Iraqis are dead. Claims of WMD and death-dealing drones are discredited. And bin Laden is still on the loose.

I stand behind no one in supporting our troops through the dangers they face every day. I grieve along with the families that have lost loved ones. The failures of post-war Iraq lay squarely on the Bush administration for recklessly sending this country—sending our men and women—to war, a war that should not have been fought, a war in the wrong place, at the wrong time, and for the wrong reasons.

Mission accomplished? The mission in Iraq, as laid out by President Bush and Vice President Cheney, has failed. Even more disturbing, the disdain for international law, and the military bombast of this cocky, reckless administration have tarnished the beacon of hope and freedom which the United States of America once offered to the world.

How long will America continue to pay the price in blood and treasure of this President's war? How long must the best of our Nation's military men and women be taken from their homes to fight this unnecessary war in Iraq? How long must our National Guardsmen be taken from their communities to fight and to die in the hot sands of Iraq? How long must the mothers and the fathers see their sons and daughters die in a faraway land because of President Bush's doctrine of preemptive attack? How long must little children across our great land go to sleep at night crying for a daddy or a mother far away who may never come back home?

President Bush typified the Happy Warrior when he strutted across the deck of the USS *Abraham Lincoln* a year ago this coming Saturday. He was in his glory that day. But on this May 1, we will remember the widows and the orphans who have been made by his fateful decision to attack Iraq. We will be aware of the tears that have been shed for his glory. How long? How long? How long?

Source: *Congressional Record*, April 29, 2004, S 4628–4630.

IRAQ/NIGER CONNECTION (JULY 2003)

On January 28, 2003, President Bush gave a State of the Union address in which he laid the foundation for military action against Iraq. In his speech, the president spoke of weapons of mass destruction and Iraq's intention to use them against the United States. One piece of intelligence he used to support this claim was a report stating that Iraq had tried to purchase uranium from Niger to make nuclear weapons. It soon became apparent that this intelligence report would be difficult to confirm, and some suspected that it could have been exaggerated or fabricated entirely. When the insubstantial nature of this claim came to light, the president avoided most questions regarding the issue and said that a simple mistake had been made.

It is mistakes such as these, and other intelligence mishaps regarding Iraq and its alleged possession of weapons of mass destruction, that have been a source of increasing concern among Senate and House Democrats. The Niger uranium connection was just one in a series of intelligence blunders that have called into play the effectiveness and abilities of the U.S. intelligence apparatus, as well as the credibility of the administration.

BUSH'S REMARKS FOLLOWING DISCUSSIONS WITH PRESIDENT YOWERI KAGUTA MUSEVENI OF UGANDA AND AN EXCHANGE WITH REPORTERS IN ENTEBBE, UGANDA (JULY 11, 2003)

Q. With all due respect, Mr. President, can you take a question, sir?
President Bush. Sure.

Q. Why—can you explain how an erroneous piece of intelligence on the Iraq-Niger connection got into your State of the Union speech? Are you upset about it, and should somebody be held accountable, sir?
President Bush. I gave a speech to the Nation that was cleared by the intelligence services. And it was a speech that detailed to the American people the dangers posed by the Saddam Hussein regime. And my Government took the appropriate response to those dangers. And as a result, the world is going to be more secure and more peaceful.

Source: *Public Papers of the Presidents of the United States: George W. Bush* (Washington, DC: Government Printing Office), 901–902.

AMERICANS SHOULD KNOW THE TRUTH ABOUT IRAQ (JULY 14, 2003)

Mr. Maurice Hinchey (D-NY). Mr. Speaker, the decision to go to war is the most profound decision that any nation can make. It should be done, of course, judiciously and only with the utmost of care and only as a last resort. This is especially true of democratic republics such as ours, when the actions of the government must be with the consent of the governed.

In order for the governed to give their consent, that consent, of course, must be informed. And it is the responsibility of the government to inform its citizens in an honest and straightforward way with regard to the background and information that it has that causes it to make such profound decisions.

On January 23 of this year, the President of the United States in this room addressed the Joint Session of the Congress as well as the people of the United States. And in that address he made a number of assertions with regard to the state of Iraq and why it was important for us to engage that country in hostility. Among those statements he made was one with regard to the importation of processed uranium from Niger. The President said in his statement that the British Government had informed them that the Government of Niger was importing processed uranium, and that was in the context of Iraq's trying to develop a nuclear weapon.

Now, we know that the President had that information on a first-hand basis. He did not have to quote any information from the British Government. He had it on a first-hand basis because the Vice President of the United States back in March of last year went to the Central Intelligence Agency and asked them to conduct an investigation as to whether or not Iraq was importing processed uranium from Africa.

The Central Intelligence Agency then asked former Ambassador Wilson, who had a long and distinguished career in the Foreign Service including positions in West Africa, asked Mr. Wilson if he would go to Niger to discover whether or not it was possible for Niger to export processed uranium to Iraq for the purpose of building a nuclear weapon.

Ambassador Wilson went there. He spent a considerable amount of time, something in the neighborhood of close to 2 weeks. He interviewed dozens of people. He came back and reported to the Central Intelligence Agency that he found no reason to believe whatsoever that any processed uranium has been exported from Niger. Why? Because the uranium companies there are owned by essentially European countries and the controls are very, very strict and rigid. He examined a number of people who were involved in the companies and their controls, as well as people in the Niger Government. He came away believing there was no way that processed uranium could be exported from Niger to Iraq.

He reported to the Central Intelligence Agency. The Central Intelligence Agency obviously then reported to the Vice President of the United States, who we can only imagine and expect reported to the President of the United States.

Nevertheless, the President then came here before the House and said that Niger was exporting processed uranium to Iraq when the government, our government, the administration knew, based upon firsthand information as a result of a CIA-sponsored investigation, that that was not the case. In addition, though, now we know that is not the case because we have the report of Mr. Wilson and we have other information that can only compel us to conclude that the President was wrong in his statement; and, in fact, he has admitted he was wrong in that statement, blaming Mr. Tenet.

Also in that address before a joint session of the Congress, the President mentioned the presence of vast quantities of chemical and biological weapons that were also in Iraq, according to his statement to that joint session. He also said that there were delivery mechanisms that were in Iraq and that those delivery mechanisms could be armed very, very quickly with those biological and chemical weapons and they could be used to bring those weapons into conflict against countries in the surrounding region, including Israel, against others, and that this constituted a direct threat to the United States and to our allies.

It has been now nearly 3 months that we have been searching for chemical and biological weapons as well as the means to deliver them in Iraq, and we have found absolutely nothing.

Based upon these two sets of facts, one has to question, what else did the President say that was false and why did we go to war in Iraq? This Congress needs to initiate a full and complete congressional investigation as to the causes surrounding our entry into that war and the prosecution of that war, and it must do so forthwith.

Source: *Congressional Record,* July 14, 2003, H 668.

ABUSE OF IRAQI PRISONERS AT ABU GHRAIB PRISON (MAY 2004)

On April 28, 2004, *60 Minutes* reported a continuation of a story done by Seymour Hersch about prisoner abuse in Abu Ghraib prison. The report told of U.S. soldiers from the 372nd Military Police Company torturing Iraqi prisoners and was accompanied by pictures of the torture taken by the soldiers themselves. The United States Army began an investigation of prisoner abuse in January 2004 but did not make it public. Finally, in response to the public outcry, seventeen soldiers and officers were removed from duty and seven were charged with aggravated assault, maltreatment, dereliction and battery by a military court. Seven soldiers faced court martial and were dishonorably discharged. The only officer involved, Brigadier General Janis Karpinski, was demoted to the rank of colonel.

The torture inflicted by U.S. soldiers on their Iraqi charges took on many forms from physical to mental abuse. The physical was probably the most outrageous to the international community, all the more so since it could be seen in the pictures that were broadcast on television and newspapers across the world. The physical abuse took many forms: putting electrodes on prisoners, physical beatings that included jumping on gunshot wounds, pouring acid on prisoners, urinating on them, and mass forms of intimidation. Prisoners were even put on dog leashes and walked while military guard dogs were made to back them into corners. The most demeaning form of intimidation came in the form of using female guards to lead around naked male detainees and forcing them to simulate acts of sodomy with each other.

The international community was outraged at the actions committed by U.S. forces. Furthermore, they called for an immediate investigation into U.S. actions in Iraqi prisons. The Arab and Muslim communities across the globe equated these crimes with Saddam Hussein's abuses at the Abu Ghraib prison. Many nations called for the immediate withdrawal of the U.S. troops. On the domestic front, the majority of American citizens were outraged at the photographs and asked how this could happen without anyone's knowledge. Secretary of Defense Donald Rumsfeld was quoted saying, "These events occurred on my watch as Secretary of Defense. I am accountable for them. I take full responsibility, I feel terrible about what happened to these detainees" (*The Congressional Record, May 7, 2004*). In President Bush's speech, he announced the start of an investigation, but stopped short of apologizing or claiming responsibility for the acts.

Congresswoman Kaptur called the actions in Abu Ghraib an atrocity and asked why Congress was finding out more information from the media than from the president and the Department of Defense. She called for the resignation of Rumsfeld, Lt. General Richardo Sanchez, Major General Geoffrey Miller, and White House Counsel Alberto Gonzalez. She questioned the lack of information coming from the administration, as well as the lack of accountability coming from the top. The congresswoman called for a full out investigation to determine where the orders truly came from and to make sure that all those responsible were held accountable. The actions at Abu Ghraib prison continue to cast a shadow over the U.S. presence in Iraq and, many feel, remain unresolved.

BUSH'S INTERVIEW WITH ALHURRA TELEVISION (MAY 5, 2004)

Q. Mr. President, thank you for agreeing to do this interview with us. Evidence of torture of Iraqi prisoners by U.S. personnel has left many Iraqis and people in the Middle East and the Arab world with the impression that the United States is no better than the Saddam Hussein regime. Especially when this alleged torture took place in the Abu Ghraib Prison, a symbol of torture of——

The President. Yes.

Q. What can the U.S. do, or what can you do to get out of this?

The President. First, people in Iraq must understand that I view those practices as abhorrent. They must also understand that what took place in that prison does not represent America that I know. The America I know is a compassionate country that believes in freedom. The America I know cares about every individual. The America I know has sent troops into Iraq to promote freedom—good, honorable citizens that are helping the Iraqis every day.

It's also important for the people of Iraq to know that in a democracy, everything is not perfect, that mistakes are made. But in a democracy as well those mistakes will be investigated, and people will be brought to justice. We're an open society. We're a society that is willing to investigate, fully investigate in this case, what took place in that prison.

That stands in stark contrast to life under Saddam Hussein. His trained torturers were never brought to justice under his regime. There were no investigations about mistreatment of people. There will be investigations. People will be brought to justice.

Q. When did you learn about the—did you see the pictures on TV? When was the first time you heard about——

The President. Yes, the first time I saw or heard about pictures was on TV. However, as you might remember, in early January, General Kimmitt talked about a investigation that would be taking place about accused—alleged improprieties in the prison. So our Government has been in the process of investigating.

And there are two—more than two investigations, multiple investigations going on, some of them related to any criminal charges that may be filed. And in our system of law, it's essential that those criminal charges go forward without prejudice. In other words, people need to be—are treated innocent until proven guilty. And facts are now being gathered.

And secondly, there is investigations to determine how widespread abuse may be occurring, and we want to know the truth. I talked to the Secretary of Defense this morning, by the way. I said, "Find the truth, and then tell the Iraqi people and the world the truth." We have nothing to hide. We believe in transparency, because we're a free society. That's what free societies do. They—if there's a problem, they address those problems in a forthright, upfront manner. And that's what's taking place.

Q. Mr. President, in a democracy and a free society, as you mentioned, people investigate, but at the same time, even those who are not directly responsible for these events take responsibility. With such a problem of this magnitude, do we expect anyone to step down? Do you still have confidence in the Secretary of Defense?

The President. Oh, of course I've got confidence in the Secretary of Defense, and I've got confidence in the commanders on the ground in Iraq, because they and our troops are doing great work on behalf of the Iraqi people. We're finding the few that wanted to try to stop progress toward freedom and democracy. We're helping the Iraqi people stand up a government. We stand side by side with the Iraqis that love freedom.

And—but people will be held to account. That's what the process does. That's what we do in America. We fully investigate. We let everybody see the results of the investigation, and then people will be held to account.

Q. If your State Department issues a human rights report about practices around the world and abuses, and we call upon countries every once in a while to——

The President. Right.

Q. ——try to put pressure on them to allow International Red Cross to visit prisons and detention center, would you allow the International Red Cross and other human rights organization to visit prisons under the control of the U.S. military?

The President. Of course we'll cooperate with the International Red Cross. They're a vital organization, and we work with the International Red Cross. And you're right, we do point out human rights abuses. We also say to those governments, "Clean up your act," and that's precisely what America is doing.

We've discovered these abuses. They're abhorrent abuses. They do not reflect—the actions of these few people do not reflect the hearts of the American people. The American people are just as appalled at what they have seen on TV as the Iraqi citizens have. The Iraqi citizens must understand that. And therefore, there will be a full investigation, and justice will be served. And we will do to ourselves what we expect of others.

And when we say, "You've got human rights abuses, take care of the problem," we will do the same thing. We're taking care of the problem. And it's—it is unpleasant for Americans to see that some citizens, some soldiers have acted this way, because it does—again, I keep repeating, but it's true—it doesn't reflect how we think. This is not America. America is a country of justice and law and freedom and treating people with respect....

Source: *Public Papers of the Presidents of the United States: George W. Bush* (Washington, DC: Government Printing Office) 786–789.

ABU GHRAIB SCANDAL: WHERE DOES THE BUCK STOP? (MAY 10, 2005)

Ms. Marcy Kaptur (D-OH). Mr. Speaker, I rise tonight to discuss a vital issue that has not received nearly as much attention as it should, and that is the full accountability of those responsible for the prison abuse at Abu Ghraib prison in Iraq and likely other abuses in other locations.

Last week, 1 year after the shocking pictures of prisoner abuse became public, a military judge declared a mistrial in the case against Private First Class Lynndie England, and I emphasize private first class.

England, one of just a few enlisted personnel charged in the case, attempted to plead guilty in order to receive a more lenient sentence. But Judge James Pohl threw her guilty plea out and the court-martial after determining that Private England could not have realized her actions were wrong. Maybe that is because exactly 1 year ago today, Private England told the media that she was ordered by her superiors to pose naked with Iraqi prisoners at Abu Ghraib prison.

The case has more questions about Abu Ghraib than it answers, Mr. Speaker. Who was really in charge at Abu Ghraib prison? Who ordered the torture, abuse, humiliation of those prisoners? Why have only a few enlisted personnel, and very low-ranking ones at that, and one Reservist officer been punished? What was the real chain of command? Were contractors involved at any point? And how did their involvement compromise the normal chain of command?

According to the Christian Science Monitor, a study by the Army Inspector General, not yet released but reported last week by the media, has exonerated all senior Army officers in Iraq and elsewhere. How about that? Exonerated them all, except the single brigadier general in charge of U.S. prison facilities in Iraq. Why does the Pentagon refuse to look up the chain of command, only trying to place blame at those at the very bottom? Does anyone really believe that these soldiers acted on their own?

The Philadelphia Inquirer editorialized: "No one at the top...is blamed for wrongdoing," even though the "climate was fostered from the top down that tolerated, even encouraged, the abuse at Abu Ghraib."

In February, 2004, the International Red Cross released a report detailing dozens of serious human rights violations that occurred in Iraq between just March and November of 2003, including electrocution, forced nudity, and other lewd sex acts, forcing detainees to wear hoods and more.

Who should be held accountable? First, Secretary of Defense Donald Rumsfeld. He is at the top of my list. Personally authorized similar abusive interrogation techniques for prisoners held in Guantanamo Bay, Cuba, including the use of dogs for intimidation, the removal of clothing, the hooding of prisoners, and "non-injurious physical contact." He ordered several prisoners in Iraq, though not at Abu Ghraib, to be hidden from the International Red Cross so the organization could not monitor their treatment. Are we supposed to believe that such actions at Abu Ghraib were a mere coincidence and not orchestrated by anyone who had the power to order from the top down?

How about Lieutenant General Ricardo Sanchez? He is second on my list. Two Army investigations, one of which he stated he "failed to ensure proper staff oversight" of Abu Ghraib, but he has yet to be officially sanctioned, punished, or charged.

Third, Major General Geoffrey Miller. According to the Center for American Progress, he was sent to Abu Ghraib to "Gitmoize" the place. Under his command, the International Committee of the Red Cross found interrogation techniques at Guantanamo "tantamount to torture."

Fourth, White House Counsel Alberto Gonzales. When he served in that capacity, he advised President Bush that laws prohibiting torture do "not apply to the President's detention and interrogation of enemy combatants" and an interrogation tactic only constituted torture if it resulted in death, organ failure, or serious impairment of bodily functions.

And last, but surely not least, President George Bush. The President is not last on this list for no reason. Harry Truman proudly proclaimed "The buck stops here." It would seem this Commander in Chief believes the buck stops far before the Pentagon, White House, or Oval Office.

Mr. Speaker, why is Congress receiving more information on these atrocities from the news media than the President or the Department of Defense? It is because they are a part of the culture of abuse that starts with loose slogans like "Bring 'em on." It sends that signal down the chain of command. They were not only operating in an atmosphere created, fostered, and encouraged by top echelon officials at the White House. They were propelled by that very behavior.

Source: *Congressional Record*, May 10, 2005, H 3088–3090.

DEFENSE OF DONALD RUMSFELD (APRIL 2006)

Since his nomination as secretary of defense, Donald Rumsfeld has been a controversial figure in the Bush administration. President Bush nominated Rumsfeld based on his years of experience under the Reagan and George H. W. Bush administrations. In April of 2006, President Bush found himself having to defend Rumsfeld as he came under attack by retired generals who served in both the Afghan and the Iraqi theatres. The generals claimed that Rumsfeld mishandled both wars, especially that in Iraq.

In 2004, when details of the prison abuse at Abu Ghraib emerged, Donald Rumsfeld took full responsibility for the actions of the soldiers; however, he stopped short of resigning from office, despite calls for this ultimate sign of contrition from various members of both Houses. On April 2, 2006, a string of retired generals began to speak out against Rumsfeld's actions and his lack of leadership. While none of them asked for his resignation outright, many hinted at it. On April 14, 2006, the president came out in support of the secretary of defense. He said that he stood by the actions and decisions of the secretary of defense. This criticism was muted until just before the 2006 midterm elections, when an editorial published in four independent military publications called for his removal. Following the Democratic Party's electoral victory the next day, President Bush announced Rumsfeld's resignation.

BUSH'S STATEMENT SUPPORTING SECRETARY OF DEFENSE DONALD H. RUMSFELD (APRIL 14, 2006)

Earlier today I spoke with Don Rumsfeld about ongoing military operations in the global war on terror. I reiterated my strong support for his leadership during this historic and challenging time for our Nation.

The Department of Defense has been tasked with many difficult missions. Upon assuming office, I asked Don to transform the largest department in our Government. That kind of change is hard, but our Nation must have a military that is fully prepared to confront the dangerous threats of the 21st century. Don and our military commanders have also been tasked to take the fight to the enemy abroad on multiple fronts.

I have seen firsthand how Don relies upon our military commanders in the field and at the Pentagon to make decisions about how best to complete these missions.

Secretary Rumsfeld's energetic and steady leadership is exactly what is needed at this critical period. He has my full support and deepest appreciation.

Source: *Public Papers of the Presidents of the United States: George W. Bush* (Washington, DC: Government Printing Office), 715–716.

CRITICISM ON IRAQ AND SECRETARY OF STATE DONALD RUMSFELD (APRIL 7, 2006)

Mr. Frank R. Lautenberg (D-NJ). Mr. President, there has been almost a raging debate around here these last couple of days on evaluations of what is taking place in Iraq, where do we stand in this war—almost a war of attrition, as I see it.

Now we have some different news that has come about to accompany those stories of horror from Iraq. Everybody now knows that the Vice President's former chief of staff, Scooter Libby, has been indicted as part of the investigation into the leak of classified material from the White House.

I remember when this controversy broke. President Bush acted incredulous that anyone would leak classified national security information. In fact, in September 2003, the President said:

"There's just too many leaks, and if there is a leak out of my administration, I want to know who it is."

But now we find out—I think embarrassingly for the President, embarrassingly for the United States—we now find out that the President himself was ordering a leak of classified material. And he leaked that classified information for political reasons. He was trying to undo some of the political damage caused by the disclosure that the intelligence community did not believe Iraq was trying to purchase uranium. There it was: the reason we went to Iraq in the first place, and substantial doubts.

People who supported that view are now challenging the intelligence that led us there, or at least the intelligence reports we got. Now, here we are, still bogged down in Iraq, with no hope in sight to fix the mess we have caused there.

Yesterday, there was debate between two of our colleagues. One was Senator Kerry, who served in Vietnam, decorated for that service, the other was the Senator from Colorado, who was harsh in his criticism of Senator Kerry's speech on Iraq.

Now, Senator Kerry and I are both veterans. I am a veteran of World War II, and I served in Europe during the war. His, again, distinguished service in Vietnam is well known. So we are both veterans, and we are very interested in the military analysis of the Senator from Colorado.

The speech of the Senator from Colorado sounded much like White House talking points: short on facts, long on innuendo and fantasy.

While politicians in Washington sometimes wear rose-colored glasses and fantasize about the situation in Iraq, American troops are dying, American troops are wounded. One need only visit Walter Reed Hospital to see how serious some of those wounds are. People have lost limbs. People lose their sight. People suffer very severely from post-traumatic stress, invisible wounds that penetrate, nevertheless, very deeply.

I have gone to many memorial services and funerals for young people from New Jersey who died in Iraq. Seventy-three soldiers from my home State of New Jersey have died in Iraq and Afghanistan. As I mentioned, I have visited Walter Reed Army Hospital here in Washington several times, and I have been struck by the incredible resilience and dedication to our country of those young Americans, those who want to be able to pick up arms again so they can do their duty. And while these brave men and women put their lives on the line, the administration is simply ignoring reality.

Paul Eaton, a former commanding general of the Coalition Military Assistance and Training Team, wrote in the New York Times on March 19, recently, that Secretary of Defense Donald Rumsfeld is—and here I quote the Times—"not competent to lead our armed forces."

Eaton further said that Rumsfeld "has shown himself incompetent strategically, operationally and tactically, and is far more than anyone else responsible for what has happened to our important mission in Iraq. Mr. Rumsfeld must step down."

This past Sunday on "Meet The Press," retired General Anthony Zinni, who just published a book, repeated the call for Mr. Rumsfeld to resign. General Zinni of the U.S. Marine Corps is a former Commander of the Central Command. He said Secretary Rumsfeld should be held accountable for tactical mistakes in Iraq.

I had the opportunity the other night to go to a testimonial for General Shalikashvili and saw films of him done with former Secretary of State Colin Powell, President Clinton—all kinds of testimonials. As I looked at General Shalikashvili, I recalled how splendidly he handled his assignment as the Chief of the joint members of the senior staff and recalled that he said that in Iraq we would need perhaps 300,000 troops or more. He was right. And we never delivered on that commitment. As a consequence, in many military circles it is believed that lack of force is responsible for some of the problems we currently see.

Several days after General Zinni spoke, President Bush dismissed calls for Rumsfeld to step down, saying he was "satisfied" with his performance.

How in the world can the Commander-in-Chief, President Bush, be satisfied with the situation in Iraq? It is chaotic. It is near a civil war. The definition of a "civil war" is that people within the same country are fighting one another. My gosh, it could not be clearer.

So how can he be satisfied with Secretary Rumsfeld's miscalculations, with his profound errors in judgment, with his stubborn unwillingness to admit mistakes?

These mistakes have had tragic consequences—tragic for the nearly 2,400 American men and women who have died in Iraq and Afghanistan, tragic for the families they have left behind.

To examine the incompetence a little bit further—I have not been in Iraq in the last couple of years. I was there then, and I met with troops, and they were asking for better body armor. They were asking for better Humvee armor. And it took 2 years to loosen up those products to protect our troops. How incompetent must one be for the President not to be up in arms?

After my visit, I said I was going to the Defense Department, and did, requesting expedited treatment for these articles that our troops needed to protect themselves and to fight the war fully.

We know that most of the claims of the Bush administration in the lead up to war were simply false. The administration claimed there was a connection between Saddam Hussein and al Qaeda. Not true.

The Bush administration claimed that there were weapons of mass destruction there. Not true.

The Bush administration claimed that the war would cost "in the range of 50 to 60 billion dollars." Not true. The wars in Iraq and Afghanistan, including the next supplemental to be brought before the Congress in coming weeks, will total a half a trillion dollars, nearly $7 billion a month spent just in Iraq.

The Bush administration said before the war the oil revenues from Iraq could bring "between 50 and 100 billion [dollars] over the course of the next two to three years." Not true again.

President Bush announced, "Mission accomplished," on May 1, 2003. He lulled the Nation into believing that it was all settled: Families, look forward to your kids coming home. Look forward to families restored. Look forward to fathers and mothers coming back to their children. He told the Nation that major combat in Iraq was over. Not true. Ninety percent of the Americans who have died in Iraq have died since combat operations had supposedly "ended."

The Bush administration claimed that the Iraq insurgency was in its "last throes." Not true. We know the insurgency has gained strength. General Abizaid recently said the number of foreign terrorists infiltrating Iraq has increased.

Since the last week of February, sectarian violence and death have reached new heights, while electricity production has dropped below prewar levels. Unemployment ranges from 30 to 60 percent.

The American people do not want their leader to deny reality. They want to hear the truth.

People on the floor of the Senate have heard me say it time and time again: I will never understand why the President of the United States refuses to let journalists, photographers, journalists who do photography, come in and take pictures of flag-draped coffins—flag-draped coffins. It is the country's last sign of honoring its dead. They are unable to take pictures of that because they do not want to tell the American people the truth about what is happening. It is, in my view, insulting to those families whose loved ones sacrificed their lives on the battlefield. Outrageous.

They do not want to tell us the truth. What they want to do is tell us untruths. Leaking information is inexcusable, when the penalties for anyone who leaks that information could be jail time.

The President of the United States, President Bush, under the guise of releasing the classification of sensitive material, had passed information, with Vice President Cheney apparently being the person who furnished it, according to Libby, who is now fighting for his freedom. So he is saying things that he can prove, I would imagine; otherwise, he would not dare say it.

We are sick and tired of this war. I am not saying what the date is that we have to leave there, but I am saying that the date has passed for the truth, for knowing what is really happening there, for knowing what our troops and their families can expect.

Last week, I went to a return-home function in New Jersey, people who have come back. They were away, some of them, 18 months—little kids running around who haven't seen their fathers or mothers for that period of time. It is outrageous. We are in a state of confusion that defies imagination, that we, this country, with all of its might and all of its wealth, can't figure out some way to deal with this problem, after having made empty promises about how easy it was going to be— "treats and sweets" was one of the expressions used—totally misunderstanding, not thinking about what it was going to take, not only to fight this war but how do you win it. And winning it means that you go home triumphant. Not so.

We see in front of us a situation that reminds us of the sad days of Vietnam, when we wanted to extricate ourselves and couldn't quite do it until the pain was so excruciating that the population could no longer stand it. We need a leader who sees clearly what is really happening and who speaks candidly—we can take bad news; we don't like it, but we can take it—about what is taking place in front of our eyes on television and newspapers in our homes. We can take the news. We will accept it and fight on to rebuild our strength and our moral conviction about what we are doing. But we need to know the truth on how to do that.

Source: *Congressional Record*, April 7, 2006, S 3370–3371.

TERRORISM AND MILITARY ACTIONS WEB SITES

ABC News Online. "Bush Pressures Afghanistan Over Christian Convert Case." March 23, 2006. http://www.abc.net.au/news/newsitems/200603/s1598715.htm

American Presidency Project. "Radio Address by the President to the Nation." November 3, 2001. http://www.presidency.ucsb.edu/ws/index.php?pid=24994

ArabicNews.com. "Assassination Attempt Claiming the Life of Qusay Saddam Hussein." November 8, 2001. http://www.arabicnews.com/ansub/Daily/Day/011108/2001110806.html

Australian Politics.com. "Bush Says bin Laden Is Wanted Dead or Alive." September 17, 2001. http://www.australianpolitics.com/news/2001/01-09-17a.shtml

BBC News. "Bush's 'Evil Axis' Comment Stirs Critics." February 2, 2002. http://news.bbc.co.uk/1/hi/world/americas/1796034.stm

———. "U.S. Expands 'Axis of Evil.'" May 6, 2002. http://news.bbc.co.uk/2/hi/americas/1971852.stm

Bencivenga, Jim. "Bush Targets bin Laden, Again." *The Christian Science Monitor*, March 4, 2005. http://www.csmonitor.com/2005/0304/dailyUpdate.html

Benedetto, Richard. "Majority Supports Bush on Terrorism." *USA Today*, March 29, 2004. http://www.usatoday.com/news/politicselections/nation/polls/2004-03-29-poll_x.htm

CBS News. "Clarke's Take on Terrorism." *60 Minutes*, March 21, 2004. http://www.cbsnews.com/stories/2004/03/19/60minutes/main607356.shtml

———. "The Fifth Estate: Conspiracy Theories, the Saudi Connection." October 29, 2003. http://www.americanfreepress.net/10_07_01/Bush___Bin_Laden_-_George_W__B/bush___bin_laden_-_george_w__b.html

———. "Plans for Iraq Attack Began on 9/11." September 4, 2002. http://www.cbsnews.com/stories/2002/09/04/september11/main520830.shtml

CNN.com. "Bush: Afghanistan Is a Victory Over Terrorism." June 15, 2004. http://www.cnn.com/2004/US/06/15/karzai/

———. "Bush: Terrorism 'Will Not Stand.'" September 12, 2001. http://archives.cnn.com/2001/US/09/11/bush.statement/index.html
———. "Iraq Insurgency in 'Last Throes,' Cheney Says." June 20, 2005. http://www.cnn.com/2005/US/05/30/cheney.iraq/
———. "Saddam Seized in Raid Near Tikrit." http://www.cnn.com/SPECIALS/2003/saddam/
Department of Homeland Security. "Threats and Protection." March 21, 2006. http://www.dhs.gov/dhspublic/display?theme=29
Federation of American Scientists. "National Missile Defense." http://www.fas.org/spp/starwars/program/nmd/
Fox News.com. "Bush Says Major Combat in Iraq Over." May 2, 2003. http://www.foxnews.com/story/0,2933,85777,00.html
Friedman, Thomas. "Foreign Affairs: Bush to bin Laden." *The New York Times*, October 12, 2003. http://select.nytimes.com/gst/abstract.html?res=F40C1EFE3E5B0C718DDDA90994D9404482
GlobalSecurity.org. "Uday Saddam Hussein al Tikriti." http://www.globalsecurity.org/military/world/iraq/uday.htm
Hersh, Seymour. "The Other War: Why Bush's Afghanistan Problem Won't Go Away." *The New Yorker*, April 12, 2004. http://www.newyorker.com/fact/content/?040412fa_fact
Hirsh, Michael, and John Barry. "The Abu Ghraib Scandal Coverup?" *Newsweek*, June 7, 2005. http://www.msnbc.msn.com/id/5092776/site/newsweek/
Miller, Sara B. "Terror-alert System: How It's Working." *The Christian Science Monitor*, August 4, 2004. http://www.csmonitor.com/2004/0804/p01s02-usgn.html
"Niger Feels Hurt by Uranium Sales Charge." September 2003. http://www.aljazeerah.info/Opinion%20editorials/2003%20Opinion%20Editorials/September/23%20o/Niger%20Feels%20Hurt%20by%20Uranium%20Sale%20Charges%20Bruce%20Stanley.htm
Sammon, Bill, and Jerry Seper. "Bush Says Terrorism on the Run." *The Washington Times*, September 10, 2003. http://www.washtimes.com/national/20030911-120003-9003r.htm
Sourcewatch. "Axis of Evil." http://www.sourcewatch.org/index.php?title=Axis_of_evil
"Terror Alert Chart." www.terror-alert.com
"Terrorism Fallout May Hurt Bush." *Sydney Morning Herald*, July 26, 2004. http://www.smh.com.au/articles/2004/07/25/1090693833424.html?from=storylhs
United Press International. "Michael Moore Plans Bush–bin Laden Film." March 28, 2003. http://www.upi.com/inc/view.php?StoryID=20030328-032440-7289r
VandeHei, Jim. "Judge Heard Terrorism Case as He Interviewed for Seat." *Washington Post*, August 17, 2005. http://www.washingtonpost.com/wp-dyn/content/article/2005/08/16/AR2005081601561.html
The White House. "National Policy on Ballistic Missile Defense Fact Sheet." May 2003. http://www.whitehouse.gov/news/releases/2003/05/20030520-15.html
———. "President Outlines War Effort." April 2002. http://www.whitehouse.gov/news/releases/2002/04/20020417-1.html
———. "Rebuilding Afghanistan." March 21, 2006. http://www.whitehouse.gov/infocus/afghanistan/

TERRORISM AND MILITARY ACTIONS
REFERENCE ARTICLES AND BOOKS

Alexander, John B. *Winning the War: Advanced Weapons, Strategies and Concepts for the Post 9/11 World*. New York: Thomas Dunne Books, 2003.
Bahmanyar, Mir, and Ian Palmer. *Afghanistan Cave Complexes 1979–2004: Mountain Strongholds of the Mujahideen, Taliban and Al Qaeda*. New York: Osprey Press, 2004.
Bodansky, Yossef. *Bin Laden: The Man Who Declared War on America*. Roseville, CA: Prima Publishing, 2001.

Boese, Wade. "Bush Pushes New Strategic Framework, Missile Defenses." *Arms Control Today* 31, no. 5 (June 2001): 18.
Bush, George W. *Our Mission and Our Moment: President Bush's Address to the Nation Before a Joint Session of Congress.* New York: Newmarket Press, 2001.
Conley, Richard. *Transforming the American Polity: The Presidency of George W. Bush and the War on Terrorism.* Englewood Cliffs, NJ: Prentice Hall, 2004.
Coyle, Phillip, and John Rhinelander. "National Missile Defense and the ABM Treaty: No Need to Wreck the Accord." *World Policy Journal* 18, no. 3 (2001): 15.
Danner, Mark. *Torture and Truth: America, Abu Ghraib, and the War on Terror.* New York: New York Review Books, 2004.
Ehrenreich, Barbara, John Gray, Meron Benveniste, and Mark Danner. *Abu Ghraib: The Politics of Torture.* Berkeley, CA: North Atlantic Books, 2005.
Gordon, Philip, and Jeremy Shapiro. *Allies at War: America, Europe and the Crisis Over Iraq.* New York: McGraw Hill Publishers, 2004.
Guillemin, Jeanne. *Anthrax: The Investigation of a Deadly Outbreak.* Berkeley, CA: University of California Press, 2001.
Ide, Arthur, and Jacob Auliff. *Jihad, Mujahideen, Taliban, Osama bin Laden, George W. Bush and Oil: A Study in the Evolution of Terrorism and Islam.* Garland, TX: Tanglewuld Press, 2002.
Joseph, R. *America Betrayed: Bush, bin Laden, 9/11 . . . Aids, Anthrax, Iraq.* San Jose, CA: University Press, 2003.
Kellner, Douglas. *From 9/11 to Terror War: The Dangers of the Bush Legacy.* Lanham, MD: Rowman and Littlefield, 2003.
Mackey, Sandra. *The Reckoning: Iraq and the Legacy of Saddam Hussein.* New York: W.W. Norton, 2002.
Moore, Robin. *Hunting Down Hussein: The Inside Story of the Search and Capture.* New York: St. Martin's Press, 2004.
Mylroie, Laurie. *Bush v. the Beltway: The Inside Battle over War in Iraq.* New York: Regan Books, 2004.
National Commission of Terrorist Attacks Upon the United States. *9/11 and Terrorist Travel: A Staff Report of the National Commission on Terrorist Attacks upon the United States.* Franklin, TN: Hillboro Publishing, 2004.
National Commission on Terrorist Attacks. *The 9/11 Commission Report: Final Report of the National Commission on Terrorist Attacks upon the United States.* New York: W.W. Norton, 2004.
Peters, Ralph. *Beyond Terror: Strategy in a Changing World.* Mechanicsburg, PA: Stackpole Books, 2002.
Ritchie, Nick, and Paul Rogers. *The Political Road to War with Iraq: Bush, 9/11 and the Drive to Overthrow Saddam.* New York: Routledge, 2006.
Scheuer, Michael. *Through Our Enemie's Eyes: Osama bin Laden, Radical Islam, and the Future of America.* Dulles, VA: Potomac Books, 2002.
Silberstein, Sandra. *War of Words: Language, Politics and 9/11.* New York: Routledge Press, 2002.
Smith, J. W. *Why? The Deeper History behind the September 11th Terrorist Attack on America*, 2nd ed. Institute of Economic Democracy, 2003.
Soros, George. *The Bubble of American Supremacy: The Cost of Bush's War in Iraq.* New York: Public Affairs, 2004.
Tanner, Stephen. *Afghanistan: A Military History from Alexander the Great to the Fall of the Taliban.* New York: Perseus Books, 2003.
Tarpley, Webster Griffin. *9/11 Synthetic Terror: Made in USA.* Joshua Tree, CA: Progressive Press, 2005.
Taylor, Mark Lewis. *Religion, Politics and the Christian Right: Post 9/11 Powers in American Empire.* Minneapolis: Fortress Press, 2005.

Taylor, Scott. *Spinning on the Axis of Evil: America's War against Iraq*. Ottawa: Esprit de Corps Books, 2003.

Thompson, Paul. *The Terror Timeline Year by Year, Day by Day, Minute by Minute: A Comprehensive Chronicle of the Road to 9/11 and America's Response*. New York: Regan Books, 2004.

Woodward, Bob. *Bush at War*. New York: Simon and Schuster, 2002.

INDEX

Abu Ghraib Prison torture, 132–33, 177–81
ACLU v. Ashcroft (2004), 41
Afghanistan. *See also* Taliban: al Qaeda in, 130; Osama bin Laden in, 130, 133–39; Taliban, 130, 131, 139–40; US attack on, 131, 139–43, 171; Zahir Shah (King), 141–43
Afghan Women and Children Relief Act (2001), 96–97, 105–8
afterschool programs, 73
Alaskan National Wildlife Reserve (ANWR) oil drilling, 32–35
Alexander, Lamar, on steel tariffs, 27–29
Alito, Samuel, 44
al Qaeda, 130, 136–43, 172–74
Andean Trade Preference Act of 2002, 8, 20–24
anthrax, 143–45
Anti-Ballistic Missile Treaty (ABM), 94, 115–17
antiviral medication, 123–26
ANWR oil drilling, 32–35
arms control, 93–94, 110–14
Arthur Andersen, 8
Ashcroft, ACLU v. (2004), 41
avian flu, 97, 121–26
Axis of Evil, 131, 145–49

ballistic missile defense system, 160–64
Baucus, Max, on navy surveillance plane in China, 98–100
Benjamin Franklin True Patriot Act, 40
Biden, Joseph, on nuclear weapons, 112–14
Bigger, Judy, on Afghan Women and Children Relief Act, 107–8
bin Laden, Osama, 130, 133–39

biological warfare, 143–45
bird flu, 97, 121–26
Bolton, John, 95–96
Bond, Christopher, on space shuttle Columbia, 78–80
Boxer, Barbara, on Enron, 18–19
Brown, Michael, 43
Bush, George W.: on Abu Ghraib Prison torture, 178–79; on Afghan Women and Children Relief Act, 105–6; on anthrax, 144–45; on ANWR drilling, 33–34; on attack on Afghanistan, 140–41; on attack on Iraq, 156–58, 165; on avian flu, 121–24; on Axis of Evil, 146–47; on Department of Homeland Security, 53–54; on Donald Rumsfeld, 182; on end of war in Iraq, 169–72; on Enron, 17–18; on Faith-Based and Community Initiatives, 45–46; on free trade, 20–21; on global climate change, 101–3; on Hurricane Katrina, 81–82; on Jobs and Growth Tax Relief Reconciliation Act, 25; military policies, 130–31; on national missile defense system, 161–62; on navy surveillance plane in China, 98; on Niger/Iraq connection, 175; on No Child Left Behind, 69–71; on nuclear weapons, 111–12; on Osama bin Laden, 135–36; on the Patriot Act, 58–59; possible ties to Enron, 16–17; on Roadmap to Peace in Middle East, 109; on September 11, 2001, 134–35; on Social Security reform, 29–32; on steel tariffs, 27; on stem cell research, 48–50; on Tax Relief Act of 2001, 12–13; on Terror Alert System, 150–52; on wiretaps, 84–85; on withdrawal from Anti-Ballistic

Bush, George W. (*continued*)
 Missile Treaty, 115–16; on Yucca Mountain proposal, 75–76; on Zimbabwe, 118–19
butterfly ballot, 3
Byrd, Robert: on Department of Homeland Security, 54–57; on end of war in Iraq, 172–74

campaign finance reform, 42
Cantwell, Maria, on ANWR drilling, 34–35
cap and trade system, 104–5
Capps, Lois, on Roadmap to Peace in Middle East, 109–10
Cardin, Benjamin, on tax cuts, 26
Center for Faith-Based and Community Initiatives, 39–40, 44–47
Charitable Choice, 39
China, 93–94, 97–100, 117
CIA, leak about, 42–43
classified information, leaks of, 182–83
climate change, 96, 100–105
cloning, 50
Coalition of the Willing, 164
Columbia (space shuttle), 42, 76–80
computer hacking, 64–65
Conrad, Kent, on Osama bin Laden, 136–39
criminal forfeiture, 63–64

death tax, 13, 15
defense system, ballistic missile, 160–64
Department of Homeland Security, 4, 39–40, 44–47, 52–58, 150–55
detention of immigrants, 66–67
diplomacy, 95–96
disasters, natural, 43, 80–83, 97, 121–26
discrimination, 61–62
domestic policy: Department of Homeland Security, 52–57; Faith-Based and Community Initiatives, 39–40, 44–47; Hurricane Katrina, 43, 80–83; No Child Left Behind (2002), 41, 68–74; space shuttle Columbia, 42, 76–80; stem cell research, 40, 47–52; USA PATRIOT Act, 57–68, 84; wiretaps, 40, 43, 65, 84–88; Yucca Mountain proposal, 41–42, 74–76
drugs, illegal, 20–21
Durbin, Richard, on attack on Iraq, 166–69

Ebbers, Bernard, 8
economic corruption, 7–8, 16–19
Economic Growth and Tax Relief Reconciliation Act of 2001, 10, 12–16
economic policy: Andean Trade Preference Act of 2002, 8; economic corruption, influence on, 7–8; Federal Reserve, 10; in free trade agreements, 20–24; immigration policy, 9; Jobs and Growth Tax Relief Reconciliation Act of 2003, 11, 24–26; oil exploration, 10, 33–34; Social Security reform, 10, 29–32; steel tariffs, 8–9, 26–29; tax cuts, 10, 25; unemployment benefits, 11
economics, supply-side, 14–15
education, 68–74
election irregularities, 2–3
Electronic Communications Privacy Act, 41
embryonic stem cell research, 40, 47–52
Enron, 8, 16–19
environmental policies: cap and trade system, 104–5; free trade agreements, 22–23; global warming, 96, 100–105; oil drilling and exploration, 10, 32–35; withdrawal from Kyoto Climate Protocol, 96; Yucca Mountain proposal, 41–42, 74–76
ESOPS, 19
estate tax, 13, 15

Faith-Based and Community Initiatives, 39–40, 44–47
federal monies and religious groups, 39, 44–47
Federal Reserve, 10
Feingold, Russell: on curtailing of civil liberties, 61–66; on immigration laws, 66–68; on past deprivation of civil liberties, 59–61; on Patriot Act, 59–68; on Zimbabwe, 119–20
FEMA, 43
FISA (Foreign Intelligence Surveillance Act), 65–66, 84–85
Florida, role in 2000 election, 2–3
flu, avian, 97, 121–26
Foreign Intelligence Surveillance Act (FISA), 65–66, 84–85
foreign policy. *See also* Afghanistan; military policies; terrorism: Afghan Women and Children Relief Act (2001), 96–97, 105–8; al Qaeda, 130, 136–43, 172–74; Anti-Ballistic Missile Treaty (ABM), 94, 115–17; attack on Iraq, 167–68; avian flu, 97, 121–26; Axis of Evil, 145–49; China, 93, 97–100; Kyoto

Climate Protocol, 100–105; nuclear weapons, 93–94, 110–14, 115–17; Preventive War Doctrine, 148–49; Roadmap to Peace in Middle East, 95, 108–10; United Nations, 95–96; withdrawal from Kyoto Climate Protocol, 96, 100–105; Zimbabwe, 95, 118–20
forfeiture, criminal, 63–64
401(k) account legislation, 18–19
Fourth Amendment, 63–65
free trade, 8–9, 20–24

gasoline supply, 32–35, 81–82
genetic research, 47–52
Gibbons, Jim, on Yucca Mountain proposal, 76
global warming, 96, 100–105

hacking (computer), 64–65
hard money contributions, defined, 42
Harkin, Tom, on avian flu, 124–26
Hawley-Smoot tariff, 9
Hinchey, Maurice, on Niger/Iraq connection, 175–76
Homeland Security, Department of. *See* Department of Homeland Security
Homeland Security Advisory System, 150–55
human rights, 22–23, 105–8, 118–20, 177–81
Hurricane Katrina, 43, 80–83
Hussein, Saddam, 42–43, 131–33, 136–39, 155–60, 165. *See also* Iraq

illegal drugs, 20–21
immigration policy, 9, 66–68
inheritance ("death") tax, 13, 15
Intelligence Authorization Act, 86–88
intelligence director, 43
international open trade. *See* free trade
Iraq. *See also* Hussein, Saddam: Abu Ghraib Prison torture, 132–33, 177–81; attack on, 42–43, 131–33, 145–49, 155–60, 164–69; Axis of Evil member, 145–46; Donald Rumsfeld and, 181–85; end of war, 169–74; Niger connection, 174–76; September 11, 2001 and, 131–33, 136–39; weapons of mass destruction, 131–32, 146–47, 156–58, 174–76
Israel and Palestine, 95, 108–10

Jobs and Growth Tax Relief Reconciliation Act of 2003, 11, 24–26

Kaptur, Marcy, on Abu Ghraib Prison torture, 179–81
Kennedy, Patrick, on Tax Relief Act of 2001, 14–16
Kennedy v. Mendoza-Martinez, 60
Kucinich, Dennis, 40
Kyoto Climate Protocol, 96, 100–105

labor policies, 22–23
Lautenberg, Frank: on Donald Rumsfeld, 182–85; on Terror Alert System, 152–55
Libby, Lewis, 42
Lieberman, Joseph, on global climate change, 103–5

McCain-Feingold Act, 42
McGovern, James P., on wiretaps, 86–88
medication, antiviral, 123–26
Meiers, Harriet, 44
Mendoza-Martinez, Kennedy v., 60
Middle East, 95, 108–10
military policies. *See also* al Qaeda; foreign policy: Abu Ghraib Prison torture, 132–33; Afghanistan and bin Laden, 130–31; Iraq, attack on, 131–33, 164–69; Iraq, war is over, 169–74; national missile defense system, 160–64
minimum wage, 23
missile defense system, 160–64
mission accomplished speech, 169–74
Moscow Treaty (SORT), 93–94, 110–14
Mugabe, Robert, 95, 118–20

Nadler, Jerrold, on Hurricane Katrina, 83
NAFTA, 22–23
narcotics, 20–21
NASA, 42, 76–80
National Drug Control Policy (2002), 41
national intelligence director, 43
National Security Agency, 43
natural disasters, 43, 80–83, 97, 121–26
Negroponte, John, 43
Niger, connection with Iraq, 174–76
No Child Left Behind Act (2002), 41, 68–74
nuclear waste, 41–42, 74–76
nuclear weapons, 93–94, 110–14, 115–17, 131–32, 174–76

Office of Faith-Based and Community Initiatives, 45
oil exploration and dependence, 10, 32–35
open borders, 9

Palestine and Israel, 95, 108–10
Pallone, Frank, Jr., on privatizing Social Security, 32
pandemic, 97, 121–25
Parker, Star, 46–47
Patriot Act. *See* USA PATRIOT Act
Paul, Ron, on Faith-Based and Community Initiatives, 26–27, 46–47
Payne, Donald M., on attack on Iraq, 158–60
Pension Protection and Diversification Act of 2001 (PPDA), 18–19
Plame, Valerie, affair, 42–43
Powell Doctrine, 131
Presidential Records Act, 41
Preventive War Doctrine, 148–49
prison, torture in, 132–33, 177–81
Privacy and Civil Liberties Oversight Board, 86
private schools, 72–74
privatization of social security, 10, 29, 31–32

racial profiling, 61–62
Reed, Jack: on national missile defense system, 162–64; on withdrawal from Anti-Ballistic Missile Treaty, 116–17
Reid, Harry: and stem cell research, 48; on stem cell research, 51–52
religious groups and federal monies, 39, 44–47
retirement accounts, 10, 18–19, 29–32
Roadmap to Peace in Middle East, 95, 108–10
Robert, John, 43
Rohrabacher, Dana, on attack on Afghanistan, 141–43
Rove, Karl, 42
Rumsfeld, Donald, 181–85
Russia, 93–94, 110–14

Sarbanes-Oxley Act, 8
school vouchers, 72–74
Secretary of Defense, 181–85
September 11, 2001: attack on Afghanistan, 130–31; attack on Iraq and, 131–33, 136–39; national missile defense system and, 161–62; Osama bin Laden and, 133–39
Shuttle Columbia, 42, 76–80
sneak and peek search, 64
Social Security reform, 10, 29–32
social services, 39–40, 44–47
soft money contributions, defined, 42

Star Wars, 130–31
steel tariffs, 8–9, 26–29
stem cell research, 40, 47–52
Strategic Defense Initiative, 130–31
Strategic Offensive Reductions Treaty (SORT), 93–94, 110–14
supply-side economics, 14–15
Supreme Court appointments, 43–44

Taliban: and Afghan Women and Children Relief Act, 105–8; and attack on Afghanistan, 139–40; beginning of, 130; and September 11, 2001, 133–39; US attack on, 139–43
tariffs, 8–9, 26–29
tax cuts, 10–16, 24–26
Tax Relief Act of 2001, 10, 12–16
Terror Alert System, 150–55
terrorism. *See also* al Qaeda; foreign policy; military policies: anthrax, 143–45; and attack on Afghanistan, 131, 139–43, 171; and attack on Iraq, 131–39, 156–58, 164–69; Axis of Evil, 131, 145–49; defined, 129; Department of Homeland Security, 4, 40, 52–58, 150–55; and end of war in Iraq, 169–74; Feingold on Patriot Act, 59–68; Foreign Intelligence Surveillance Act (FISA), 65–66, 84–85; historical overview, 129–30; and national missile defense system, 161–62; Taliban, 105–8, 130, 133–43; and Terror Alert System, 150–55; USA PATRIOT Act and, 40, 58–59; wiretaps, 40, 43, 65, 84–88
trade adjustment assistance, 23

unemployment benefits, 11
United Nations, 95–96, 156–60
USA Freedom Corps (USAFC), 40
USA PATRIOT Act: Bush on, 58–59; civil liberties under, 61–66; creation of, 40; Feingold on past deprivation of civil liberties, 59–61; immigration laws, effect on, 66–68; passage, 57–58; wiretaps, 40, 43, 65, 84–88

Valerie Plame affair, 42–43
Van Hollen, Chris, on Axis of Evil, 147–49
Vietnam syndrome, 130

War on Terror. *See* terrorism
warrantless searches, 63, 84–88

Watson, Diane, on anthrax, 145
weapons of mass destruction, 131–32, 146–47, 156–58, 174–76
Wellstone, Paul, on Andean Trade Preference Act of 2002, 21–24
Wilson, Joseph, 42–43, 131, 175–76
wiretaps, 40, 43, 65, 84–88

WorldCom, 8
World Trade Center, 44, 54, 130, 134, 137, 139, 143

Yucca Mountain proposal, 41–42, 74–76

Zahir Shah (King of Afghanistan), 141–43
Zimbabwe, 95, 118–20

ABOUT THE AUTHOR

NANCY LIND is Professor of Politics and Government, Illinois State University. She is co-editor of *The U.S. Constitution for Federal Executives* (training manual for the Federal Executive Institute, 2005), *Presidents from Reagan through Clinton, 1981–2001: Debating the Issues in Pro and Con Primary Documents* (Greenwood, 2001), and *Nonviolence and its Alternatives: An Interdisciplinary Reader* (1999). She has taught for over 20 years in the areas of public administration, organizational theory and behavior, and public policy.

BERNARD IVAN TAMAS is Assistant Professor of Politics and Government, Illinois State University. He has authored several articles and presented in the areas of party competition and the election process.